Twitter® FOR DUMMIES®
A Wiley Brand

3rd Edition

by Laura Fitton, Anum Hussain, and Brittany Leaning
@pistachio   @anum   @bleaning

with Michael E. Gruen and Leslie Poston
@gruen   @leslie

Foreword by Jack Dorsey
Inventor, Founder, & Chairman, Twitter

Twitter® For Dummies®, 3rd Edition

Published by:

John Wiley & Sons, Inc., 111 River Street, Hoboken, NJ 07030-5774, www.wiley.com

Copyright © 2015 by John Wiley & Sons, Inc., Hoboken, New Jersey

Published simultaneously in Canada

For general information on our other products and services, please contact our Customer Care Department within the U.S. at 877-762-2974, outside the U.S. at 317-572-3993, or fax 317-572-4002. For technical support, please visit www.wiley.com/techsupport.

Wiley publishes in a variety of print and electronic formats and by print-on-demand. Some material included with standard print versions of this book may not be included in e-books or in print-on-demand. If this book refers to media such as a CD or DVD that is not included in the version you purchased, you may download this material at http://booksupport.wiley.com. For more information about Wiley products, visit www.wiley.com.

Library of Congress Control Number: 2014940492

ISBN: 978-1-118-95483-6 (pbk); ISBN 978-1-118-95486-7 (ebk); ISBN 978-1-118-96009-7 (ebk)

Manufactured in the United States of America

10 9 8 7 6 5 4 3 2 1

Contents at a Glance

Table of Contents

Foreword

· ·

*L*et's be honest: You're not a dummy.

Technologies are often designed to guard against the seemingly errant desires and mistakes of the commons. What's remarkable about this technology you intend to learn is its ability to immediately expose and evolve the true desires of the commons.

Although it may seem so, simple technologies like this don't happen overnight. What looks like a story of 1 to 3 years actually has a shadow of over 15 years of work, dumb mistakes, false starts, late-night frenetic insight, and patient distillation. Twitter is a life's work built around three tenets: minimize thinking around communication, expose trends in local and global circles, and spark interaction. What you're holding in your hands describes an essence of communication upon which millions will build their own value.

While not everything can be conveyed in under 140 characters, the essence of Twitter can: "Expect the unexpected. Whenever possible, be the unexpected." I expect you to build something unexpected. Start small, start here.

Jack Dorsey
Inventor, Founder, & Chairman, Twitter
San Francisco, California

Introduction

• •

*B*y now, you've heard and seen that all the world's a-twitter. But you're probably still scratching your head and thinking "I don't get it. What's the point? Why are some people *so* into Twitter?"

Twitter is a tool that you can use to read and publish short, 140-character messages (often called *updates*). These updates can come from almost anyone, anywhere: your friends, organizations you care about, businesses you frequent, publications you read, or complete strangers you've decided to read.

As a user of Twitter, you get to choose exactly whose updates you want to read — which people you want to *follow.* In turn, other users can elect to follow *your* updates. You can post messages publicly for the entire Twitter community, send them privately from one user to another, or, with a private account, post semi-publicly only to users whom you approve. You can view these updates, called *Tweets,* on any device connected to the Internet.

Twitter has changed and enhanced almost every type of media and community imaginable, from news and sports, to entertainment, to the way that people communicate with friends and companies. Twitter has empowered users to raise money for people in need, coordinate rescue efforts in the wake of a natural disaster, and alert authorities to emergencies and illegal activities both domestic and abroad. Twitter has even powered social and political movements, altering major global events and how (and what) we come to know about them as they unfold.

Skeptical anything could do all that in just 140 characters? Give us a chance to help you understand the power of Twitter. We hope you'll use it to create something #awesome.

With some time invested in Twitter, you may also find yourself communicating more effectively. You can say a lot with a few words. Because it only takes little scraps of time to read and update, we think you'll be surprised how easily you can get value from Twitter.

About This Book

We, the authors (Laura, Anum, and Brittany), aren't employees, representatives, or shareholders in Twitter. The opinions we give in this book represent what's worked for us and our networks, but not necessarily the Twitter world at large. We've been on Twitter for quite a while, and we have a good sense about how people are using it. But Twitter is a living, breathing, and constantly changing dynamic community. Twitter itself may change its feature set, its privacy features, or general direction overnight, which changes the way that people use it.

In fact, since the first and second editions, Twitter has released thousands of changes to make it even easier to engage with the community and get value from using Twitter. Although the layout and the exact location of everything will continue to change around, the basics of Twitter likely will always be the same. After you understand how the service works, you can pretty easily find any feature that may have moved since the publication of this book. Note: When things change, keep in touch with @dummies or our personal accounts (@Pistachio, @anum, and @bleaning).

New for Third Edition

In this edition, we've added whole new chapters, trimmed old ones, created new Parts of Ten, and updated every single page of the book to reflect Twitter's extensive growth and changes in the five years since this book debuted.

As with the second edition, we've once again updated most of our screenshots and how-to's to reflect the latest changes in the Twitter.com interface. (However, remember that as an Internet product, Twitter can — and will — change at any time, so please use our guides as guides, not the be-all and end-all of the Twitter experience.) We also left in a vintage shot or two, for old times' sake.

In addition to feature changes, you'll find new case studies and examples to help you understand how the world has adjusted to Twitter. We reached out to some of the companies, not-for-profits, and individuals we feel are using Twitter in innovative and surprising ways, so look out for them in sidebars as you go through the book.

Lastly, *Twitter For Dummies,* 3rd Edition, debuts a new author team. Laura sold her startup oneforty to HubSpot, where she met rising social media stars Anum Hussain (say "un-num") and Brittany Leaning. Leslie Poston and Michael Gruen remain dear friends and incredibly important contributors due to their work on the first and second editions.

Motivation

We wrote this book to help more people understand, try out, and benefit from the incredible things Twitter makes possible. When we released the first and second editions, many still considered Twitter a fad. Trust us on this, Twitter has been outright changing lives for more than 8 years already. It's had such an incredible impact on media and journalism that we added an entire chapter just about that. Twitter can be fun, productive, supportive, and surprisingly powerful.

Just ask Laura. Before she "got" Twitter, she was practically homebound with two kids under two, trying to build her personal and professional network from scratch in a new city. Now she's a busy single mom who solo-founded, venture-capital-funded, and sold a company, wrote three editions of the book you're holding, and travels the world keynoting conferences like the Inc 500|5000. Twitter's lightning strike made all the difference. What can it do for you?

Conventions Used in This Book

In this book, we stick to a few conventions to help with readability. Whenever you have to enter text into your phone or computer, we show it in **bold**, so you can easily see what to write. `Monofont` text denotes an email address or website URL. We capitalize the names of Twitter pages and features — such as Settings. Numbered lists guide you through tasks that you must complete in order, from top to bottom; you can read bulleted lists in any order you like (from top to bottom, bottom to top, or any other way).

Note: Screenshots in this book show you what the interface was like in summer 2014. Expect that significant changes took and will continue to take place before, during, and surely, after the writing of this book.

What You're Not to Read

We wrote this book for the first-time Twitter users. If you've already created an account that's following some folks and has some followers, you can probably skip the chapters that talk about how to sign up and get moving — although you might find it useful to review the sections on how to dress up your profile. If you're a business and have already gotten rolling on Twitter, you can probably safely ignore many of the starting chapters and check out Parts III and IV. If you're a Twitter pro and could have probably written this book, feel free not to read anything and use this book as a doorstop (please recycle it when you're done!). Okay, we're kidding — it'll make a great gift for the Twitter-skeptics in your life!

Foolish Assumptions

In this book, we make the following assumptions:

- You're at least 13 years of age. (You have to be at least 13 years old to have a Twitter account.)
- You have access to a computer and the Internet (and know how to use them!).

✔ You have a working email address that you can access.

✔ You have a mobile phone and know how to send text messages (if you want to access Twitter by using your mobile phone).

✔ Bonus: You have a smartphone (if you want to use a mobile Twitter application).

✔ You can read.

How This Book Is Organized

Like other *For Dummies* books, each chapter in *Twitter For Dummies,* 3rd Edition, is self-contained, and you can read them in any order you want. However, we've organized the book into five parts; and, if you read them in order, you will gain a strong understanding of the Twitter landscape, from signing up to tweeting like a pro.

Part I: Twitter? Like Birds Do?

Part I introduces you to the very basics of Twitter, from understanding how the Twitter works to getting up and running with an account. You can figure out how to find friends and others already on Twitter, how to invite new friends to try it, and how to start communicating with your people both in public and in private. We also look at the different things that you can do with the Twitter. com interface, including some things that may not be immediately obvious.

Part II: Finding Your Flock

After you become familiar with the basics of Twitter, you probably want to know how to dig in a little deeper to find accounts and people you really want to follow, and to communicate in ways that make you look more comfortable using Twitter. We give you all that information in this part, and we provide a list of many resources that you may find useful in getting Twitter to work best for you.

Part III: Twittering in High Gear

Part III dives way into all the ways that you can interact with the Twitter interface, from desktop clients to mobile phone tricks to short-hand commands that can drastically improve the efficiency and information that you can get from Twitter. We dig a little deeper into hashtags, third party tools, and how to share visual content on Twitter.

Part IV: What's the Point? Using Twitter to Your Advantage

In Part IV, we ask you to ask the big questions about why you'd want to use Twitter and what sort of presence you might want to cultivate. We go through the different ways in which people, businesses, media, not-for-profits, and other organizations can use Twitter. We also provide case studies and examples for how brands and organizational presences have benefited other users on Twitter and themselves, and how they've successfully used Twitter to improve their brands' transparency and customer relations. There's a whole chapter on how Twitter and global media have changed each other over the past 8 years. Lastly, we show examples of Twitter's massive social and political implications, to give you a taste of some of the #awesome Twitter makes possible.

Part V: The Part of Tens

The final section is typical of every *For Dummies* book. In these chapters, we provide you with ten Tweets you can send today, ten cool ways to use Twitter, ten Twitter tools and services, and ten resources for Twitter glory.

Icons Used in This Book

Icons in this book point out important tidbits for you to look at, remember, and absorb. In this section, we go over the icons that we use throughout the book to guide you on your Twitter journey.

The Tip icon points out helpful information that's likely to improve your Twitter experience.

The Remember icon marks interesting or useful facts that we cover in detail in earlier chapters or something that's so important that you need to remember it while you're using Twitter.

The Privacy icon denotes that you should be careful about the Twitter activities that we're discussing. You may find yourself with a security or privacy concern.

The Warning icon highlights potential danger. When we use this icon, we're letting you know that you should proceed with caution.

Whenever you see this icon, rest assured that we're just letting our inner geeks run wild. Here we point out information that's interesting but not absolutely necessary to your understanding of the topic at hand. If you want all the details you can get, read these paragraphs. If you just want to know the basics, skip it.

Beyond the Book

Laura's daughter Zoe once asked her why we wrote *Twitter for Dummies* as a book instead of writing it "as a Twitter." Aside from being totally adorable, this was also a pretty good point for a first grader. We're excited that with this third edition comes significant, actionable online content to support your experience getting started on Twitter. Beyond the book that you're holding right now and of course our Twitter account (@dummies), we've created the following:

- **Cheat Sheet:** Go to www.dummies.com/cheatsheet/twitter, and you'll find our handy cheat sheet for using Twitter. We've organized the cheat sheet into several sections. You get at-a-glance guides to using Twitter's access points, defining the most commonly used Twitter mechanics, some Twitter guidelines to live by, and our short guide to what *not* to do on Twitter.

- **Extras:** On several of the pages that open each of this book's parts, you'll find links to web extras, which expand on some of the concepts discussed in that part. You'll find them at www.dummies.com/extras/twitter. The web extra for Part II helps you feel less anxious about getting started on Twitter by showing you 5 goofy first Tweets (including 2 written by your faithful authors). In the web extra for Part III, you'll find out how to rock Twitter with visual content the way Ellen DeGeneres, Bat Dad, and others have. Part IV has a web extra on how to wield Twitter like a conversational master. For Part V, we show you how to approach people you don't know yet using Twitter.

Where to Go from Here

If you haven't used Twitter before, mosey on over to Chapter 1 and start reading — we can get you up to speed in no time. If you've been using Twitter for a while and understand where everything is, but you want a better idea of how to use the service, head over to Part III, where we shift Twitter into high gear. If Part III is old hat for you, Part IV (particularly Chapters 11–14) gets into how Twitter changes business, media, socializing, and even social change. You'll find stories that can help you grow as a Twitter user.

With that, we'll see you online!

Part I

Twitter? Like Birds Do?

In this part . . .

- ✔ Learn the basics of why you may want to use Twitter
- ✔ Set yourself up with a Twitter profile that you can call your own.
- ✔ Find all the basic stuff you need so that you can get started in no time.

Chapter 1

Getting Started with Twitter

• •

• •

*Y*ou may have heard of Twitter but have no idea what it actually is. Twitter is basically a powerful social network that allows you to keep up with the people, businesses, and organizations you're interested in — whether you know them personally or not. It also lets you share what you're doing with the world — everyone from your family and friends to complete strangers. (You'll have to bear with us to find out why you would want to do that.) MIT Professor Andrew McAfee (@amcafee) describes Twitter this way: "With Twitter, my friends are never far away."

McAfee was most certainly right, because Twitter's company data in July 2014 showed that 115 million active monthly users were sending more than 53 million Tweets daily. That's a whole lot of tweeting! Additionally, of those 53 million Tweets, almost 40 percent were sent from mobile devices such as cellphones and tablets. (We talk more about tweeting from your desktop computer versus your mobile device in Chapter 4.)

Every day, we see dozens of new ideas and ways to use Twitter. In this chapter, we do our best to introduce the basic ideas and to explain how Twitter works and why it's so powerful.

Figuring Out This Twitter Thing

Twitter is a fast-evolving, surprisingly powerful new way to exchange ideas and information, and to stay in touch with people, businesses, and organizations that you care about. It's a social network — a digital abstraction that represents who you know and who you're interested in (whether you know them personally or not) — that you can access from your computer or your mobile device anywhere that has an Internet connection.

Twitter has one central feature: It lets users instantly post entries of 140 characters or less, known as *Tweets,* through the Twitter website (`https://twitter.com`), through the Twitter application on a mobile device, or by way of the numerous third-party applications that are available for both. (We talk more about the different ways to tweet in Part III.)

On the most basic level, Twitter is a communications network that combines elements of text messaging; instant-messaging communication tools, such as iMessage on Apple devices; and blog-publishing software, such as Blogger and WordPress. As with blogging, your Tweets are generally published to the world at large, and anyone can read them on Twitter.com (unless you make your account private to protect your Tweets so that only those you choose can see what you share). Unlike blogging, Twitter limits you to just 140 characters. As with instant messaging, you can communicate directly with people (through direct messages), but each public message has its own unique resource locator (URL), so each message is actually a web page. Instant messaging also lacks the social network "following" features of Twitter and basic ideas such as "publish-subscribe" and one-to-many broadcasting of messages.

Think you can't say anything meaningful in 140 characters? Think again. *Twitterers* (people who use Twitter) are not only innovating clever forms of one-liners, haiku, quotes, stories, and humor, but also including images and links to things like websites and blog posts, which carry a lot more information and context. Writing 140-character messages seems trivial. But writing headlines and very short advertising copy is famously hard to do really well, and the right words can be quite powerful. Consider: "Man Lands on Moon."

Twitter sounds simple — deceptively simple. When you think about how millions of people around the world are posting Twitter messages, following other people's Twitter streams, and responding to one another, you can start to see the significance behind Twitter's appeal. In fact, Twitter has noticed that it acts like a "pulse of the planet," a record of what everyone is thinking about, talking about, doing, and feeling — right now. Now, that's pretty interesting!

True, Twitter can look like it's full of noise. But once you find interesting people and accounts to follow, your Twitter stream shifts from a cascade of disjointed chatter to one of the most versatile, useful online communications tools yet seen — that is, if you take the time to find out how to use that tool correctly.

Twitter is a great way for you or your company to connect with large numbers of people quickly and personally, just as though you were having a conversation. In tech-speak, Twitter is a microblogging tool; however, you can more easily think of Twitter as a giant cocktail party with dozens of conversations you can join (or start) at any moment. Or, if you prefer a work metaphor, Twitter is like the office water cooler, where any number of informal (or formal) conversations can take place.

If you're familiar with blogs, instant messaging, and web-based journals, you can start to understand what makes Twitter so unique. The web offers a lot of information. Twitter can turn those long articles, lengthy conversations, and far-reaching connections into easily digestible facts, thoughts, questions, ideas, concepts, and sound bites. In other words, when you have only 140 characters, you have to be succinct.

The origins of Twitter

Twitter connects a wildly diverse array of people from all over the world, erasing all barriers and boundaries. Some of the media hype has called Twitter nothing short of revolutionary. And because Twitter is so easily customizable and open-ended, it has continued to become more and more popular with people and companies.

But Twitter's beginnings, like those of so many other digital innovations, were humble. Twitter was built in 2006 by four technology entrepreneurs: Evan Williams, Biz Stone, Noah Glass, and Jack Dorsey. All four were then employed by a San Francisco–based web company called Odeo, which specialized in publishing software for *podcasting* (audio broadcasting over the web). Dorsey was the one who came up with the original concept, and the four subsequently built it as an internal tool for Odeo employees. At first, they had no idea that it would catch on the way it did.

A management shakeup led to Twitter's and Odeo's reincorporation into a new company, Obvious Corp. Shortly thereafter, Twitter was released to the public. Already a favorite among Silicon Valley's geek elite, Twitter had its real coming-out party at the South by Southwest Interactive Festival (SXSWi) — an annual confab of tech and media innovators in Austin, Texas — in March 2007, when it was about a year old. Not only did it win the conference's Web Award honor, but also, its rapid-fire messages became the de facto coordinating and communicating tool for thousands of SXSWi attendees. The company became the digital world's new darling.

Shortly after SXSWi 2007, Twitter was spun off once again, becoming its own company separate from Obvious Corp.: Twitter, Inc.

Now millions of people use Twitter to keep in touch with family and friends, to launch and expand careers, to connect businesses and reach customers, to build a brand, to report the news, and to do a whole lot more. No two people or businesses use Twitter exactly the same way, and that fact is part of the secret to Twitter's success. You might argue that there isn't really a wrong way to use Twitter (as long as you mind the terms of service and don't try to actively do harm), so you get to tool it to your own needs.

How Individuals Use Twitter

I'm starting to think Twitter has nothing to do with birds.

— *Comedian Jim Gaffigan via Twitter February 15, 2012*
(https://twitter.com/JimGaffigan/
status/169975951118172160)

Looking at Twitter for the first time, you may be compelled to ask, "But *why* are all these people, many of whom seem like just random strangers, talking?" At first glance, Twitter seems flooded with disjointed conversations, interactions, and information. You can find news headlines, political debates, observations on the weather, and requests for advice. The idea of Twitter can be a bit confusing for new twitterers.

People have many reasons for using Twitter:

- ✔ **To connect:** Most people start using Twitter to forge connections and be part of a community. Others just want to be heard. Twitter lets millions of people around the world hear what you have to say; then it lets you connect with the ones who want to hear from you or talk to you about your passions, interests, and ideas.

  For more on the social side of Twitter, check out Chapter 13.

- ✔ **To record:** Some people tweet as a way to take notes on life. They use Twitter at conferences or events, or just while walking around to jog their own memories later about something that happened or what they've discovered. If you're walking down the street and notice a new restaurant you want to check out when you have more time, you might tweet about that. Now you have a way of remembering to go back to that interesting-looking place. Even the Library of Congress records Tweets. Yes, that stuff you publish on your humble little new account will end up in the Library of Congress. Whoa.

- ✔ **To share:** Some people use Twitter to share what they think, read, and know. They may tweet links to great articles or interesting items, or they may tweet original thoughts, ideas, hints, and tricks. Some people tweet quotes from speeches or classes, and others share choice bits of their inner monologue. Even when this information can get pretty obscure, with millions of listeners, someone's bound to find it informative or interesting.

- ✔ **To stay in touch:** Whole families and groups of long-term friends use Twitter to stay in touch. Twitter can send public or private notes to your friends, and it stores all sent messages, which means that you don't lose your thoughts when you close your browser (or your desktop or mobile application). Connecting on Twitter is a great way to preserve an initial contact with someone you've just met, such as at an event or conference, in a way that lets you gradually get to know that person more over time.

Twitter is pretty easy to use, meaning that everyone from your 13-year-old cousin to your 92-year-old great-grandma can figure out how to use it to say hello. Because you can access Twitter by using a computer or mobile device (or both!), it fits into mobile lifestyles and brings you closer to the everyday thoughts of those you're interested in.

How Organizations Use Twitter

This #September, clean water means dignity and health in India. Watch the video and be a part of the story: http://youtu.be/6bH7SPNdSt4

— charity: water's September campaign announcement via Twitter, August 21, 2013 (https://twitter.com/charitywater/ status/370181463133528064)

charity: water is a New York City–based charity working in 22 developing countries around the world, bringing clean water to people in need. Every September, the organization runs a campaign to solicit donations and raise awareness. Every year since 2008, Twitter has played a huge role in the success of the campaign, helping charity: water share educational materials about the cause as well as live updates during in-person fund-raising events.

Although charity: water has a huge reach of 1.4 million Twitter followers, the power of Twitter works for much smaller organizations, too. Groups such as churches and local charities can use Twitter to provide an additional way for members to connect, plan, and reach out beyond their immediate community. Preachers tweet about their planned sermons, youth group directors tweet about events, and local soup kitchens tweet when they need help. Whether it's extra hands for a project, far-reaching assistance with a fundraiser, or some other big idea, Twitter can enable organizations operating on a budget to think on their feet.

New organizations have also sprung up through Twitter. As Laura did for charity:water in December 2008, it's become very common for people to start their own donation campaigns on Twitter and encourage other Twitter users to donate and then tweet about it. But Twitter isn't just for charities. Enthusiasts of just about any interest have banded together on Twitter. You can find organizations for food and wine lovers who share recipes and swap restaurant reviews on Twitter. (You can search for the subjects that interest you at https://twitter.com/search-home.)

Musicians use Twitter to spread the word about concerts, song releases, charitable efforts, and their daily lives as celebrities. (Britney Spears' official Twitter account: @BritneySpears is one of the most widely followed) John Mayer (@JohnMayer) live-tweeted the Grammy Awards even back in 2010. Musicians working hard to make a name have used Twitter to engage thriving, and involved, fan bases.

Twitter has also been a big help for community efforts. Whether it's Amber Alerts, fund-raisers, searches for kidney donors, or the effort to "Bring Back Our Girls," 230 schoolgirls kidnapped by Boko Haram Terrorists (#bringbackourgirls), Twitter shines as a tool for social good. Plenty of people in the world want to lend a helping hand, and Twitter's platform makes it easy to do so, in real time, with a global network of connections.

How Businesses Use Twitter

> *#coffee is trending. It's like twitter understands not only what we need, but what really gets us going. #tweetfromtheseat*
>
> — *Charmin via Twitter, August 6, 2014* (https://twitter.com/Charmin/status/497009506455658496)

If individuals, community groups, and nonprofit groups can use Twitter (as we discuss in the preceding sections), businesses large and small can use it, too.

Discount airline JetBlue uses Twitter to advertise fare specials, put out weather alerts, and conduct customer service (@JetBlue). Coffee retailer Starbucks uses Twitter to connect with customers and spread company culture (@Starbucks), as does online shoe retailer Zappos.com (@zappos). Early on, computer manufacturer Dell started a Twitter account (@DellOutlet) to promote special deals on returned equipment. It announced in June 2009 that its Twitter account had generated more than $2 million in revenue. Predictably, Dell now has many more accounts: @Dell, @DellCares, and @DellEnterprise, just to name a few.

So why would a business want to establish a presence on Twitter? There are several reasons:

- ✔ To network with customers and see what they're saying.
- ✔ To answer questions.
- ✔ To finely tool a company image.

✔ To poll and pull in feedback.

✔ To bring in new leads or customers.

✔ To take advantage of an innovative form of 140-character advertising. (If you have a limited quantity of something to sell in a short amount of time, you can't find a better channel than Twitter to make it known.)

Even a business with no customers on Twitter can take advantage of the off-platform benefits that we talk about in Chapter 11.

But none of these reasons really scratches the surface of why so many people use Twitter. Whether you want to use it for mostly personal or mostly business reasons, or even a blend of the two, you'll find that your reasons for tweeting multiply over time while Twitter becomes more and more useful to you. Each chapter in this book clearly explains why Twitter has caught on like wildfire and how you can join in the fun (and enjoy the business benefits) of this microsharing service.

If you're not sure where to begin, you'll be glad to know that many professions are comparing notes about the best ways to use Twitter. Twitter's Business blog (`https://business.twitter.com`), for example, shines the spotlight on businesses that are using Twitter to grow awareness and drive results. Here, you can find dozens of industry-specific blog posts and guides on how to use Twitter most effectively.

For more on putting Twitter to use for your business, turn to Chapter 11.

The Twitter Ecosystem

Excited to add a new line to my Twitter bio . . . grandfather-to-be! @hillaryclinton and I are so happy for Chelsea and Marc!

— Bill Clinton, 42nd president of the United States, via Twitter, April 17, 2014 (`https://twitter.com/billclinton/ status/456901920935149568`)

When you log in to Twitter.com, you see a small box on the left side that says Compose New Tweet. Sometimes, this Twitter prompt has users stuck in a rut, freezing up out of self-consciousness, concerned that they're not doing it right, or stuck with just plain old 140-character writer's block. You know these Twitter accounts when you see them: The twitterers end up tweeting only about what they had for breakfast, posting that they're leaving the office to go home and watch *House of Cards,* or making various other mundane life updates that don't spark much conversation. Many of these Twitter users don't end up getting involved in the Twitter culture, and some then stop using Twitter altogether.

How Twitter differs from Facebook

"Facebook is closed, Twitter is open. Facebook is structured, Twitter is scattered. Facebook is people you've known, and many you might have wanted to forget; Twitter is people you never knew, but might have wanted to meet. And because of all of that, barring an acquisition or failure to execute . . . Twitter will overtake Facebook and become the backbone of the real-time web."

— *Brightidea.com CEO Matthew Greeley* (@Brightidea)

If you're a regular Facebook user, you may be wondering how Twitter is different from the status updates that are part of Facebook. The main way in which Twitter differs from Facebook is that with Facebook, most of the time you're broadcasting your status updates to people you've allowed to be your friend and view your profile on Facebook. Currently on Facebook, you can make every update public if you wish, but it's still not the norm. On Twitter, you're by default sharing your updates with anyone in the world. You can protect your Twitter updates so that only people you allow can see them, but that's not very common. Instead, most people leave their Tweets open to the public, which means anyone who's interested in what you're saying can follow you — and you can choose to follow them back or just ignore them. You don't have to know the people you follow, and your followers don't have to know you.

Replies work differently on Facebook, and as a result, the system is much less dynamic. On Facebook, when people reply to your status update, their replies appear as comments that are connected to your update itself, which moves farther and farther down in the feed until eventually, it's not even seen anymore. (These replies, however, are preserved in the profiles of the users who initially shared something.) On Twitter, the most recent replies are always at the top of the stream, which means the conversation continues to be relevant and visited for as long as people are talking.

On Twitter, people frequently repeat your Tweets for their own followers. This practice is commonly called *retweeting*. If your band is playing at a club on Friday, you might tweet, "MyBand rocks out Blondie's, 123 Main St, LA, Fri 9/3 @ 9 pm www.myband.com for tickets." If any of your followers wants to spread the word, he might tweet, "RT @yourname: MyBand rocks out Blondie's, 123 Main St, LA, Fri 9/3 @ 9 pm www.myband.com for tickets." That *RT* is shorthand for *retweet,* and by putting your name after RT, he's letting his followers know that you're the one who originally posted it (and that you're the one whose band is playing at Blondie's). If you want to encourage people to retweet something, you can even put something like "Please RT" in the Tweet. What all this means is that your Tweets can spread like wildfire, and you can get the word out (fast!) about the things you want to share.

To make retweeting even easier, Twitter has a Retweet button right next to the Reply button, which will take a Tweet verbatim and make an exact copy to share with your followers.

It's really striking to see how much faster, farther, and more easily messages spread on Twitter. Sharing and passing along information are what make Twitter a sensitive global news detector, a powerful tool for social change or marketing, and an interesting and dynamic flow of ideas and information.

Instead of Compose New Tweet, Twitter's prompt used to say What's Happening? Before that, the prompt read What Are You Doing? As more people were using Twitter, the company realized that many of its active users were ignoring the former question and instead tweeting about news stories, how-to articles, cartoons, promotions, and other things that weren't necessarily about what was happening or what they were doing in their personal lives. To that end, Twitter is inherently flexible and open-ended, so you don't need to stick to a rigid set of rules. In effect, Twitter is what you make it. Feel free to compose a new Tweet right now and tell all of us "what's happening" in the world around you.

If you're brand-new to Twitter and ready to try it out, turn to Chapter 2 for information on how to sign up, customize your profile, and adjust your settings. Chapter 3 fills you in on the Twitter.com interface; it's sort of a road map of the site that shows where everything is.

You can get much more value from Twitter — and have a lot more fun — if you just let yourself relax and talk about what's on your mind. Passionate about aardvarks? Send out a few Tweets of aardvark facts and see who talks back to you. Have a burning desire to change careers from accounting to roadie for a rock band? Talk about it! You can probably get a response or two.

Thinking in 140 Characters

We'd like to thank you in 140 characters or less. And we just did!

— Twitter co-founder Jack Dorsey, accepting Twitter's Web Award honor at the South by Southwest Interactive Festival in March 2007

Simply put, a *Tweet* is what you call the 140-character message that you send out onto the web by using Twitter.

Why call it a Tweet? It's convenient, tying into the whole theme of birds chirping. Also, like much of the Twitter vocabulary, *Tweet* is a term coined by the users, rather than the company — evidence of the playful loyalty that avid users have toward the Twitter brand. In fact, it wasn't until late winter 2010 that Twitter officially changed their references to "updates" to "Tweets" based on how the world talked about tweeting.

Twitter limits the length of Tweets to 140 characters (letters, numbers, symbols, and spaces), a length that may seem short at first. And it is. How in the heck are you supposed to say anything in this tiny bit of space? How can you distill your company pitch into 140 characters, review a book, or summarize a movie in so few words? With time, you get used to this length restriction.

Perhaps one of the coolest things about Twitter is that the more you use it, the easier it is to write short, sharp, clear Tweets. As you get more accustomed to tweeting, you find that squeezing thoughts into 140 characters makes you refine the point in ways you wouldn't have thought of before.

Some Twitter users have reported becoming better salespeople offline or better writers because Twitter's mandated brevity forces you to focus your thoughts into concise, direct sound bites. Because Twitter's communication format encourages brief but engaging ideas, Twitter sparks conversations faster than almost any other Internet conversation format.

Where the name "Twitter" comes from

We want to get this out of the way: Yes, Twitter is a silly name. It calls to mind images of birds chirping or the all-night gabfests at junior-high sleepovers. But to be fair, a whole lot of web services have silly names. In an industry peppered with companies that have names such as Meebo and Veoh, a company called Twitter doesn't stand out as having a particularly odd moniker. (Bing and Google are chuckleworthy too, if you think about it.) Co-founder Jack Dorsey has argued from the start that Twitter is a fitting name for the service. In an early interview, when Twitter was still owned by Obvious, Inc., founders Jack Dorsey, Evan Williams, Noah Glass, and Biz Stone answered a question about where the name came from. Dorsey said, "If you look it up in the dictionary, it's actually just [a] short burst of activity, and it's something that birds do. It's just like chirping." In this case, the name reflects the short bursts of noise (or Tweets) that Twitter users make when they conduct their digital banter. (If you haven't made the connection already, this definition explains why Twitter's logo is a cartoon bird. To watch a video of the interview in its entirety, go to `www.podtech.net/home/?s=obvious%2C+twitter`.)

Chapter 2

Welcome to the World of Twitter

Twitter is a deceptively simple yet powerful conversation platform that enables users to broadcast short messages to the world and to connect more closely with people they care about. Intrigued about why this simple-looking tool is so well-loved and popular? This chapter is the place to get your feet wet. It usually takes using Twitter for a while to get what about it could be really interesting and valuable to you. Luckily, Twitter is not only easy to use, but also quick to set up and a piece of cake to get going.

In this chapter, we go over the very basics of Twitter: getting a username, beautifying your profile, finding people to communicate with, and getting yourself situated and ready to start tweeting like a pro in no time.

Signing Up

With many web services, signing up is the easiest part of an otherwise-complicated process. With Twitter, using the site is just as easy as signing up.

To sign up for a Twitter account, follow these steps:

1. **Use your web browser to navigate to the Twitter website at** `https://twitter.com`.

   The Twitter splash screen appears, as shown in Figure 2-1.

2. **Click the large yellow Sign Up for Twitter button.**

   The signup screen appears, as shown in Figure 2-2.

Figure 2-1:
The Twitter
splash
screen.

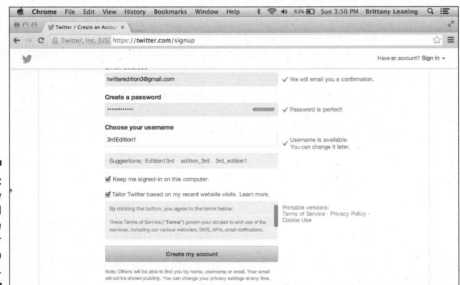

Figure 2-2:
The very
short and
simple
Twitter
signup
screen.

3. Type your desired username and basic information in the appropriate fields.

The only information Twitter requires from you is your name, a unique email address where Twitter can contact you for notifications, a password of your choice, and a username. (You'll probably take longer to decide on a username than to actually sign up. We cover how to choose a good Twitter name in the following section, and you can change it later.)

4. **Consider two additional options.**

   You see two check boxes: Keep Me Signed-In on This Computer and Tailor Twitter Based on My Recent Website Visits. By checking the first box, you're saying that this new account will be your default account that you want to be logged in to at all times. By checking the second box, you're agreeing to let Twitter give you suggestions about people you might enjoy following, based on information from your recent visits to websites that have integrated Twitter buttons or widgets. You can choose to check one box, both boxes, or neither box, depending on your preference.

5. **Click the large yellow Create My Account button.**

   Twitter now takes you to a setup screen, or sometimes, a CAPTCHA screen (see Step 6), or refreshes the screen in case you didn't fill out any of the fields correctly, as indicated by a red marker. (In most cases, the red marker appears because you're trying to sign up for a user account that's already taken or you've mistyped your email address.)

   By clicking the Create My Account button, you're agreeing to Twitter's terms of service. You see a link at the bottom of the screen that lets you read those terms of service, if you like, or you can go to `https://twitter.com/tos` to read them.

6. **Type the CAPTCHA code in the field, if you're prompted to do so.**

   This step is a standard web tactic to prove that you're a human and not a spam program (see Figure 2-3). For more information on this code, see the "What's up with the CAPTCHA?" sidebar later in this chapter.

Figure 2-3:
Are you
human?

7. Follow the onscreen tutorial to find people you know.

To jump-start your Twitter experience, the sign-up process includes a way for you to find people you may want to follow based on category and to automatically connect with people you know. (We cover how to find people to follow and invite people to join later in this section.) If you like, you can follow the onscreen wizard. If you want to get straight to Twitter, click the Next button on the left side of the screen until you get to the main Twitter screen. You'll know it when you see it (see Figure 2-4).

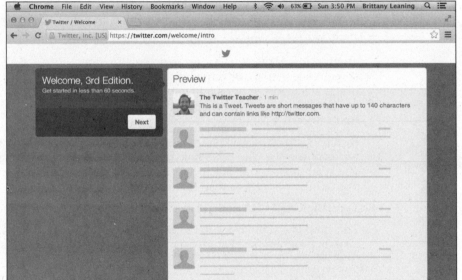

Figure 2-4:
The Twitter welcome. It's magical!

When you've gone through the instructions on building your timeline, you're taken to your newly created Twitter account, where you need to confirm your email address (see Figure 2-5).

8. To confirm your email address, log in to the email account you used to sign up for your Twitter account.

You should see an email from confirm@twitter.com.

9. Open the email, and click the blue Confirm Your Account Now button or click the link in the email (see Figure 2-6).

Did you know you can register for Twitter on the go? Get started while you're away from a computer through the Twitter app, which is free to download in the App Store or Google Play, by visiting `https://twitter.com` in the web browser on your mobile device, or simply by texting to 40404 (in the United States). (We talk more about using Twitter on your mobile device in Chapter 4.)

Figure 2-5: Your Twitter account. Almost there!

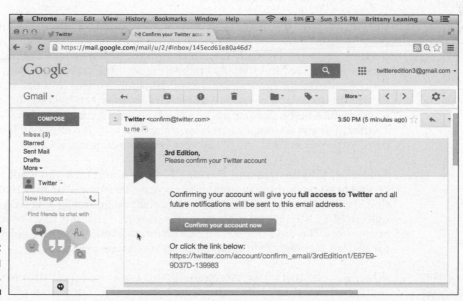

Figure 2-6: Getting confirmation.

What's up with the CAPTCHA?

A CAPTCHA is a quick check to make sure that an actual person, rather than a computer program, is using the website. Web applications use CAPTCHA (which stands for Completely Automated Public Turing test to tell Computers and Humans Apart) as a standard defense against spam and automatically generated user accounts.

You may find the CAPTCHA a bit tricky to read, but that's largely the point. Computers have a hard time reading text that's distorted in any way, but humans can adjust rather quickly.

Sometimes, you run into a hard-to-read or ambiguous CAPTCHA. If you're having trouble reading the CAPTCHA, Twitter uses the popular reCAPTCHA tool, which can easily generate another CAPTCHA for you. Just click the refresh arrows icon above the sound and question icons to get another CAPTCHA. There is an audio version of the CAPTCHA on Twitter, but it doesn't seem to work well.

If you can't read a CAPTCHA after a few tries, you may be a computer. If you think that you may, in fact, be nonhuman, please consult your doctor or trusted medical professional.

Picking a Username

On Twitter, your username is your identity. Laura's Twitter name, or *handle,* is @Pistachio (her business name at the time she joined), and it has become the way that many people know her. She's met tens of thousands of people in real life after initially connecting with them through Twitter, and it's not unusual for her to hear "Hey, Pistachio!" from across the street or across the room at a party. @Pistachio has, in effect, become her nickname. If you want a quick glimpse at the search engine optimization (SEO) value of Twitter, just run a Google search for the word *pistachio,* and you'll find that her Twitter account is one of the very first search results. Crazy.

That story emphasizes that you should think about how you want to be perceived both on and off Twitter and how your username fits into that perception. Twitter is a far-reaching service, and if you get really involved in the culture of Twitter, it undoubtedly spills over into real life, like the rest of the social web. The days of choosing anonymous handles such as sexybabe44 for instant messaging programs or chat rooms are long gone.

When we refer to Twitter usernames in this book, we follow the convention of putting an at sign (@) before the name because that's how you refer to other users on Twitter. (If you want to tweet that you're reading Laura's book, for example, you might say, "Reading @Pistachio's book." That way, people who follow you on Twitter can easily click over to Laura's Twitter profile in case they want to follow her, too!) But when you're actually choosing a username, the @ isn't part of it. The only characters you can use are uppercase and lower-case letters, numbers, and the underscore character (_).

If you can sign up for Twitter by using your full name or a variation of it as your username (assuming that somebody else isn't already using it), we recommend doing so. It makes your experience with Twitter much easier when the line between online and offline blurs.

If your name is John Ira, you may want to pick a Twitter username such as @johnira, @jira, or @john. If users have already claimed those monikers, Twitter recommends a variation of the username you were interested in. You could also add an adjective or descriptor, such as @bostonjohn or @johnthepainter. If you prefer that people not know who you are, you can choose a name that's a bit more generic. You can use a handle that you've established on other websites. You may also want your username to match your email address. If your email address is doglover1980@example.com, you may decide to use @doglover1980 as your Twitter name.

Using Twitter for your business? You can use your company or business name as your username, and you can fill in that business name in the Name field on the Settings screen for your account. If you do, you may want to include the name of anyone who handles the company Twitter account in the 160-character Bio field on the Settings screen for your Twitter profile. (We cover how to customize your profile in the "Customizing Your Profile" section, later in this chapter.)

If you're looking to be a bit more removed and really prefer to use a nickname rather than your actual name, your company, or your product name, choose a username that's friendly and accessible to the people you want to interact with. On Twitter, you want people to respond to you, not to be put off by a risqué or otherwise questionable handle. (If you want to be risqué, go for it, but understand that you'll limit the other users who will be willing to interact with you.) Likewise, if you run into your Twitter pals at networking events or other real-life social situations, you want to make sure that you don't mind having your username written on your name tag or shouted out in greeting.

Why @Pistachio?

Believe it or not, people constantly ask where the username @Pistachio came from, so here goes. Laura's first office was painted an unfortunate green color — that precise, indescribably ugly shade of her grandma's favorite ice cream on summer nights at Friendly's restaurant by the rotary (or roundabout, if you're not from the northeastern United States) in Gloucester, Massachusetts. Laura first adopted the color as a company name in 1997, and over the years, it has become part of her identity. Thus, she now is @Pistachio.

Lean toward using a short Twitter username. Tweets are only 140 characters, so when people are replying to you, if you have a longer name, you leave them less room for message content. Twitter limits your username to just 15 characters for this very reason. (For more on how to reply to another person on Twitter, turn to Chapter 5.)

Your Twitter name has power and influence in *search engine optimization* (SEO), which affects how close to the top of a search results list you appear in a search engine such as Google or Bing. A business should consider using the name of the company as its Twitter name so people searching can find it.

Finding Contacts

When you sign up for Twitter, you're prompted to check whether your friends are also on Twitter (see Figure 2-7) on the Find Friends screen. Finding contacts on Twitter can be a lot of fun! The easiest way to find your friends is to import your friends and contacts from other services that you already use (such as Gmail, Yahoo! Mail, Hotmail, and AOL). You may be pleasantly surprised by how many people you know are already busy tweeting away.

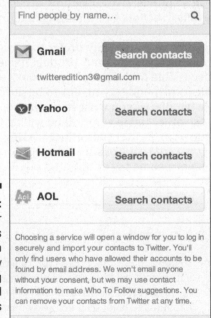

Figure 2-7:
See whether your friends are on Twitter by importing your email address book.

To import contacts and make them part of your Twitter world during the registration process, follow these steps:

1. **Select the email account type from which you want to import on the left side of the Find Friends screen.**

2. **Click the Search Contacts button.**

3. **Type your email credentials in the Username or Email and Password fields.**

   Twitter looks at your contact list from your email account and gives you a list of all the people from your address book who are already on Twitter.

   Having Twitter automatically find your contacts involves entering your email account password. Although Twitter has established itself as a trustworthy service, in general, be very cautious about sites that ask you for your email address and password.

4. **Select the people you want to follow.**

   If you click the Follow #Selected button, everyone in your address book will be automatically followed for you. If you want to follow only some of the people in your address book, simply clear the check boxes of the people you prefer not to follow.

   When you follow people on Twitter, you see their updates on your Twitter home screen.

5. **Repeat these steps for all your other email networks, if you have them.**

6. **Invite friends, family, and co-workers to join Twitter.**

   Alternatively, if you didn't find all the people in your address book that you want to follow, you can invite them by using the Invite Friends via Email field below the address-book prompts. (For more on inviting people to join Twitter, see "Inviting Contacts," later in this chapter.)

If you're inviting multiple friends to join Twitter, remember to separate email addresses with commas to help Twitter identify each of the email addresses as individual units.

If you skip inviting friends and family to join Twitter during the registration process, you can always go back and do this later. Just search for people by first name, last name, or email address by clicking the #Discover tab at the top of any Twitter screen.

Using useful people-finding tools

Jumping into random conversations is a great way to find like-minded Twitter users, but it's not the only way. You can use a few tools to discover people on Twitter who share your interests or live near you.

One of the more interesting tools out there, TwitterLocal (`http://twitterlocal.net`), helps you find Twitter users by geographic location. It's a great way for people who are interested in real-life meetups, as well as those in localized industries (such as real estate and car sales) who use Twitter to drum up business, to contact one another.

Twellow (`www.twellow.com`) is another handy tool for widening the scope of your Twitter universe (which, yes, some call a *Twitterverse*). Twellow sorts Twitter users by categories based on keywords in the Bio sections of their profiles. Users can also claim Twellow profiles for any Twitter usernames that belong to them by proving who they are. Claiming lets you edit the entry to add categories or remove incorrect categories. Twellow is searchable by name, location, or category, similar to an online yellow pages for Twitter (hence, the name *Twellow*).

We talk more about third-party tools and applications in Chapter 8.

Searching by using Twitter Search

Twitter also has its own search engine, known as Twitter Search, which you can access by typing in the search field at the top of any Twitter screen or by going to `https://twitter.com/search-home`. You can enter any keyword of your choice in the Twitter Search field, and Twitter not only brings you results in chronological order (with the most recent at the top), but also lets you know when people have made new Tweets that match your search criteria and gives you the option to refresh the search results.

You can use Twitter Search to find new people on Twitter by typing keywords connected to your interests or profession in the field. Bonus: Because Twitter Search sorts results based on how recent they are, the people you discover through this search are likely to be very active Twitter users.

Twitter Search was originally built by another web startup called Summize, which earned special access to Twitter's application program interface (API) to create a search engine for the microsharing service. Although Twitter acquired Summize and long ago renamed it Twitter Search, the Summize name was used casually for several years before dying out.

Making sure you don't follow too many people

Be cautious when following new people. You can easily get excited and start following a ton of random people, but this approach has some potentially negative consequences. It takes time and genuine interaction to build relationships on Twitter, so many of the people you follow initially (who don't personally know you) may not opt to follow you back immediately. As a result, you may find that you're following many more people than are following you, and your follower/following ratio is skewed heavily to the following side.

Twitter has a rigid follow limit: Every account can follow no more than 1,000 users per day or 2,000 total. If you follow 2,000 people in two days, you reach a cap based on your current following/follower ratio. The only way to lift that cap is to wait for your following/follower ratio to even out. In other words, you'll need to gain more followers.

An account that's following 500 people with only 1 or 2 people following it back always looks like a spam account — and you don't want people to think that you're a spammer. Take a relaxed approach, following a few people at a time, talking to them, and giving them time to follow you back before increasing your follower circle. Over time, your numbers swell on their own just because you're building a network and interacting with it.

Twitter users are often interested in meeting and talking with new people, and want to hear fresh voices. If you talk about your passions, interact with people in and out of your network, and are genuine, you'll have no trouble finding people to follow and getting them to follow you back.

If you have a blog or website, use it to introduce yourself to people you follow or who may want to follow you, and link to that page in your Twitter bio so that it welcomes curious new people. Companies that tweet should include Follow Me buttons on their websites or blogs so that it's clear that their accounts are authentic.

Inviting Contacts

During the registration process, after you import your contacts from your email address book, you have the option to invite any of your contacts who aren't yet using Twitter.

The process is really simple:

1. **On the Find Friends screen (refer to Figure 2-7), paste or type the email addresses of all the people you'd like to follow, separated by commas.**

2. **Click the gray Invite Friends button.**

   An invitation to join Twitter is sent to the people you selected, letting them know that you're on Twitter and that they can follow your updates by signing up for Twitter themselves. (If you're concerned, Twitter allows you to preview that email if you click the See What You'll Send Them link below the Invite Friends to Twitter via Email field.)

If you haven't found friends whom you know are on Twitter via email, you can search for them by hand by using the #Discover tab. Follow these steps:

1. **On the top navigation bar of any Twitter screen, click the #Discover tab.**

   The tabbed navigation loads below the navigation bar.

2. **Click Who to Follow.**

   A list of Twitter accounts appears, with a search bar at the top of the list.

3. **Enter the name or username of the person or company you're looking for.**

   If you're looking for co-author Brittany, you might just try searching for *Brittany Leaning* or *@bleaning*. Just start typing in the Search Using a Person's Full Name or @Username search field and then click the gray Search Twitter button.

You can also search for people outside the #Discover tab by using the search bar at the top of your Twitter account. The quick way to search for a person you know is on Twitter is to type the person's name or username in the top search bar, as shown in Figure 2-8.

Figure 2-8: Find people to follow by searching for them.

If you don't opt to invite people during the registration process, or if you want to invite people down the road, you can always email people you know whom you think would most enjoy or benefit from Twitter, sending them a link to your Twitter profile and writing a note explaining what Twitter is. You might also consider sharing the link to your new Twitter profile on other social networking sites, such as Facebook and LinkedIn. Many people choose this approach when they first join Twitter so that they can keep the invitation process personal.

It's become commonplace for many Twitter users to put Twitter handles on business cards, blog posts, presentation slide decks, and in email signature lines. These actions are indirect invitations for the people who meet us in real life or interact with us in business to connect with us on Twitter as well. The more people who join you on Twitter, the more effective your network becomes.

Getting Comfortable: Just Tweet It!

> _Tis my first twitt-er. Or tweet? Twit? Or tweet? "Twit or tweet everybody." Is this anything?_
>
> — _Ellen DeGeneres' first Tweet via Twitter, March 10, 2009_
> _(https://twitter.com/TheEllenShow/_
> _statuses/1306777707)_

If you click the Me tab on Twitter's top navigation bar, you see your Twitter profile with a Choose Your First Tweet prompt. In this section, Twitter suggests a couple of ideas for your very first Tweet: "Hello Twitter! #myfirstTweet" and "Just setting up my Twitter. #myfirstTweet." Using the hashtag #myfirstTweet helps other users find and engage with you.

You also have the option below these suggestions to write your own Tweet from scratch. If you'd like to see what other people's first Tweets were, you can go to https://discover.twitter.com/first-tweet and type any person's Twitter handle to see his very first thought posted to Twitter.

The entire premise of Twitter used to be framed literally as answering the question "What's happening?" in 140 characters or less. So go ahead! Tell Twitter what's happening around you right now. Type a message in the Compose New Tweet field on the left side of your home screen or in the field below your Me tab, keeping under the 140-character limit. When you're done, click the Tweet button. Congratulations! You've just made your #FirstTweet.

You may be thinking, "Wait — that's it?" That's right: That's it. Tweeting is that simple. Though your first Tweet was probably something mundane (such as "Trying out this Twitter thing" or "Hello there, Twitter. I'm reading _Twitter For Dummies!_"), you start to add more of your personality and information to your Tweets as you get the hang of it.

As you add more and more Tweets, people begin to see what's going on in your life and what you're thinking about. Twitterers following you or searching for keywords in Twitter in all likelihood start talking to you about what you're doing. The conversation starts with those simple exchanges. Talk about your favorite band's new album, your mechanic and how she fixed your car's catalytic converter, or really anything at all. If you've already found your contacts on Twitter, they probably will respond to you pretty quickly. If you don't have any followers yet, don't worry; they'll come.

We discuss suggested Twitter etiquette, culture, language, and all that stuff in Chapter 7. This chapter simply tells you how to get your Twitter profile up and running so that it reflects who you are and what you want to get out of Twitter.

Your Tweets, right now, are publicly visible and searchable even if you delete them immediately after clicking the Tweet button. This situation isn't life or death, but be careful. If your updates are unprotected, what you tweet ends up in Twitter Search and in search engines, sometimes even if you delete it almost immediately. (Chapter 8 discusses search tools in depth; Chapter 10 explains how to protect your Tweets.)

Customizing Your Profile

Your public page on Twitter, also known as your *profile,* gives other Twitter users their first impression of you, and it can make a big difference in whether they decide to follow you. Take a few minutes to dress it up a little! Making sure that it reflects you or your business makes all the difference when it comes to whether people will follow you to see what you have to say.

After you sign up for Twitter, one of the first things you should do is personalize your profile. Make sure that you have

- ✔ A profile photo (a picture that shows up to the left of your Tweets, representing you or your company)
- ✔ A header photo (a picture that people see when they view your profile directly or when they see you in their followers/following lists)
- ✔ A background image or background color for your home screen
- ✔ A bio that's 160 characters or fewer
- ✔ A link to anything else you want to share

Some of the best profile pages on Twitter are the ones that give you a look at that user's personality. Someone who loves to ski might upload an image of his favorite mountain range as the profile background and pair it with a profile photo that depicts him in ski goggles. You don't have to bare your soul, but people on Twitter want to know something about you, and the public page is where they can first discover it.

After you log in to Twitter, you can customize your profile at any time by clicking Settings in the top-right navigation bar.

Changing your profile photo

Your profile photo is displayed to the left of all your Tweets, so it's your official face on Twitter. Some Twitter users change their profile photos regularly to post different photos of themselves, some users leave their photos the same all the time, and still others change their photos according to a specific occasion (holiday-themed for Christmas or Halloween, for example). Your profile photo is your face, some other picture, or the default egg icon. It's your choice.

People don't like following you back if your profile photo is just the default egg icon. Show your smiling face, and set others at ease!

To change your profile photo, follow these steps:

1. **Sign in to Twitter, and click the Me tab on the menu bar.**

2. **Click the gray Edit Profile button on the right side of the header section of your profile (see Figure 2-9).**

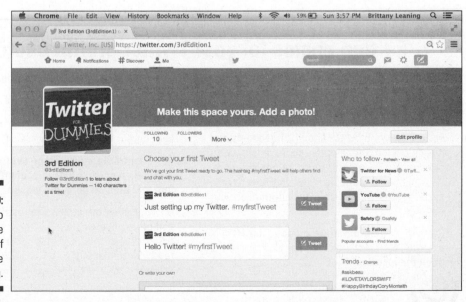

Figure 2-9: Show who you are instead of using the default egg.

3. **Click the square Change Your Profile Photo icon.**

4. **Click the Upload Photo button. If you'd prefer to take a photo instead, click the Take a Photo button.**

5. **Once you've selected a file from your computer, click Open.**

   Your photo appears in the center of the screen.

6. **Use the slider to adjust the size of your photo.**

7. **Click the Apply button when you finish adjusting your photo.**

   Your picture is uploaded to Twitter.

Currently, Twitter supports the .jpg, .gif, and .png file formats but not animated .gifs.

The size of your profile image is restricted to 700KB (which is a rather large image), and Twitter crops it automatically into a square for your public profile. Choose an image that's square or close to square, or make sure that the part of the image you want featured in your profile photo's thumbnail version is in the center of the image.

Try to find or crop a picture that's at least 73 x 73 pixels — the correctly optimized size that Twitter suggests for profile images.

If you upload a photo and it doesn't look quite right, don't panic! Just find a new picture (or adjust the original file) and try uploading it again. You can upload a new picture at any time.

Editing photos for your Twitter profile photo

Many of the photos that you want to use for your Twitter avatar may include other people whom you want to crop out, or the picture composition just may not allow you to get a good head shot. Fortunately, both Macs and PCs have tools that let you put together a profile photo quickly without needing third-party photo-editing software. As a bonus, these tools show you how to take *screen shots* (pictures of what appears on your screen).

Start by finding a picture on your hard drive, the web, your cellphone, or digital camera, and open the picture.

If you use Mac OS X, follow these steps:

1. **With the picture file open and visible on the screen, press ⌘+Shift+4.**

   Your cursor changes into a crosshair.

2. **Click and drag your cursor over the area that you want to include in your profile picture and then let go of the mouse.**

   On your desktop, a new file (usually titled something like Screen Shot 2014-05-11 at 10.21.18 PM) appears, ready for uploading.

On a Windows computer, follow these steps:

1. **With the picture file open and visible on the screen, press the Print Screen button on your keyboard.**

   This button may be labeled PRNTSCR or a similar abbreviation.

2. **Press Windows+R.**

   The Run dialog box appears.

3. **Type** mspaint **at the prompt, and click OK.**

   MSPaint opens.

4. **Press Ctrl+V.**

   A screen shot is pasted into MSPaint. By default, the Move tool is selected.

5. **Drag the screen shot up and to the left to mark the top-left corner of the picture you want to use as your profile photo.**

6. **Click outside the selection rectangle to deselect the screen shot.**

7. **Scroll to the bottom-right corner of the image.**

   A small dark blue box appears directly outside the bottom-right corner of the image.

8. **Click and drag that tiny blue box up and to the left.**

   Stop where you want to mark the bottom-right corner of the image.

9. **Choose File⇨Save As.**

   The Save As dialog box appears.

10. **Save the file as a** .jpg, .gif, **or** .png, **give it an appropriate name (such as** twitterprofilephoto**), and save it in a place where you can find it later.**

    You're ready to go!

Changing your header photo

Your *header photo* is the large image displayed on the top of your Twitter profile. This large image welcomes people to your personal profile and illustrates a bit more about you that maybe you couldn't fit into your 160-character bio. Many people use this space to showcase a picture of a place or cause they identify with, an extracurricular activity they enjoy, or something else that demonstrates what they're passionate about.

To change your header photo, follow these steps:

1. **Sign in to Twitter, and click the Me tab on the menu bar.**

2. **Click the gray Edit Profile button on the right side of the header section of your profile.**

3. **Click the camera icon in the center of the screen (see Figure 2-10).**

Figure 2-10:
Show your
followers
what you're
all about.

4. **Click the Upload Photo button.**

5. **Once you've selected a file from your computer, click Open.**

   Your photo appears in the header area of your screen.

6. **Use the slider to adjust the size of your photo.**

7. **Click the Apply button when you finish adjusting your photo.**

   You should see a prompt saying that your header photo was success-fully uploaded to Twitter.

Twitter's recommended dimensions for your header photo is 1500 x 500 pixels. If you size your image to these dimensions before uploading it to Twitter, you get the desired fit without any trial and error.

Using your header image to expand your profile

Because Twitter's user profiles are so limited, some avid Twitter users take advantage of the header image to add more information or personal links than Twitter allows for in its short bio section. In many cases, a Twitter user includes a short professional biography, accompanied by more links and ways to connect with that user. This idea is a great way to let people know where else they can find you.

To customize your header image, you need to use a custom template application or create your own template from scratch by using a program such as Adobe Photoshop or a free image editor such as Canva (www.canva.com). You can also use Microsoft PowerPoint.

Changing your personal background

In addition to changing your avatar, you can change the background of your home screen from the default to another color or pattern. You can even upload an image of your choice (or do both). You can *tile* an image (make it repeat, like tiles on a floor), make an image large enough to cover the entire background, or choose a smaller image that doesn't cover the entire background and leaves a solid color behind it. Think of your home-screen background as the background that covers the desktop on your computer; it's a nice way to customize your space, but only you will really see it.

To change your background, follow these steps:

1. **Sign in to Twitter, and click the Settings icon on the top-right menu bar.**

2. **Choose Settings from the drop-down menu.**

   The Settings screen opens.

3. **Select the Design tab.**

4. **Select a premade background, or use your own image or pattern.**

   The premade Twitter backgrounds appear in square thumbnail images inside the Design tab.

   If you don't want a standard Twitter look and want to use a background image or pattern from your computer, click the gray Change Background button below the pattern images. Choose the option titled Choose Existing Image from the drop-down menu, and browse through the images on your computer.

5. **(Optional) If you want your image to tile, select the Tile Background check box.**

6. **Select the side that you'd like your image to align on: Left, Center, or Right.**

7. **If you want to change only your image, click Save.**

8. **(Optional) To customize your text and links, click the Background and Theme color fields.**

   You may want to make your Twitter page match the color scheme of your blog or website. If you can access the hexadecimal codes on your blog's color scheme, you can enter those same hexadecimal codes in the appropriate fields. When you finish, click Save Changes to update your colors. If you mess up before you save your changes, you can always click Cancel or navigate away to retain your current color settings.

Hexadecimal codes are the six-digit codes used in website design to assign colors; each combination of numbers and letters corresponds to a different shade. The code 000000 is black, for example, and FFFFFF is white. Plenty of places on the web offer easy-to-understand guides to hexadecimal color codes. Check out Adobe's Kuler (`https://kuler.adobe.com`) if you're looking for a nice color palette.

9. **Select a black or white transparent overlay.**

10. **When you're happy with your color scheme, click Save Changes.**

If you're using Twitter for business purposes, use your theme colors to reflect your company's identity, matching the identity you've selected for your profile and header images.

If the default themes or images don't appeal to you, or if you're looking for something simpler or more casual, you can find free background images at a site such as COLOURlovers (`www.colourlovers.com/themeleon/twitter`). COLOURlovers offers a variety of pattern graphics and color schemes, all of which are sized specifically to fit Twitter profiles. If you're feeling adventurous, you can hunt online for interesting background images on your own and upload them yourself. Just make sure that they're the right shape and size.

Your background image is almost always overlaid with your Twitter stream, so you usually won't be able to see the middle of the image. Your screen width dictates how much of your background you actually see.

Chapter 3

A Tour of the Twitter Interface

In This Chapter

▶ Reading the feed on your Twitter home screen

▶ Making a Twitter conversation personal by using @replies and direct messages

▶ Marking your Twitter favorites

▶ Viewing who you're following and who's following you

▶ Reviewing your past Twitter updates

*F*or the power it wields, Twitter is one of the simplest and, we think, most elegant websites for mass communication. The interface makes interacting with other people — some you already know and others you'll meet — incredibly easy, and it cleanly organizes a lot of information.

As you use Twitter more and more, you may want to know where to locate things quickly and how to manage your communication flow more intelligently. In this chapter, we dive into each Twitter screen, showing how it relates to the conversations going on around you and the conversations you're having directly.

Navigating Your Home Screen

When you first log in to Twitter, the home screen is your first stop. After you set up your account, you go to this screen to touch base with your followers and the people you're following. On the home screen, you also see tabs and icons in the navigation bar: Home, Notifications, Discover, Me, Direct Messages, Settings, and Compose New Tweet. (We talk about using these tabs and features later in this chapter.)

Additionally, the Settings and Help tab along the top of the home screen lets you change your settings, update your profile, upload your avatar and more. Chapter 2 covers most of these setup features, so flip back if you'd like to learn more about this tab specifically.

The home screen, shown in Figure 3-1, has a standard layout. The header has a navigation bar of links that appears on all Twitter screens. Those links' names and icons describe where they take you.

Figure 3-1: The Twitter home screen, where you'll spend a lot of time.

The areas on the left and right side of most Twitter.com streams (your profile snapshot, Trends, Who to Follow) is called the *sidebar*. It's both a reference for the main content area and a controller for the website, and it's configured a little differently in each view.

Twitter is a living web application. Its interface changes from time to time, so if you can't find something immediately, it's likely taken on a different name or moved to a different location in the interface. For up-to-date information about what's going on with Twitter, visit the company's blog (`https://blog.twitter.com`).

Your profile snapshot

Now that you've had the tour of the Home screen, let's head over to your personalized, public-facing profile. This is where you showcase who you are, what you're interested in, and why someone should follow you.

✔ **Your information:** When you're logged in to Twitter and viewing your home screen, you see only a profile snapshot — not your whole profile. The first things you see in your profile snapshot are your profile picture, header image, name, and username. Other information included in your full profile — such as your location, website URL, and bio — appears only on your profile page, on the Me tab. You can click your profile picture (also known as an *avatar*), the Me tab, or any username link for your name to see your profile page.

✔ **Your stats:** Below your basic information are the total number of Tweets you've posted since signing up for Twitter, the number of people you're following, and the number of people who are following you. These numbers could quickly tell someone how active a user is on Twitter, whether they're influential or worth following, and whether they might be willing to follow you back. @ConanOBrien, for example, has 11 million followers, but follows only 1 person in return. With that ratio, chances are good that if you follow him on Twitter, he won't follow you back.

Tweet interface

If you continually use Twitter's web interface to post updates, you'll become very well acquainted with it. Directly atop the left column, below your profile snapshot, you find a text field in which you can post your latest update (or Tweet). The text in the field says Compose New Tweet. You can expand the field by clicking it. When the field is expanded, you see a camera icon, a pin icon, the number 140, and a Tweet button. The camera icon allows you to attach a photo to your Tweet. The pin icon lets you include a location in your Tweet so other users know where you're tweeting from. The number shows you how many characters you have left in your message. When you finish composing your Tweet, you can click the Tweet button to send it immediately.

While you type your message, the 140 number decreases, letting you know how many more characters you can type before you go over the limit. When you get to 20 characters remaining, the number turns burgundy, and when you get to 10 characters remaining, the number turns red. If you go over 140 characters, the number starts counting into the negatives. If you can't click the Tweet button, you've likely gone over the limit, so be succinct!

As soon as you type a new Tweet and click the Tweet button, your Tweet appears in the area directly to the right of the Compose New Tweet field. This area is your main Twitter stream, showing Tweets by the people you follow (including yourself).

If you included a long URL in your last Tweet, you may notice that it was shortened, with an ellipsis (. . .) at the end. You can click the ellipsis-shortened URL to go to the web address you intended. Additionally, the time stamp saying how long ago you posted that update in fact contains that update's *permalink* (a URL that points to a specific web page). Click that link, and a page dedicated to that Tweet — and that Tweet alone — opens. Cool, huh?

Permalinks are a big part of what makes conversations on Twitter different. Unlike instant messages or chat rooms, Twitter makes it possible to bookmark, link to, reply to, and archive every single Tweet. Right now, you can go online and view famous Tweets that represent historical turning points for Twitter, such as @jamesbuck's "Arrested" at `https://twitter.com/jamesbuck/statuses/786571964` or @jkrums's "There's a plane in the Hudson . . ." at `https://twitter.com/jkrums/status/1121915133`, both of which permanently changed the world's understanding of what Twitter means for media, liberty, and human rights.

Trends

You can see what the rest of the world is tweeting about on Twitter's Search page and in the new Trends part of the home screen. If a new movie is coming out, the World Series is on TV, or a major news event is happening somewhere in the world, you're likely to see it as a Trending Topic.

- ✔ **Trends:** This field contains Trending Topics, the most commonly tweeted words and hashtags at any given time. The Trends view is a surprisingly powerful peek at what's going on in the world (at least, the world according to Twitter users) at any given moment.

  You can customize this field to feature tailored trends, which are trends based on topics you tweet about and people you follow, or you can set it to a specific city or country, or even worldwide. To change your Trends settings, click the Change link in the top-right corner and then select or type your location. If you prefer tailored trends, click Change and then click the Get Tailored Trends button in the bottom-left corner.

- ✔ **World Cup 2014:** This was a temporary section that Twitter installed due to extraordinarily heavy interest in World Cup news, schedules, scores, and more during the 2014 tournament. It let fans view Tweets about specific upcoming matches or view all Tweets to the #WorldCup hashtag in general.

Who to follow

As you're setting up your profile, it's important to start following the people who share your specific interests. This field helps you identify people you may know or may be interested in following, based on connections you've already made or topics you've already tweeted about.

To navigate this section, simply click the Follow button if you'd like to follow one of the suggested users listed. If you prefer not to follow any of the users listed, click the X button to the right of the user's Twitter handle, and a new suggested user pops up. The nice thing about this feature is that it displays who in your network is currently following said user, so you can get a more complete picture and connect some networking dots. If you want to see more than just three suggested users at a time, click the View All link in the top-right corner of the field to display an extended list of suggested users that includes each person's Twitter bio. This feature helps you gain more context about users before you decide to follow them.

You can also find more people you know by importing your contacts from Gmail or other email accounts (see Chapter 2).

Your Twitter stream

All the action on Twitter, appropriately, lives front and center on your screen. Officially called Tweets, this stream of Twitter updates contains your Tweets and the Tweets of those you follow in a (mostly) chronological order, with the most recent Tweets at the top. The exception to the chronological rule is when someone retweets a Tweet (see "Retweets" later in this chapter).

The Tweets section of your home screen goes by several names, including *stream, timeline,* and *feed.* Some people who follow thousands of Twitter users call it a *river.* The Tweet stream flows faster the more people you add to your list of friends and the more people you follow.

The stream "flows" only when you refresh your web browser or click the gray View *X* New Tweets bar at the top of your stream; it doesn't automatically display new Tweets. Words such as *stream* and *flow* most likely derive from the dynamic moving displays of many third-party Twitter clients.

This area is where the conversations happen; it's your home base for connecting with people and businesses on Twitter. By reading your stream, you can find new people to listen to (friends of your friends and connections) and can also jump in and participate.

Each Tweet appears in its own little field. If you hover your cursor over the field, arrow, continuous arrow, and star icons pop up on the right side of the Tweet. If the Tweet is yours, you also see a trash-can icon; not surprisingly, clicking it lets you delete the Tweet from the feed. We discuss what these icons mean in the next section of this chapter.

Viewing Your Notifications Tab

See who's interacting with you directly through *@replies* and *@mentions* (Tweets in response to or generally mentioning individual users), *favorites* (ways to positively acknowledge or bookmark Tweets), and *retweets* (sharing content that has already been posted by another Twitter user).

Favorites

Clicking the star icon, or Favorites button, adds that Tweet to your Favorites list (which you can get to by clicking Favorites on your Me tab). When you mark something as a favorite, you make it easier for yourself to find that Tweet in the future. The Favorites button also acts as Twitter's version of a Like button, which you may know from social networks such as Facebook and LinkedIn. We discuss different uses of favorites in "Revisiting Your Favorite Tweets" later in this chapter.

Retweets

You can forward the Tweet you're reading to your Twitter followers by clicking the continuous-arrow icon, also known as the Retweet button. Your followers see that Tweet as coming from the user who first posted it, along with a note along the top of the Tweet mentioning that the retweet came from you. (If the Tweet was by a user who protects her updates, this feature is unavailable. You have to retweet the old-fashioned way, described in Chapter 5.)

@replies and @mentions

The little arrow icon that appears when you hover your mouse over a Tweet on the home screen is the force behind one of Twitter's most powerful conversational features: @replies. Taking its format from a syntax used in chat rooms, @replies is a Tweet that, although public and visible to all Twitter users, is directed specifically to one Twitter user. Twitter has ramped it up by automatically detecting when an @ symbol is placed directly in front of a word (with no space in between) and adds a link to the Twitter user who uses that word as his handle. More than just ways to direct a Tweet to one person, @replies can help you find new people to add to your network when you see one of your contacts conversing with someone you don't know and decide to check that person out.

For every publicly viewable Tweet that includes a user's handle, that user can view those Tweets in the @replies link. So any time your @username appears in a Tweet, it gets collected here. Some heavy users don't like this setup because it can get cluttered fast if you're lucky enough to get mentioned a lot. Even though the screen is now technically considered the Notifications tab, most Twitter users still call these sections of Twitter.com @replies or @mentions.

If you hover your cursor over a Tweet that you want to respond to, the arrow icon and Tweet menu bar appear; click the arrow icon to reply to that Tweet. Once you've clicked, you'll see a Tweet field pop up with the username of the person you're replying to. See the Tweet button on the bottom right side of the field? That's the button you'll need to click in order to publicly share your reply. If you reply instead of composing an entirely new message, Twitter then associates your reply with the original Tweet. The person can see what Tweet prompted your reply by clicking the Details link at the bottom of your tweet to him. This Details link will take you directly to the Tweet's permalink (mentioned earlier in this Chapter).

Here are some tips on making the most of your Notifications tab (see Figure 3-2):

✔ **Send @replies any time.** You can send an @reply to someone by just typing the @ symbol and, without a space, her username (for example, @bleaning). Then type your message and click Tweet. (See Chapter 5 for more on replying.)

If you make your reply manually (as opposed to clicking the Reply button of a specific Tweet that you want to reply to), your reply won't be linked to any particular Tweet. @replies actually do initiate a conversation as much as they act as actual replies. But if you really want to reply to a specific Tweet, you're usually better off clicking the Reply button.

Figure 3-2:
The Notifications tab, where you can join the conversation.

> ✔ **Join a conversation.** If you see that one friend or colleague on Twitter has responded to someone in her network who wants to know where to get the best pizza in Boston, and you have a recommendation, you can share it. You just have to click the Twitter handle that your friend is @replying to and throw in your two cents' worth. By starting conversations with friends of your friends, you bring new people into your own stream.

Keep in mind that @replies are public tweets. Other people can always read your @replies, and they'll be stored by search engines. If you have something private that you need to tell someone, use another feature of Twitter: the direct message (see the next section).

In Twitter's early days, any time you sent an @reply to someone, all your followers would see that reply in their Tweet streams. Some time ago, Twitter adjusted the way that @replies work. Suppose that you're following Bill and Christy, but Christy isn't following Bill. If you send an @reply to Bill, that reply won't show up in Christy's feed. If Christy did follow Bill, however, she would see that reply in her stream. Twitter is set up this way to prevent disjointed conversations and so that some of the most frequently @replying Twitter users don't flood their followers' feeds.

Direct Messages

Direct messages (DMs) let you send your contacts private notes through Twitter. Just like regular Tweets and @replies, they're limited to 140 characters. Unlike with regular Tweets and @replies, the only person who can see a DM is the recipient.

You can send a DM only to a Twitter user who's following you (but you don't have to be following that user), a setup that's designed to prevent spamming and other unwanted messages by ensuring that people get DMs only from people they want to follow.

The easiest way to see whether someone is following you, and to send them a DM while you're there, is to go to that person's profile page. You can get to the profile page by clicking that person's username anywhere you see it or by typing `https://twitter.com/username` in your web browser's address bar. If you see Follows You next to the person's username, you're free to DM that person. To double-check, click the gear icon next to the Follow button while you're viewing the user's profile. If you see Send a Direct Message listed on the drop-down menu, you're free to click it and start typing away.

If you want to see all your private interactions (both sent and received DMs), click the little envelope icon on the top-right side of the main navigation bar. A screen pops up, displaying your Twitter "inbox" full (or not so full) of DMs (see Figure 3-3). To see all interactions with an individual user, click the gray field that surrounds her message. If you click the user's name or avatar, you see a snapshot of the user's profile instead of the message thread. Once you've clicked into a conversation with someone, you'll see a field to send a direct message. Just start typing as you would in the Compose New Tweet field, and click Send Message when you are ready to send your private message.

Figure 3-3: The Direct Messages panel lets you have private Twitter conversations.

Sending DMs is easy, but proceed with caution! Many Twitter users have embarrassing tales of DMs that they accidentally sent as public Tweets because they formatted the Tweets incorrectly or sent them from the Twitter home screen instead of from the users' profile pages (best bet) or the Direct Messages pages. Double-check just to be sure.

Touring Your Discover Tab

This tab helps you get a better view of what's happening in the world, based on your interests.

Tweets

This tab was once called Stories and focused on showcasing the most popular news articles. Today, the tab is called Discover and showcases the top

Tweets based on a particular user's interests and tailored trends. The majority of the accounts featured in this section are different from those you see in your home feed. The Discover tab aims to help you find new accounts that you're not following yet, rather than showing you Tweets from accounts you already follow.

Activity

On your home screen, you see a lot of Tweets, retweets, @replies, and @mentions. What you don't see are interactions such as favorites, follows, or list additions. If you're interested in seeing more of these interactions, you can find them in the Activity section. These actions often get unnoticed by the masses because they tend to be more intimate, one-on-one types of interactions.

Who to Follow

Guess what! The Who to Follow section under the Discover tab is exactly the same as the Who to Follow section you'll see in the sidebar on your home screen, which was mentioned earlier in this chapter. We're not trying to trick you; there are a couple of ways you can get to this section, and we want to show you every way possible.

Find Friends

Similar to the Who to Follow section, the Find Friends section, located under the Discover tab, can also be found through the sidebar on your home screen. See Chapter 2 to find out more about connecting Twitter with your email address book.

Popular Accounts

Do you love music? Are you a big sports fan? Are you picking up photography on the side? Twitter's got topic experts for those activities. If you click Popular Accounts on the Discover tab, you see a grid of suggested Twitter accounts, listed by topic or interest (see Figure 3-4). You only see each user's avatar, so click that avatar if you want to find out more about or follow a particular user.

Figure 3-4:
Discovering
popular
accounts.

Twitter Search

You may notice a search bar at the top of the screen labeled Search Using a Person's Full Name or Username. This search feature happens to be the same as the search feature in the top navigation bar, which you can also find at `https://twitter.com/search-home`. If you want to find a specific account, find out more about a particular hashtag, or see who's tweeting about a certain topic, you should try searching for it by using the search bar.

If you protect your Tweets, searching with Twitter Search doesn't work because the Tweets aren't indexed in the search engine. It's a small price to pay for privacy.

You can also search for specific Tweets by using Bing, Google, or another search engine. Bing and Google actually purchase data from `Twitter.com` and offer advanced search terms so that you can really focus the search. Additionally, Google's and Bing's search interfaces make it possible to see who is talking about your Tweets, in addition to the Tweets themselves.

Google and Bing do such a good job of indexing Twitter that search engines remain (at this writing) the best way to find out whether someone is on Twitter. At `Bing.com` or `Google.com`, run a search for *first name last name Twitter,* and usually, you can find out right away whether a person is a tweeter. Bear in mind that very famous people who appear to be tweeting may be fan pages or other hoaxes, though (unless @DarthVader actually does exist, in which case be very afraid!).

Your public tweets are indexed by search engines. You can delete your tweets on Twitter by clicking the trash-can icon, but if you don't do it within a few seconds, Bing and other search engines, as well as Twitter's own search tool, will already have indexed those tweets. Sometimes, tweets are forever. On one hand, indexing is good for your visibility online. Because Bing and other search engines index your tweets, those search engines can bring more people to your Twitter profile, which can possibly bring those people to your website.

Be cautious: If you're tweeting as yourself, we advise not saying anything on Twitter that you wouldn't want your mom, your boss, or your child to stumble across later while searching for something else. Also take great care with names, because Tweets about a person may show up closer to the top of search results than mentions of her name on other types of websites.

If you imagine that someone whose opinion you value is looking at what you write, you can avoid getting into any trouble. Twitter is so easy to use that it's equally easy to slip up, and because of its conversational nature, you can sometimes forget that it isn't a private room. One public-relations executive upset his client when he tweeted a snide remark about the client's city upon landing there for a meeting. Oops! Remember the context you're tweeting in; also remember that people may assume that you're talking about them when you're not. You may not be thinking today about what may be findable weeks, months, and years from now.

Checking Out Your Me Tab

Here's where you can find your personal profile page, which showcases much more than just your profile snapshot.

Your Tweets

You can see what you've tweeted in the past in a variety of ways, but the first place to check is your own profile. Click the Me tab on the navigation bar (or just click your avatar in your profile snapshot) to open your profile page. Your profile page, in addition to displaying your short bio and profile information, displays a feed of all your public Tweets in chronological order. Just like the screens showing your followers and who you follow (which you can read about in the preceding sections), older posts are listed at the bottom.

Your profile is a publicly accessible URL. If your username is @dummies, for example, you would navigate to https://twitter.com/dummies to jump to your profile page.

If you're looking for a specific Tweet, you can look for it by using Twitter's Search page: `https://twitter.com/search-home`. Do a search for your username. If it's a common name, you might want to include the @ symbol and a keyword from the Tweet. The Tweet you're looking for will most likely appear in the search results. Figure 3-5 shows a Twitter Search results page.

Figure 3-5:
Twitter
Search
results.

Photos/videos

If you ever decide to attach an image to your Tweet or share an animated GIF, you'll see all these Tweets in one particular tab of your profile page. All your Tweets (both media and text-based) show up in the Tweets tab of your profile, but these media files are also set apart on their own tab. That way, your more visually inclined followers can get a snapshot of what you'll be tweeting about without needing to read anything. We discuss photos and videos in much more detail in Chapter 9.

Seeing Who You Follow

After you start using Twitter to its full potential, you may want to see a list of who you follow. To find this section, click the Following tab in your profile, and you see a list of profile snapshots featuring users' avatars, header images, and bios (see Figure 3-6). You may find yourself digging through this tab if you're looking for a particular user or want to visualize the types of people you're following.

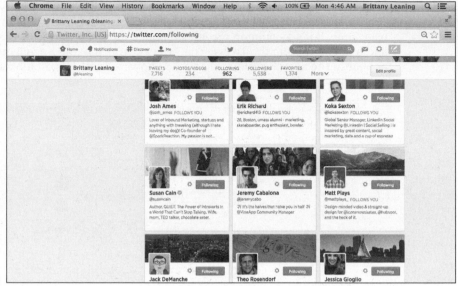

Figure 3-6:
Check
out all the
Twitter
users you're
following.

If you have a particular user in mind and aren't sure whether you're following her, go to that person's Twitter page. If you're following her, you see Following below her avatar. If you're not following her, you see a Follow button, which you can click to follow her.

After you follow more than 100 people, you probably want to use another method to figure out who you follow. You can find out who you follow in a few ways, using third-party applications built on Twitter's API, such as Wefollow and justunfollow (more details on these in the next section).

Figuring Out Who's Following You

You may want to see who's following you on Twitter. Maybe you want to find new people to follow, or you're just curious who's reading your Tweets. You can pull up the list of your followers on any Twitter page. Find the sets of numbers in your profile in the tab labeled Followers. Twitter sorts the list with the people who've started following you, the most recent at the top.

You have to scroll through the Followers list bit by bit. Chapter 17 suggests some tools, such as Wefollow (http://wefollow.com) and justunfollow (www.justunfollow.com), that can show you both who you're following and who's following you, which is considerably easier than scrolling through your followers in small increments.

Organizing with lists

Santa's not the only one who gets to check things twice these days. Twitter users also get to make lists of people. Being added to a list is kind of like being followed, in that a user has identified you as a person to follow. Instead of giving you a new follower, Twitter identifies you as *Listed* and adds that info to the Settings and Help tab or the More section of your profile.

Someone may have listed you for a few reasons. You may have gone to school with that person. You may have met the person at an event, and she thinks you have entertaining Tweets. Maybe you're just a stellar Twitter user and the person wants to recognize you for it. In any case, you must have done something right for someone to have listed you!

To see who's listed you (and what lists you've been put on), click the Lists tab below Settings and Help; then click Member Of. You see the title of the list, who created it, how many members it has, and the list creator's Twitter avatar (see the figure below).

What's particularly neat about this feature is that if you click the list name or visit https://twitter.com/dummies/authors, you'll see the stream of Tweets written by the people in that list.

Lists add a little bit of complexity and subtlety to the Twitter experience, and they can be powerful tools to help you manage your Twitter experience. We go into lists a bit more in Chapter 4.

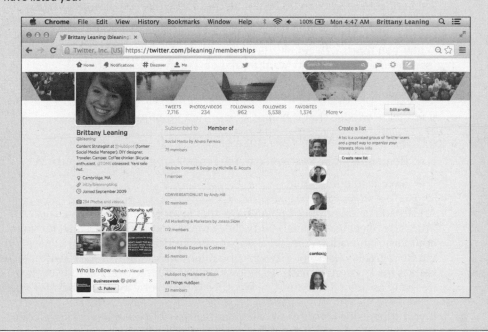

If you don't want to have to use a website to keep up with your followers, you have several options:

- **Turn on email notifications in the Settings area.** Click the Email Notifications tab. You see a section titled Email Me When. Select the check field titled I'm Followed by Someone New, and click Save Changes at the bottom of the screen. The email notification authorizes Twitter to send you an email alerting you about each new follower. Then you can just click a link in the email to that user's profile and see right away whether you want to follow that person back.

- **Try to send a user who may be following you a DM.** If he's following you, you're able to send that DM. If he's not following you, you get a User Does Not Follow You error message. Then you have to decide whether you want to try to get that user's attention in another way.

Revisiting Your Favorite Tweets

As mentioned earlier in this chapter, one of the icons that appear when you hover your mouse over a particular Tweet is the star icon, or Favorites button. This feature started as Twitter's equivalent of a bookmarking tool. When you mark a Tweet as a favorite, it appears on your Favorites screen (see Figure 3-7). You may want to mark a Tweet as a favorite to

- Save it for later.
- Acknowledge that it helped you or that you found it amusing.
- Mark it so that you can reply to it later.
- Remember it so that you can reference it in a blog post or article.
- Save it to quote later.

Ari Herzog (@ariherzog) pointed out that favorites are untapped opportunities to collect testimonials and other Tweets that may have value for your company. Innovation software company Brightidea (@Brightidea) uses it to curate a great collection of Tweets about innovation, drawing on Twitter search results for keywords related to innovation. Don't limit yourself to using favorites only as literal favorites. Use favorites whichever way works best for you!

If you start using favorites on a regular basis, you'll soon have a large collection of Tweets that you can gather data from for various projects or reference when you need to remember a particular joke or comment. You can also use it to bookmark links to visit later. Many of your best links and referrals will come from your fellow Twitter users.

TIP

One way to find more people on Twitter is to visit your friends' profile pages on Twitter and look at *their* favorites, to see which Tweets they liked most. If your best friend marked a particular Tweet as a favorite, and you're not yet following the person who posted that Tweet, you may want to start following that person.

Figure 3-7:
Your favorite Tweets are stored forever.

Searching favorite Tweets

At the time we're writing this book, Twitter doesn't offer a way to search your favorite Tweets and hasn't announced any plans to do so. While your list grows, you may want to find some way to catalog your Tweets. Some people use Microsoft Excel or Google Docs. Others keep a record of their favorite Tweets' permalinks (permanent URL) pages and tag them by topic, using bookmarking services such as Pocket (https://getpocket.com) and Evernote (https://evernote.com).

Indexing your favorite Tweets takes a bit of hacking:

1. **To get to a Tweet's permalink, find the Tweet in your Twitter stream, and click the small link below it that shows the time when the Tweet was sent.**

   That link loads the Tweet on its own page, which you can bookmark because that page has a standard URL that always leads to that Tweet.

2. **Add that URL to your favorite bookmarking service.**

   Follow your bookmarking service's directions for adding a URL.

3. **If the option is available, tag the link so that you can search by topic later to find it again.**

After you have a system in place for keeping track of Tweets that you want to save, you can find them whenever you need them.

Chapter 4

Using Twitter Wherever You Think Best

Twitter is a great tool for providing friends, family, and followers updates on what's going on in your life. But as you've probably noticed, life occurs in a lot of places, not just on the computer. Don't worry, though, because Twitter's got you covered. The folks at Twitter have designed their application so that you can use it in multiple ways and in multiple places.

Some Twitter users prefer not to access the service through a browser window, need a few more organizational options than the webpage affords, or just want to share Twitter on an external website or blog. If you want to get the most out of Twitter, you need to figure out how you prefer to access the service. Some people use the Twitter website, the Twitter mobile application, or any number of third-party services built with Twitter's application programming interface (API). You can use widgets, gadgets, browser plug-ins, and a huge array of other ways to interact with Twitter at your convenience and on your terms.

In this chapter, we go over all the ways that you may want to use Twitter, and we also give you some pointers for maximizing the application based on your needs.

The Desktop Experience

Like most users, you probably started by logging in to Twitter.com and using the basic web interface, shown in Figure 4-1, to manage your Twitter stream and communicate with your contacts. It's simple, no-frills, and convenient.

Most of what you need is right there on the top toolbar. But what if you need more functionality, mobility, or versatility, or you just want more bells and whistles?

Figure 4-1:
The web interface, which is just one of the ways you can use Twitter.

If you want to stick to using Twitter on your desktop, but you're interested in becoming a super-user someday, you may want to try a desktop client. We share a couple of examples of desktop clients later in this section, but feel free to jump to Chapter 17 for more tools and services.

Desktop clients

You can access Twitter through one of the many downloadable desktop applications that third-party developers have created with Twitter's API. We cover these desktop clients more thoroughly in Chapter 8. The most popular application is TweetDeck (shown in Figure 4-2), which became so popular that Twitter acquired it.

Basically, a Twitter client allows you to use Twitter from your desktop without having a browser open. Many of these clients also offer features that Twitter doesn't, including the ability to thread Tweets and track conversations, create lists, filter content, open simultaneous accounts, and delete direct messages.

Figure 4-2:
You can get
your Twitter
info by using
TweetDeck.

These services work by talking to Twitter to get the information they need, so they don't work if Twitter isn't working. They rely on it to gather and relay the data you see and use.

Browser plug-ins

A third-party application created for Twitter is Twitter for Chrome (https://chrome.google.com/webstore/category/apps — search for "Twitter"), which is a plug-in that you can use with the Google Chrome web browser. *Plug-in* just means that a specific feature of the application gets installed right into the browser and runs from there. This particular plug-in won't run with Mozilla Firefox, Apple's Safari, or Internet Explorer, and you can't use it if you don't use Google Chrome.

Although most plug-ins and add-ons made for Twitter are safe to put on your computer, always be careful any time you install something new. A good way to tell whether an application is okay is to ask your friends on Twitter whether they use it. Most active Twitter users are happy to provide tips and recommendations.

Chrome, Firefox, and other browsers approve plug-ins that have been submitted to their developer programs. Plug-ins that prove not to be harmful are endorsed by these browsers.

Putting Twitter on your site

You may want to go a bit beyond run-of-the-mill widgets if you're hoping to put Twitter on another web page seamlessly. If you have technical expertise or access to a good web developer, you can build your own widget or plug-in that uses the Twitter API. You can find details on building a widget at https://dev.twitter.com.

If you're not a computer programmer or developer, you probably won't ever touch the Twitter API directly, but you'll be using it — without even knowing it — every time you use a third-party application.

Widgets and gadgets

Twitter and other sites offer widgets that let you embed information from a service such as Twitter onto other sites — all so that you can share Twitter more easily. Sometimes, widgets come in the form of HTML code that you can copy and paste into your home screen or a blog template. At other times, they come in the form of an application that you have to install on a social network platform, such as Facebook. You can use dozens of official and unofficial widgets for Twitter. Anyone can build a widget by using free widget-building tools, so there's no telling how many Twitter widgets actually exist.

Twitter has an official page where you can find the code for an embeddable widget, complete with step-by-step instructions for installing it. Just go to https://twitter.com/settings/widgets/new. Here, you'll find code for embedding a user's timeline, favorites, a list (which we go over later in this section), a keyword or hashtag, or a photo collection that you create — all in real time.

You can find an official Twitter application for Facebook, too, which means that you can make your Twitter updates show up as your Facebook status updates, or you can display a badge of your Tweets on your Facebook profile. You can find the Twitter application for Facebook at https://apps.facebook.com/twitter.

Lists that improve your desktop experience

We mention lists a few times in this chapter with regard to using TweetDeck or specific widgets. Twitter creates lists to help you see only the updates you want to see while allowing you to follow as many people as you'd like.

When you start following more than 100 people on Twitter, your timeline may start to feel a little overwhelming. You'll start to see Tweets flying past you before you can read them all. This list-building feature helps you segment your Twitter followers into more manageable chunks.

Take Brittany's list Boston, MA as an example (`https://twitter.com/bleaning/lists/boston-ma`; see Figure 4-3). She created this list manually to see which updates are local, as opposed to Tweets from all over the world.

Twitter list

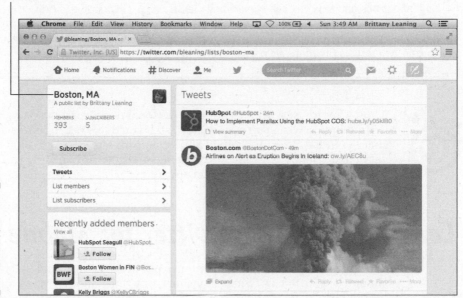

Figure 4-3:
You can
segment
your follow-
ers by using
Twitter lists.

Create lists ahead of time and add a few people every day rather than adding all list members in one sitting. Lists are meant to be added to over time. The easiest way to do this is by creating a habit — once you've followed someone, also add him to a specific, customized list.

To create a list of your own, follow these steps:

1. **Click the Me tab on the toolbar of any Twitter screen.**

   Your profile page appears.

2. **Click the More tab on your profile page.**

   A drop-down menu appears.

3. **Choose the Lists option from the menu.**

   A screen for creating and managing your personal lists appears.

4. **Click the Create New List button on the right sidebar.**

5. **In the resulting field, fill out your list title, description, and privacy settings.**

6. **Click Save List.**

   Your list is created.

Subscribing to lists

If you prefer, you can subscribe to someone else's public list instead of creating your own. The great thing about this option is you can check in on list updates periodically without following every individual Twitter user in the list. If you refer to Figure 4-3, you see a Subscribe button in the left sidebar. If you click that button, you see Brittany's Boston, MA list in your list of lists (how meta!) at (`http://twitter.com/username/lists`). If you choose to subscribe, this doesn't mean that you've followed every person on that list; you've followed the list itself.

TIP

If you want to use a list for your own personal purposes, you should select the Private option when you create your list. If you'd like other people to see and share your list, select the Public option instead. A private list could consist of very close friends, whereas a public list could consist of people you work with or networked with at a conference or event.

Leaving the Nest: Twitter for Mobile

In our experience, the key to Twitter happiness is Twitter mobility. You should be able to use Twitter anywhere, any time, and any way you want, particularly on your phone. You can get this mobility via the Twitter mobile application, the Twitter mobile website (`https://m.twitter.com`), or SMS text messages. Depending on which mobile device you're viewing the mobile site on, the interface may be missing a few of the regular, web-based Twitter site's features (you can't see your widgets on a mobile device, for example), but you can use it pretty much as you do the normal site.

If you have a smartphone, such as an iPhone or Android phone, you can try a few downloadable Twitter apps. The iPhone has a nice interface for Twitter, and you can download several apps from the iTunes App Store or Google Play that make using Twitter on the go even easier. Some of these apps are free, some cost a few bucks, and some have both free and paid versions.

People tend to swear by the apps they love best, and no user group is more enthusiastic than the iPhone and Android crowds, whose debates about apps such as Twitter, Buffer, justunfollow, and more can keep a conversation going through several pints of beer at a tweetup.

These mobile Twitter apps barely scratch the surface of what you can find, and new ones are created fairly regularly. There's no real consensus on which is best. Try a few to see which ones you prefer.

The API difference

Twitter's API fuels its flexibility, and that flexibility is a big part of what keeps Twitter users loyal. The API is so customizable that you can create a new service for Twitter on a whim, based on what you want to do with it — a big plus, especially if you plan to mold Twitter to fit a specific company goal or make it a big part of a marketing campaign or promotion. If you can't find an existing application that works with Twitter to make it do exactly what you need, you can make one yourself or hire someone to do it. Full customization is rare on the web, but you can mold Twitter to work anywhere you need it to: at work, at home, or even while rock climbing.

The Twitter mobile app

If you're interested in live-tweeting events, sharing updates about life around you, or reading Tweets as you travel to and from work, the Twitter mobile app is for you. In fact, you wouldn't be alone: The majority of Twitter's users now access the platform from mobile devices. The mobile app is relatively robust, so nearly everything you see on the desktop website, you'll see on the mobile app (see Figure 4-4). This app, created by Twitter, is the best basic app out there for navigating Twitter on the go.

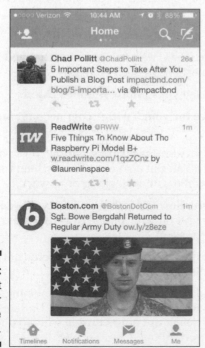

Figure 4-4: The robust Twitter iPhone application.

If you don't have a smartphone, but you'd still like to get Twitter notifications on your phone, you can set up SMS delivery. (This is actually where the 140-character limit was derived from — using Twitter on your cellphone — since a text message would break into two separate messages if you typed more than 140 characters.) We go over how to do this in the next section of this chapter.

Text messages (SMS delivery)

It's fairly simple to opt in to receiving Twitter via text messages (SMS delivery). First, you have to set up a mobile device so that Twitter knows where to send your Tweets. To do so, follow these steps:

1. **Click the gear icon in the top-right corner of your Twitter.com home screen.**

2. **Click Settings in the drop-down menu.**

   The Settings screen opens.

3. **Click the Mobile tab.**

4. **Select your country/region, enter your mobile phone number in the text field, and then click the Activate Phone button.**

   You're given the word GO and instructed to text this word from your phone to 40404.

5. **Send GO from your phone as a text message to 40404.**

   You'll receive a text message from Twitter confirming that your device has been verified and SMS alerts have been enabled.

6. **Refresh the page until you see your phone number listed.**

7. **Turn on SMS device updates for your Twitter.com account and then click Save Changes.**

   Now you can choose to have text-message notifications on or off, or to receive direct messages only. You can also opt to have them turned off during a specific time (say, while you're sleeping or at work).

   From the Device Updates drop-down list, choose On if you want to receive Tweets as text messages on your phone or Direct Messages if you want to receive direct messages.

8. **(Optional) Select a sleep period during which you prefer not to receive updates, and click Save Changes.**

   If you're enabling device updates but don't want them coming in 24 hours a day, in the Sleep section, select the Turn off Updates During These Hours check box and select the hours during which you don't want to receive updates on your phone.

Make sure that your cellphone carrier has an unlimited text-messaging plan — or that you're willing to pay for a lot of extra texts — before setting Twitter device notifications to On. Twitter doesn't charge for texts, but your carrier might!

You don't automatically receive device updates from everyone you follow on Twitter. You have to turn these device updates on manually for each person. To see if you've turned device updates On or Off for any given person, take the following steps:

1. **Go to that user's profile on Twitter.**

   You can access a user's profile by clicking the user's username in one of her Tweets.

2. **Click the gear icon next to the Following button.**

   A drop-down menu appears.

3. **Turn the person's device updates on or off by choosing Turn on Mobile Notifications or Turn off Mobile Notifications.**

   Make sure that you've enabled all device updates on your phone first.

Part II
Finding Your Flock

Still feeling a little nervous about taking the plunge and sending your first Tweet? Check out five #FirstTweets that remind us that everyone was once a Twitter dummy at www.dummies.com/extras/twitter.

In this part . . .

- ✔ Find the people you want to communicate with.
- ✔ Find the people you may know outside of Twitter on Twitter.
- ✔ Identify and connect with new people who share your interests.
- ✔ Identify other personalities and brands that you may want to connect with using Twitter.

Chapter 5

So How Do I Start Twittering?

In This Chapter

▶ Scouring Twitter for interesting people to follow

▶ Following people

▶ Replying to messages, privately and publicly

▶ Attracting new followers

*O*ne of the neatest byproducts of the Twitter experience is that your conversations, your followers, and your ability to interact with your network extends far past the `Twitter.com` interface into nearly any web page, thousands of applications on any mobile or computer platform, and into the real world. Hashtags and usernames adorn advertisements, television segments, stages, and every conceivable form of media. But equally important to accessing your Twitter account from virtually anywhere is understanding how to interact as a good citizen in the global Twitter community.

In this chapter, we go over the nuts and bolts involved in discovering, managing, and interacting with people and brands via Twitter. We help you better understand how to relate to the people you follow and interact with on Twitter, and to the people who follow and interact with you. We give you some hints about how to play well with others within the Twitterverse so that you can start having conversations right away!

Finding People to Follow on Twitter

A key part of getting the most out of Twitter is knowing where and how to find people whose Twitter streams are of interest to you. Most people start by following their friends, associates, and people they know, and many find that interacting within their networks can be the most rewarding part of Twitter. Given the hundreds of millions of people who use Twitter, it's well worth searching `Twitter.com`, `Google.com`, and every publication you read online or offline for other people to follow who can add value to your stream.

You can easily find and follow people on Twitter. The onboarding process gives you a natural start, and `Twitter.com`'s own account discovery tools can be revisited any time you'd like to find some fresh voices.

Check the byline of nearly every article you read online for the author's name, and if a link to his Twitter account isn't readily available, simply search his first and last names and the word *Twitter* in any search engine to find his account. You can also search for people within `Twitter.com`'s own interface, but we've found search engines to sometimes provide better results more conveniently.

During the course of reading and interacting on Twitter, you can easily browse people's profiles by clicking the link on their username when you find something they say to be interesting or relevant to you.

As you start accumulating updates from the people you follow, you'll quickly realize that it's important to organize and manage your decisions about who's worth following and how you'd like to receive their updates. That process can become complicated because of the size and diversity of the Twitter ecosystem.

Avid users have countless theories and strategies about the best ways and reasons to follow others. But Twitter is for your use, so you can make up your own rules as you go along, creating your own criteria for managing your Twitter experience.

Used well, Twitter is very personalized. No two people use Twitter in exactly the same way, and no two people follow a given account on Twitter for exactly the same reasons. Quite literally, no two people experience the same Twitter because everyone is consuming different streams, publishing to, and interacting with different sets of readers.

If you start to get overwhelmed by Twitter, remember that you are able to shape your experience by selecting who you listen to and interact with directly, who you put on lists, and who you block or report for spam if you encounter difficulties.

As you become more familiar with Twitter and more comfortable shaping your entire Twitter experience, you naturally develop and change your own guidelines for building your network. Luckily, Twitter is built to allow for these changes, so you don't have to miss a beat.

Whether you're looking for business associates, news sources, friendly conversation, or pretty much anything else, Twitter lets you surround yourself with people, publications, and other brands that enrich your life. Finding Twitter to be boring? Maybe you just haven't tuned in to the right channels yet.

Seeing who's talking

When you want to start looking for people to follow, see whether anyone's already interacted with you. If you've already posted some Tweets, people may have replied to you. (If you haven't yet tweeted, what are you waiting for? Dive in and start tweeting! Not sure how to start? Feeling shy? See Chapter 15 for Tweets you can send today.)

When someone wants to address you directly on Twitter, that user does so by replying to one of your Tweets or by mentioning you.

To reply to a Tweet, Twitter users click the Reply button, compose their Tweet, and click Tweet to post. Notice that these Tweets — from anyone — become a part of the comments stream of the original Tweet and can by found by anyone looking at the full conversation around that Tweet.

Your reply will also show up as its own Tweet but is visible only to others who are following the person you replied to or who have clicked to view all Tweets from you, including replies.

To mention you, Twitter users simply put the @ symbol before typing your Twitter handle somewhere in the Tweet. That's all it takes for a Tweet to end up on your Mentions tab.

If you're completely new to Twitter and you've only posted a handful of Tweets, you probably won't have any mentions yet. That's okay! You have plenty of other options for finding people to follow (see the next sections).

Searching for people

You can search for people on Twitter itself many ways. The simplest is by using the search field — look for the magnifying-glass icon and the words *Search Twitter* inside an oval — present in the navigation bar at the top of every Twitter page. Run your search using any name, keyword, industry, title, and so on, and then look for a link in the left navigation bar to the People subset of results in that search.

Twitter currently has three main pages aimed at helping the new user find new people to follow: Who to Follow, Find Friends, and Popular Accounts. You can find these sections by clicking on the #Discover tab in the top left navigation at `Twitter.com`. Here's what you can expect from each.

✔ **Who to Follow** (`https://twitter.com/who_to_follow/ suggestions`) starts by looking at who you are already following, as well as what's newly popular and related right now, and provides you a customized list of accounts you might also like.

✔ **Find Friends** (`https://twitter.com/who_to_follow/import`) does exactly that, but beware: You might end up sending out a bunch of random requests to join Twitter to everyone in your address book if you don't pay attention when you are using this page.

It's perfectly safe to authorize Twitter to search contacts for any of the services displayed on this page, and Twitter will tell you what it's going to do next. What it does next is show you the list of your contacts who are already on Twitter and ask if you'd like to follow them. For the most part, this is probably a good idea, but you should probably review the list before giving Twitter the go-ahead to do so.

Next, it asks if you want to invite the rest of your contacts to come try Twitter. Here's where you should tread lightly. Depending on how you use the web and the third-party service you've clicked, this could be a lot of random people. You probably don't want to blindly invite them all to join Twitter. Don't be afraid here, but also don't just click all the way through the options like some kind of robot.

✔ **Popular Accounts** (`https://twitter.com/who_to_follow/interests`) is a descendant of Twitter's early experiments with a Suggested Users list, which were less successful than the more customized suggestions it gives today as Who to Follow. It's still pretty useful, though, because it divides Twitter's most popular and most interesting accounts into a little more than two dozen categories and suggests roughly 50 to 200 good accounts within the category.

You'll also find that as you use Twitter, suggested accounts pop up here and there throughout the experience. Maybe you've just followed a new account, and a few "similar account" suggestions pop up. Maybe in the sidebar you notice some new faces under Who to Follow (currently on the right side).

Finally, if you're looking for accounts by topic, you might be best served running a Google search that will find articles and blog posts discussing great accounts to follow, as in this example:

Top film directors on Twitter

Another really popular way to find people on Twitter is to simply use your favorite search engine. Because Google indexes every public Tweet, you can use it to find twitterers by interest or by name. To use Google to find people you might want to follow, either search their first names, last names, and the word *Twitter*, or do a slightly more specific search this way:

1. **Type your keywords or the username you're looking for in the text field.**

2. **Add** site:Twitter.com **at the end of your search query.**

3. **Click the Search button.**

   See what pops up!

You probably want to conduct people searches and keyword searches periodically to make sure that you continue to cultivate your Twitter experience's richness and value with new voices. Although Twitter is great for reconnecting with old friends and keeping up a conversation with existing business associates, it's also a fantastic way to reach out and find new people and companies to listen to.

A great way to get started following people on Twitter is to import your contacts from your web-based email account (such as Yahoo! Mail or Gmail). We cover this in detail in Chapter 2.

Doing a simple search

Twitter's main search page (`https://twitter.com/search-home`) is great for advanced searching. But sometimes, a quick search is what you need. Twitter makes it easy to do this, as well as save that search for immediate future use.

In the preceding section, we discuss the Search Twitter oval that lives at the top of every Twitter page. You can type anything you want there, and when you press Enter or click the magnifying glass, your Twitter feed turns into a live search result of all the Tweets that match your search query. Figure 5-1 shows a live Twitter search for louisck.

Figure 5-1:
Fast Twitter
search for
louisck.

If this is a search you think you'd be doing often, you can save it by clicking Save to the right of the Results For heading, on the upper-right corner of the feed. That search term sits inside of your right sidebar for quick access to live search results. (You can find it under the search field.)

Inviting people personally, through Twitter

Another option for inviting people to Twitter is to do it personally, directly to their individual email addresses. This page is called Find Friends (`https://twitter.com/who_to_follow/import`), and you can get back to it anytime from the top navigation bar by clicking #Discover (`https://twitter.com/i/discover`) and looking for the Find Friends link to the page in the main menu there.

As mentioned earlier, you should be very careful when you decide which of your "not yet on Twitter" contacts you should invite using these automated emails. We are not big fans of them. If you really want to convince someone to join Twitter, write them a personal email approaching the subject and telling them why. If eight years of news coverage and recent near-ubiquity in all kinds of media has not convinced someone to join, the robo-email you send is unlikely to help.

Twitter doesn't offer you a chance to customize what the email says. The person or company you invite gets a generic email that mentions your Twitter handle and some basic information about how to sign up for an account.

The main drawback to any of the invitation options in Twitter's web interface is that none of them offer a custom message option. If you know people whom you want to invite, and you think they'd respond better to a private or more personalized note, just shoot them a normal email that includes a link to the Twitter main page or even to your profile page on Twitter (`www.twitter.com/username`) and a note about why they might benefit from signing up and joining in. It's often more effective to email them a link to an article that is going to help them understand what uses of Twitter they may find valuable. Eight years on, Twitter definitely remains a minute-to-learn, lifetime-to-master type of system.

Checking out Twitter Lists

One of Twitter's more flexible and powerful features is the ability for users to create lists of accounts. Unsurprisingly, they're called Twitter Lists, and they can provide some structure to how you want to read and interact with others on Twitter. Lists allow you to categorize accounts and view their most recent Tweets, whether or not you even follow them.

A community leads

Twitter users have come up with an interesting way of recommending people to follow — something called FollowFriday. It uses a community-driven system called hashtags, which we cover in Chapter 8. Our friend Micah Baldwin (@micah, pronounced *Me-ha*) started it, and he has this to say about it:

In January of 2009, I sent a simple Tweet: "I am starting FollowFridays. Every Friday, suggest people to follow, and everyone follow him/her. Today its @jeffrey and @dannynewman." After a suggestion to add the hashtag #followfriday and four folks retweeting it, FollowFriday was born.

After a few months, more than 100,000 Tweets with more than 300,000 recommendations are sent each Friday (it actually begins on Thursday U.S. time because it's Friday overseas!) and it's growing each week.

FollowFriday mirrors what happens in the real world. One person suggests a book to read, or a restaurant to go to, or a person you should meet, and if you trust her, you take her word. The concept is very simple: Write a Tweet listing two or three people you follow that you think others should follow as well, and provide a bit of an explanation. (Remember: It's only 140 characters, so be brief both with your recommendations and with your explanations!) For example,

"@Pistachio, @micah, and @gruen are three people that make me laugh every day. #followfriday." That's it!

If you're new to Twitter and you're looking for people to follow, you can search for #followfriday, or #ff, at https://twitter.com/search-home to see people who have been recommended. Note, the results might be overwhelming. If so, stick to paying attention on Fridays to the folks you already follow, and see which accounts they recommend.

The original intention behind FollowFriday is exactly what makes Twitter great. It gives you the ability to participate, it's easy, and you can share people you're proud to know (even if it's just on Twitter) with other people. After all, Twitter is about sharing information and experiences with people you're proud to be associated with, in a very easy, participatory way. In practice, many abuse the idea. It's still worth trying out, especially where it comes to paying attention to individual #FF Tweets from people you respect, as opposed to the whole flood of #FF Tweets.

Why Fridays? Fridays seem to work well because it's the end of the week, and people have the time to think about whom they would like to recommend. Plus, FollowTuesday just doesn't have the same type of ring, now does it?

For example, you may have a few different types of people you're interested in hearing from. Some are celebrities, some are friends you went to school with, and others are people you work with. By using the Lists feature, you can organize those people into lists. You can view these lists as discreet Twitter streams so that when you view them, the only Tweets that show up are from the people in that list.

You can use this feature to your advantage when finding other Twitter users to follow. For example, if a classmate of yours has found you on Twitter, you may visit her profile and notice that she's created a list of people who went to your alma mater. By clicking that list, you can see the usernames of everyone she has found on Twitter who went to your school. Or your news-junkie friend may have a list of the best breaking-news Twitter accounts. You can go into that list, curated by your friend, and select the breaking-news outlet that works best for you.

In short, you can use other people to help find accounts that can add value to your experience.

If you find a list that you really enjoy, you can add that list to your own Twitter List collection.

We cover lists in depth in Chapter 4.

Following back

By default, Twitter sends you an email every time someone follows you. This is a useful starting point for finding people to follow because there's likely a reason why he followed you in the first place. It may be because he knows you, or it may be because he thinks you're a good person to follow. No matter what, it's nice to know when someone's following you. Unfortunately, new followers can also sometimes be spam, a robot, or other malicious accounts.

Yes, Twitter, like any popular online communication tool, has spammers. Although Twitter — both the company and the community of its users — tries to aggressively fight spam accounts, there is almost an arms race at any given time.

They're often pretty easy to spot, especially if you click through to their profile page and check their ten most recent Tweets. These might be offering you the usual fare of online deals or bedroom-related drugs, they might be the same Tweet over and over and over with @mentions to various influencers, or they might be some creative new approach. You can safely ignore them. If you'd like to help Twitter identify these accounts, you can click the Block and Report for Spam button on their profiles.

If you find receiving Twitter notices a bother, you can turn them off:

1. **Click the gear icon and select Settings from the menu that drops down.**

   The Settings screen opens.

2. **Click Email Notifications in the left sidebar (see Figure 5-2).**

   You see a list of email notification options.

3. **Select any of the emails you'd rather not receive.**

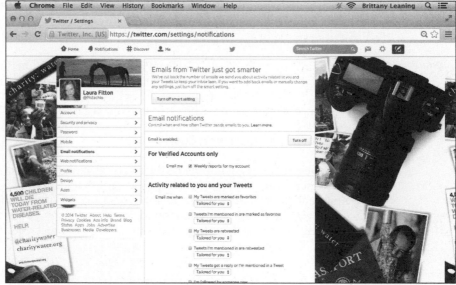

Figure 5-2:
On the Email
Notifications
screen, you
can choose
which, if
any, emails
are sent
to your
mailbox.

Following People

Following people on Twitter is dead simple. After you navigate to a person's Profile page, click the Follow button. You're done! Give it a shot:

1. **Browse to** `https://twitter.com/dummies`.
2. **Click the Follow button.**

   The button changes to the word *Following*. Cool!

Many different extensions and features of Twitter make it possible to follow someone from almost anywhere. For example, in a news article you might find buttons, sidebars, or other features that give you the option to click follow without ever leaving the article page of the publication you are reading.

You might find the "follow me (or us) on Twitter" call to action anywhere, including print advertising and billboards. Unfortunately, click-to-follow technology has not come to print advertising yet, so you'll have to remember that username (if it was provided!) long enough to write it down somewhere for typing later. If the advertiser forgets to tell you their username, and this happens much more often than it should, you can always use Google, Twitter Search, or a visit to their website to try to figure it out on your own.

Alternatively, you can submit your follow request to Twitter by texting 40404 (in the United States; short codes for your locality may vary) and typing `follow username` or `F username`.

Back in the day, typing `F username` in any Twitter interface functioned as a command for Twitter to follow the username that followed the letter F. This no longer works for Twitter.com, Twitter apps, or anything other than texting via 40404 or your local short code. Don't use that old shortcut because it's very awkward to have "F username" show up as a Tweet in your timeline. Not that we would know from experience. Cough.

The experience of following people on Twitter is straightforward. On the most superficial level, you just have to pay attention to keep on top of interesting news and information people might be sharing. Twitter is full of thousands of conversations going on all around you. If you open yourself up to them, you may find excellent people who are thrilled to meet you.

Using the Follow button

When you're operating on Twitter time, sometimes you may feel that it takes you too long to decide whether or not to follow someone when you see his username show up in your Twitter feed. For these reasons, Twitter added the Follow button essentially everywhere in its many interfaces. You no longer have to go all the way to someone's profile page to follow him. Instead, you are offered the chance to do so nearly anytime you see a new user.

The Follow button is really straightforward. In many of the places that Twitter shows you a user's name and avatar image, it also provides a gray button labeled *Follow.* Click that button once to follow and a second time to unfollow if you change your mind.

The first time you click a user's name or username from anywhere in the Twitter interface, a smaller window pops up, showing you a preview of her profile. You can see some basic information, some recent Tweets, and a Follow button. If you click her name again, you go all the way through to her actual profile page. We personally prefer the profile page itself if we're curious about getting to know someone well enough to decide on subscribing to her updates or not.

Replying to Tweets

So, what happens when you receive an @reply, and you want to respond — or if you just want to respond to any Tweet, for that matter? See the faint gray *Reply, Retweet,* and *Favorite* words and icons in the bottom of the Tweet? Hover your mouse cursor over the Tweet and these words will darken and become clickable.

Each individual Tweet, when you click the time stamp to go to the URL for that Tweet alone, has a similar menu, showing Reply, Delete, Favorite if it's your own Tweet (as shown in Figure 5-3) or Reply, Retweet, Favorite if it's someone else's.

Reply arrow

Figure 5-3:
Don't miss
the Reply
arrow!

Clicking the star icon bookmarks that Tweet as a favorite, which we cover in Chapter 3. But clicking the arrow icon sets up the Twitter entry field so that you can reply to that individual Tweet. When you send your response, it appears in a conversation thread below the original Tweet and includes a live link to the stand-alone page (also known as a *permalink*) for the Tweet you responded to.

You may find these permalinks helpful even though Twitter itself is now much better at threading Tweets together by conversation. If you're familiar with a set of @replies and the links associated with them, you can much more easily navigate the conversation later. When you know how to access the individual page for each Tweet, you can also link to that Tweet directly if you choose to respond to it in a longer format outside Twitter, such as a blog post.

You can reply to any Tweet that you can see, and the procedure is the same, whether you're following the person or not. But assuming your Twitter account is public, your @replies are public, too. If you want to use Twitter for private messages, the protocol is a little different, as we discuss in "Sending Direct Messages" later in this chapter.

Go ahead and jump right in

Given the casual and conversational tone of Twitter, you can pretty easily jump into an existing conversation on Twitter, and (unless you're trying much too hard) you won't look like you're barging in. Twitter users are aware that this is a public forum and contributions can come from anywhere and at any time. Start by clicking one of the usernames involved in the conversation, or enter one or both usernames manually in the Update window. (Remember: The format for addressing a Twitter user is *username*.) Then chime in by saying something relevant to their discussion.

Don't rush to be conversational to the point that you end up being irrelevant or spammy. If the conversation is about something you don't know anything about, hold off. But if it's about a movie that you've seen or an idea you're really excited about, pipe up!

It may take a few tries with a few different people to get the ball rolling. Don't be discouraged if you send out a few @replies and don't

get responses; many Twitter users, especially relatively new or very famous ones, don't pay close attention or respond to @replies either from people whom they're not following or those who don't seem particularly perceptive to them. Many people on Twitter, however, respond very quickly to new voices because, for many on Twitter, the point is still to simply be conversational.

Be patient about expecting replies to questions that are easily answered using Google or other resources. Also, please be patient with people that a lot of people interact with. Jennifer Lopez, for example, may still be Jenny from the block, but there's no way she can converse with many — if any — of the thousands of people an hour mentioning her Twitter handle @JLo in their Tweets. To see how busy her @ mentions tab is, just search @JLo (`https:// twitter.com/search?f=realtime&q =%22%40jlo%22&src=typd`) and click All.

Retweeting

In the early days of Twitter, it was commonplace for people not to just reply to Tweets they liked, but to forward that Tweet on to their own followers by simply copying the text in the original Tweet and pasting it in a new Tweet. This practice grew to be known as retweeting (RT for short) and was so popular that Twitter built that functionality directly into their interface.

Retweeting a link

To retweet a link, follow these steps:

1. **Find the word *Retweet* and the Retweet icon on the tweet that you'd like to forward to your followers.**

2. **Click the word *Retweet* or the two-bent-arrows icon.**

   A confirmation dialog box pops up.

3. Click Retweet.

That Tweet will be forwarded to your followers.

To your followers, that Tweet looks as though it came from the person who wrote the Tweet in the first place, complete with his avatar picture and username. To credit you for the retweet, Twitter places your name directly above the original writer's name and specifies that you retweeted the Tweet.

If the user has marked her updates as private, you won't see the word *Retweet*, and clicking the Retweet icon won't do anything. You could technically retweet her by copying and pasting, but unless you've gotten her specific permission to share what she wrote, you're violating her privacy and copyright by doing so. You're also just not being nice.

Retweeting the old-fashioned way

Although the Retweet feature is pretty neat, some users prefer the old way of doing things. To retweet someone's Tweet the old-fashioned way, simply retype or copy and paste that Tweet into any tweeting window and add characters to format it, like so:

RT @dummies This Tweet was written so you can practice retweeting.

Twitter etiquette strongly dictates that you make every effort to credit the original author of the Tweet. Because many will only read the beginning of the Tweet and ignore the end of it, anything in parentheses, and so on, it's more polite to recognize the speaker up front.

Commentary on the retweet

Retweeting the old-fashioned way has some advantages. One compelling reason is that users can comment on the original message. If you use Twitter's built-in retweet function, that's not possible because the original message is preserved and forwarded as-is. Therefore, to add commentary, you must either write it in another Tweet and link to the original, or use the old RT method if there's room for comment.

For example, one might imagine the following (fictional) exchange:

@neilarmstrong: That's one small step for man, one giant leap for mankind.

Only to be retweeted with addendum:

@buzzaldrin: That was supposed to be "a man." Sheesh! RT @neilarmstrong That's one small step for man, one giant leap for mankind.

When you're quoting someone, such as a line he wrote in an article or a phrase he spoke at a live event, you should simply use quotes around his words, and keep it short enough that you can follow the quotes with his username. Try these, from Laura's favorite crush, we mean, comedian Louis C.K.:

"I would rather be with my kids than anybody else." `@louisck`

"Everything's amazing. Nobody's happy." `@louisck https://www.youtube.com/watch?v=rqk3GdOkqPY`

Notice in the second one, we provided a link so that readers can see more context for the quote, and in this case watch a typography experiment video of the interview the quote comes from.

Sending Direct Messages

Private messages on Twitter are called direct messages (DMs). Like any other kind of Tweets, they're limited to 140 characters in length. Except with certain business Twitter accounts that allow any follower to send a DM (replies, of course, are not guaranteed), you can't send a DM to someone unless that Twitter user is following you. Likewise, only your own followers can send you DMs.

Because of overlap between the unsavory parts of human nature and the technological specifics of Twitter, DMs have been particularly vulnerable to outbreaks of malicious attacks. Phishing scams — in which bad actors try to get you to give them private information like passwords by making a site look legitimate — are particularly prevalent.

Be very, very, very wary of any DM that includes a URL. Most of the time people won't include a URL in a legitimate DM unless they have already established with you that they are sending you one for a particular reason. The scammers are clever, though, and they will play to your ego (*"OMG ROTFL have you seen this (picture/video) of you?"*). Or they will go after common fears (*"I am shocked what this post is saying about you online"*) to get you to click.

Fortunately, Twitter has cracked down and now allows very few URLs to be shared via DM. We hope this will make the following paragraphs sound quaintly outdated before the book even makes it into stores. Then again, it's better to be safe than sorry.

If the face on the DM in question is unfamiliar to you, for example, someone you followed or followed back without knowing him very well, don't click that URL without checking in with him and confirming he sent it and it's legitimate.

But even if you recognize them, don't click yet.

Sometimes scams look legitimate — and spread more quickly — because they come from people you know very well whose accounts are acting without their knowledge. Maybe they clicked a bad link or entered their login data somewhere insecurely, or their Twitter account has been compromised in some way.

When it's from a familiar face, it's really tempting to click the link included, so think carefully and ask yourself: Did I expect a message on this topic from this person? Does the message sound like how this person usually communicates with me?

If you're not certain a URL in a DM is legitimate, either ask the sender, or copy some of the text in the DM and paste it into a search engine like Google. com just to check for any reports of it actually being a scam. You can even test the URL from the DM by copying it and pasting it into Twitter's own search field and evaluating whether legitimate accounts are sharing it or whether it's only being shared by bots, spammers, and scammers.

What do you do if you want to get in touch with someone privately on Twitter but that person isn't following you? New Twitter users are often tempted to send @replies to that person saying "tried to DM but you don't follow" or something of the sort. Some Twitter users don't mind receiving those kinds of Tweets, but many others see them as rude or as blatant attempts to get new followers.

So if you're trying to get in touch with someone who doesn't follow you, you have some options:

- ✔ **Check the user's profile page.** See whether he has made available some other form of contact information — a website URL, an email address, or a blog. You can often find this info in a user's short bio section. If there is a URL on his profile, click it. If it goes to his website, look for a contact us page or link there. If it goes to an identification service like about.me, use that service's email feature to try to send an email to him.

- ✔ **Conduct a web search.** Try searching for the user on your favorite search engine. Just type her full name and a couple (or more if it's a very common name) of keywords that help narrow it down to her.

- ✔ **Tweet a polite question publicly to the user.** While the you-don't-follow-me approach is a little obnoxious, most twitterers will make a reasonable effort to respond if you respect their time and make it clear why they should answer you. Follow the person, and then send a message to his username expressing why you're requesting his time and attention, and ask that he respond privately. For example, you might try writing *username you don't know me but please follow back temporarily or DM me your email if you're able to answer a question?*

Please be polite if you try this. Bear in mind that just because you have the ability to reach out to someone does *not* mean you have the right to demandingly expect a response.

Direct-messaging shorthand

If you use Direct Messages a lot, you start to find going to the Direct Messages page every time you want to send someone a message a bit tedious. Fortunately, there is shorthand to send a DM without going to any particular part of the interface:

1. **Click in any Twitter composing window or field.**

2. **Type** d, **followed by a space and then the username of the person to whom you want to send a direct message.**

3. **Type a space after the username and then write your message.**

   The update should have this form: d dummies Hey, there!.

4. **Click Send button to send the DM.**

One word of caution if you plan to send direct messages from a phone or by typing d and the username of the recipient: On a small keyboard, you can very easily make a typing error, such as misspelling the username, accidentally posting a letter other than d, pushing two d's, or something else. Look twice before you send your message to make sure that it's truly private and not a public Tweet by accident, especially if it contains personal information that you don't want the whole Internet to know (such as a phone number, an address, or unkind or embarrassing words of any sort).

Should I @ or DM?

When you try to decide whether to respond to somebody on Twitter by using a public @reply or a private DM, you should consider the following criteria:

✔ **Questionable content:** If your mother, grandmother, boss, or kid were looking over your shoulder at what you just started typing, would that be a problem? Really try to imagine the worst possible person who could read the message, even if he is not on Twitter. If the answer is yes, perhaps a direct message is in order. Even then, be careful. DMs can be — and have been — accidentally posted as public Tweets when people miss something in composing the DM.

✔ **Volume:** If you're a power user who posts to Twitter many times a day, every Tweet that does not start with the character @ goes into your followers' streams and contributes to the noise. You should be sensitive to this fact. If you Tweet often, give your followers a break and save those one- or two-word responses, such as "oh @Pistachio LOL" or "hey @dummies How?" for a direct message.

✔ **Sensitive information:** If you're supplying contact information, addresses, phone numbers, or other personal information that you don't want just anyone on the Internet to have access to, it's the right time for a direct message. Keep in mind that not everybody has the same standards regarding privacy and openness on the web, so if you're sharing any information pertaining to anybody else's contact information or whereabouts, err on the side of caution and use a DM.

If you haven't protected your Tweets, remember that although you can delete Tweets, whatever you write may already be indexed in Google and other search engines for all time. Even if a search engine didn't see it, an angry reader might have and might snap a screen shot (an image of the mobile or computer screen containing what you wrote) and publish it elsewhere. So think twice!

Encouraging More Followers

Twitter is a very receptive environment for forging connections with new friends and contacts, so amassing a list of followers is relatively simple. Typically, you gain followers in the natural course of using Twitter, but here are a few guidelines to follow:

✔ **Be real.** Being genuine goes a long way, and you're likely to gain followers without even trying.

✔ **Be interesting.** You don't have to fascinate with every Tweet you type, but do try to Tweet about things more relevant to the world at large than what you just ate for lunch or the heinous traffic on your morning commute. Talk about your interests instead. Talk about what's in the news. Or talk about what you think *should* be in the news. The related point is that it's better to be the good kind of interesting rather than the bad kind. Praise, enthusiasm, and kindness go far on Twitter. Drama, complaining, and self-centeredness do not.

✔ **Be involved.** The more into a topic you are, the more people will respond to your enthusiasm. Say that you're really into classic cars. Don't talk just about your own fascination with them, but try to help other people on Twitter who might have questions on the subject, and make it your business to be a source of great links to images, videos, and articles about the topic. It's even okay sometimes to engage in passionate conversations and debates, too. Position yourself as someone who has some valuable information on your chosen issue. This will help you grow your following the natural way and with relevant people who are less likely to leave later on.

Estimates in early 2014 indicated that 80 percent of world leaders — including the Pope (@Pontifex) and Barack Obama (@BarackObama) — are active on Twitter. In every field, exceptionally influential people use it to share and spread ideas. Heck, now that Oprah Winfrey (@Oprah) tweets, it's almost proof enough in and of itself just to mention her.

If you'd ever become lucky enough that @Oprah posts a Tweet with your username in it — perhaps replying to an @Oprah message you sent to her — you'd be barraged by new followers who've seen your username in connection with that famous person's.

Bear in mind that the most popular Twitter users have, at this writing, tens of millions of followers and thousands of people @replying to them per hour, so don't count on a response from a famous twitterer as a way to get your foot in the door.

It's also just rude to use someone. If you wouldn't interrupt the person next to you in line at the store with your question, it's probably not nice to interrupt someone with a lot of demands on her time with it. Conversation is two-way and most effective when it's generous to the listener, not selfish for the speaker.

Some Twitter users try to lure followers by offering contests, giveaways, or other incentives to reach certain pseudo-milestones, such as number of Tweets or number of followers. This approach is cheesy and can look like you're desperate for new followers. Your return on the time invested in Twitter will be much better if you cultivate carefully and just allow your network to grow organically.

Regardless of how you get people to follow you, make sure to keep your Twitter interactions genuine. What you post on Twitter and contribute to the conversation, along with your ability to listen, determines your authority more than any follower count ever could.

We can't stress the importance of listening enough. The more you listen and hear what people have to say, and then respond thoughtfully, the more you can find out about people and the more well-rounded your experience (and the experience of your followers) becomes. Listening is the golden ticket of Twitter; make sure to do it every day that you log in. And log in often.

One way Laura breaks it down in her conference keynote speeches is what she calls her four word guide to Twitter:

Listen. Learn. Care. Serve.

Pay attention to what you're hearing. Learn from it and from your experiments and try new things as a result. Show in your efforts that you truly and genuinely care about what you are writing and the people you are writing to. Above all, try in all your efforts to be of service to others.

If we had to summarize all of the contents of this entire book in just two words, we would cite Laura's *two* word guide to Twitter:

Be useful.

Chapter 6

Who's Using Twitter

*B*ecause Twitter is so open and direct, it can open doors and grant astonishing access to people you can't otherwise approach. It's become an effective tool for reaching out to people, companies, and even celebrities, both on- and offline.

Have you ever thought "I wish I could talk to someone higher up the ladder and get a real solution to this problem!" or even "I'd love to be able to tell this person or that company what a good job they do, but I don't have their contact info!"? Well, Twitter can help you bridge that gap.

It's no longer surprising to see which companies, people, and brands have jumped onto Twitter. If anything, it's surprising to find holdout professionals and brands not on it. In this chapter, we cover some popular types of Twitter accounts, provide examples for each type, and show you how to find others. When you're finished with this chapter, you'll be able to see whether the person or company that you want to find is on Twitter.

Tweeting with Regular People

After it gained a foothold among the digital-media enthusiasts at the South by Southwest Interactive Festival in 2007, Twitter was a fast-growing playground for techies and geeks. Over time, people from all walks of life have discovered Twitter and embraced it. Twitter allows a user to communicate effectively with one person or many, and the benefits can work for anyone.

Twitter has become a quick and easy way to stay connected to family, friends, and coworkers. People at all levels of any kind of business can use Twitter to easily interact with customers and potential clients, and get real-time engagement and feedback.

We highly recommend that you make a point of trying to use Twitter to talk to people whom you already know in real life, such as your family and friends, especially when you are starting out. From there, branch out a little to meet your friends' connections and other like-minded people. You can also meet some very unconventional people you may find incredibly interesting. On Twitter, you'll encounter everyone from celebrities to local community leaders to great-grandparents to young teens. You never know who you may come across from day to day, which is part of Twitter's charm.

But by far the biggest asset of Twitter is the sheer mass of everyday people sharing their thoughts, discussing and spreading everything from their lives to global news and, of course, socializing and networking. You can easily discover at least one new thing from someone on Twitter every day just by logging in.

As superficial as a relentlessly flowing stream of 140-character messages may seem, the Twitter community is a thriving way for real people to connect in the real world, too. You can easily set up and promote events through Twitter on fairly short notice, so many twitterers find their online connections often turn into offline friendships and business. It doesn't matter if you identify as introverted, extroverted, or any mix of both; the on- and offline social jumble that is Twitter is a great way to meet people.

So before we dig deeper into who's using Twitter in future chapters, in this chapter, we'll cover the basic types of accounts you might want to follow, and how to find them.

Just because a Twitter user isn't one of the most prolific people on the service doesn't mean that person isn't worth your time. Some of the most interesting twitterers post less than others, waiting to add their two cents' worth until they think they have something worth saying. Keep an eye out for those people and follow them when you get the chance. You'll likely get more value following a highly selective account that only shares a few valuable things than following someone who posts 20 times a day about stuff that's not important to you.

Regardless of whom you know or want to get to know on Twitter, you may want to set a few boundaries first. Twitter is a wide-open community of people from all walks of life engaged in every human pursuit imaginable. Yes, there are bad actors. Yes, there are things you don't want to see, and there are definitely things you don't want your kids to see. You will want to take your time to be selective about who you follow and who you follow back of those who follow you. Also remember that unless you create a private Twitter account, Google indexes your Tweets, so the whole Internet can see what you say, even, in some cases, if you delete it. Exercise caution! Never blurt out sensitive information — say, your home address or phone number — in public Tweets. Save those for Twitter's private direct messages or, better still, for exclusively private communications like texting or email. You may even feel more comfortable starting with a private account. If you do, still use careful judgment about what you post. Many initially private users later take their account public, sometimes without considering that what they wrote when it was still private will now be out there for all to see.

Popular Accounts

Throughout this chapter we're going to make numerous references to something Twitter calls Popular accounts. We'd like to introduce this feature right up front because it's the easiest, fastest way for anyone to find good accounts to follow.

Twitter realized pretty early on that a Twitter account with nobody interesting to follow was not a very compelling Twitter account at all. One attempt to help new users get up and running was called the Suggested User List. Over time, this idea developed into a more specific, topic-sorted subset of Twitter accounts that is built right into the navigation as Popular accounts.

To view these accounts, click the #Discover tab and then click Popular Accounts in the left navigation bar. Figure 6-1 displays the list of Popular Accounts categories you should now see.

Figure 6-1: Popular accounts index page.

Twitter staff personally select these lists to find a relatively small number of high quality accounts on the various topics. That way, you're not just blindly following the most famous person you can think of, whether or not they are providing any value on Twitter.

Not to be confused with Popular accounts, Twitter also has another type of account — Verified accounts — that we will explain in the next section. The biggest difference is the Popular accounts (which are likely also verified) were chosen for their editorial value, whereas Verified accounts just tell users that the account is representing who it claims to be.

Verified Accounts

As Twitter expanded in popularity, so did the number of fake Twitter accounts claiming to be well-known people. To combat hoaxes and other impersonators with bad intents, Twitter very selectively verifies accounts of extremely public companies and individuals. Generally, if the account is having trouble with impersonators already, or is extremely prone to being impersonated, it can qualify to become what is called a Verified account.

Verified accounts are accounts that the Twitter staff have verified as being who they claim to be. You can tell whether or not an account is verified by the small light blue circle with a check mark in it, visible next to the account's name in a variety of Twitter profile interfaces. To see what we mean, navigate to Laura's profile page (@Pistachio) and look for that small round powder blue circle with a check mark that designates a verified account.

If you are still unsure, Twitter follows all of its verified users from its @verified Twitter account and organizes some of its verified users into a set of categorized Twitter lists on that account. These lists are another pretty handy place to find users you might want to follow; see https://twitter.com/verified/lists.

If something that looks like the verified logo is in a user's avatar or header photo or positioned somewhere different, that account is likely someone who wants to trick you into thinking they are verified. This is silly. Verification doesn't mean anything particularly special; it just means this person was at high risk of impersonation and his identity has been verified. It's human nature that if there is a badge out there, everyone wants it. Don't sweat whether or not you ever get this one.

To all the musicians, executives, actors, authors, and others who aspire to having a verified account as if that were an achievement, it's not. It's just a way to protect unwitting users from being tricked. In fact, we have a confession: Before the days of verified accounts, even we got it wrong from time to time. In the first edition, we listed Tina Fey as a celebrity to follow on Twitter. Unfortunately, the @tinafey account at the time was not Tina Fey, as revealed early in 2009. At this writing, she's still — famously — not on Twitter. Bummer, because we really like Tina Fey.

Becoming a Verified account (or not)

Though it's somehow almost universally tempting, pretty much nobody should try to become a Verified account. As you can see in the figure below, Twitter does not accept verification requests from the general public. You don't apply for verification; it simply applies (or doesn't) to you. It's something Twitter does when there is a spoofing problem or a high probability that a real account will be spoofed. Verification isn't Twitter, Inc., saying certain accounts are special; it's about protecting the Twitter community from bad actors. Officially, it's not open to the general public.

All you can do to establish clearly that your Twitter account is really you is to be sure to display your Twitter account prominently on your official web presence (website, Facebook page, and so on) so that any potentially confused people can cross-reference it. Then, if your account ever encounters severe enough spoofing problems to qualify for Twitter verification someone from Twitter can verify that it is you.

The process is extremely tricky, severely backlogged, and has changed many times due to excessive and frivolous requests and end-user abuse. For more information, please see `https://twitter.com/help/verified`. Be forewarned! If you even slightly suspect you might *not* be eligible for verified account processing, you're not. Be grateful; this is actually good news!

Building Company Relationships with Twitter

Many companies have found value in Twitter as a way to build brand awareness, run contests, build community, strengthen relationships with customers, provide better and more immediate customer service, gather and nurture leads, promote events and webinars, boost sales, drive foot traffic to stores, encourage referrals, and do dozens of other business uses. Companies' presences on Twitter range from individual Twitter accounts belonging to employees or executives to official corporate accounts for the brand run by teams of marketing or public relations representatives.

Here are some of the most famous examples of companies that were very early adopters and got lots of positive buzz for their presence on Twitter:

- **Zappos.com:** This online retailer (@Zappos), founded during the dotcom boom, is now owned by Amazon.com and based in Las Vegas. It is very rightly very famous for fully integrating Twitter into its corporate structure. Long before most other companies, Zappos CEO Tony Hsieh was a Twitter regular, hundreds of Zappos employees tweeted, and the company began to use Twitter for customer service and feedback. Hsieh encouraged every Zappos.com employee to participate on Twitter because he wanted Zappos employees to get to know one another better, hang out more, and feel more closely connected as a team. As a byproduct to this widespread employee use, and official "Zappos on Twitter" web pages listing the Zappos-affiliated accounts, brands, and employees on Twitter, Zappos' Twitter presence kept the world posted on what's going on in the company.

- **Comcast:** After serious issues with negative connotations to their brand name, this cable company took Twitter by surprise (although they had been actively listening to Twitter for two months when they did) and established the Comcast Cares account (@comcastcares), then run by Frank Eliason, the company's director of "digital care." Eliason has moved on and is currently with @Citi, but @comcastcares still has a team of employees on Twitter who handle customer service, helping as many as they can by escalating problems directly to Comcast's executive customer service department. Scale is a very real issue here. We've always wondered why Comcast doesn't focus more on improving their core customer service offerings to catch problems long before they become Twitter problems. As of this writing, Comcast continues to be plagued by its fundamentally bad customer service reputation. A giant Twitter patch, no matter how famous it made them at the time, wasn't enough.

These days, companies in pretty much every industry have found effective uses of Twitter. What follows is just a tiny sampling of some companies and resources for finding companies in some really popular industry categories.

Food, drink, and nightlife:

✔ Foodspotting (`@foodspotting`)

✔ Epicurious (`@epicurious`)

✔ Alton Brown (`@altonbrown`)

✔ Top Chef (`@BravoTopChef`)

✔ Food & Drink (`https://twitter.com/who_to_follow/interests/food-drink`)

Major retailers:

✔ Target (`@Target`)

✔ Walmart (`@Walmart`)

✔ Peapod (`@PeapodDelivers`)

✔ Macy's (`@Macys`)

✔ Amazon (`@amazon`)

Publishing and media:

✔ Books, as shown in Figure 6-2 (`https://twitter.com/who_to_follow/interests/books`)

✔ News (`https://twitter.com/who_to_follow/interests/news`)

✔ Wiley Tech (`@WileyTech`)

✔ For Dummies (`@ForDummies`)

Figure 6-2:
Popular
Accounts:
Books.

Travel:

- Johnny Jet (@JohnnyJet)
- Adventure Girl (@adventuregirl)
- TripAdvisor (@TripAdvisor)
- Kayak (@KAYAK)
- Expedia (@Expedia)
- HipMunk (@thehipmunk)

Finance, taxes, and banking:

- Capgemini (@Capgemini)
- H&R Block (@HRBlock)
- QuickBooks (@QuickBooks)
- QuickenLoans (@QuickenLoans)

Millions of businesses large and small are using Twitter. To learn more about using it for your business, check out Chapter 11 of this book for a deeper dive on using Twitter for business.

Talking Politics with Actual Politicians

Politicians took to Twitter as a means to connect with their constituents and, um, converse (sometimes it gets pretty shrill and hostile) with their fellow politicians quite slowly at first. Those days are long gone. Twitter is now a major outlet for politicians at all levels, including at least 80 percent of world leaders.

This doesn't surprise us. Twitter is a great way for politicians to communicate ideas, argue a position on issues, attempt to influence any constituency, stay on top of debates and breaking news, and give a more intimate look into their lives at a time when *transparency* is one of the most positive buzzwords around. In the United States, the Democratic Party was early to jump on the bandwagon, and many users started exploring Twitter in the midst of Barack Obama's tech-savvy and successful 2008 presidential campaign. It's everywhere now, worldwide, particularly with some countries such as Indonesia where a sizeable portion of the population uses Twitter. Don't believe us? Recent figures show 6 percent of all global Twitter usage comes from Indonesia, and as a result, its president, S. B. Yudhoyono (@SBYudhoyono), with 5.35 million followers as of August 2014, is the third most-followed head of state behind the current American President Barack Obama (@BarackObama) and India's Prime Minister Narendra Modi (@narendramodi).

Government employees and office holders have to deal with privacy and legal issues that most other twitterers don't, so you may find politicians occasionally seem a bit on the quiet side when tweeting.

Here are some accounts and resources to get you started:

- ✔ Government, as shown in Figure 6-3 (`https://twitter.com/who_to_follow/interests/government`)
- ✔ U.S. Democratic Congressional Campaign Committee (`@dccc`)
- ✔ U.S. National Republican Congressional Committee (`@NRCC`)
- ✔ U.S. President Barack Obama (`@BarackObama`)
- ✔ California Governor Jerry Brown (`@JerryBrownGov`)
- ✔ The Office of British Prime Minister (Currently David Cameron) (`@Number10gov`)
- ✔ Former Vice President Al Gore (`@algore`)
- ✔ The White House (`@WhiteHouse`)

Note that some of these accounts aren't maintained by the people whose name appears on them. Barack Obama's account, for example, is a mix of Tweets from the president himself and updates posted by staff members.

Figure 6-3:
Popular
Accounts:
Government

Following Celebrities on Twitter

It's nearly impossible to watch more than a few minutes of television without being exposed to a hashtag, a username for a Twitter account, actual Tweets displayed on the screen, someone who is talking about Twitter, or even someone asking viewers to answer a question or share their thoughts via Twitter.

The list of the top 100 most-followed Twitter accounts is dominated by celebrities for pretty obvious reasons. When you have a gigantic fan base, it's really easy to build a gigantic Twitter following. That said, you will still find celebrities on Twitter's top 100 who have far more Twitter followers than celebrities who are as famous in general, but who do not make good use of Twitter.

Now more than ever, celebrities use Twitter heavily. There are many reasons why, so we'll give you a few of our favorites:

- ✔ **To connect with fans:** Whether announcing new projects, releasing a new video, asking for opinions on new tracks, or answering fan questions, the possibilities of using Twitter to go direct to fans are limitless.

- ✔ **To get personal:** Basketball star Shaquille O'Neal (@SHAQ) made Twitter his absolute playground early, opening himself to surprise tweetups, meals, and other meet-and-greet opportunities with fans.

- ✔ **To share interests:** Actor George Takei (@GeorgeTakei), who Star Trek fans knew as Sulu, uses his Twitter stream to share popular stories, viral online content, and causes he feels strongly about.

- ✔ **To inspire:** Oprah Winfrey (@Oprah), and Arianna Huffington (@AriannaHuff), post rich streams full of tremendously inspiring articles, ideas, quotes, and photographs.

- ✔ **To make money:** Ellen DeGeneres' (@TheEllenShow) famous selfie turned out to be part of a highly orchestrated influencer marketing program paid for by Samsung to promote its new phone. It's a great photo, and people have had a lot of fun with it, but it was also an advertisement — a point that stirred up some controversy when other high-profile selfies were discovered to be part of the program.

- ✔ **To be real:** Singers Lady Gaga (@ladygaga) and Sara Bareilles (@SaraBareilles) tweet just like the rest of us, gushing in excitement over successes and complaining about tired feet and other mundane life moments that make their lives seem a whole lot more "real." They are just two of probably millions of musicians — celebrities and up and comers — who have taken to Twitter to reach out to fans. For more ideas of musicians to follow, check out Figure 6-4.

Figure 6-4:
Popular
Accounts:
Music.

Bear in mind, as living and breathing humans, celebrities also use Twitter for some pretty awful stuff. They argue, they gossip, they have breakups (we miss how much fun Ashton Kutcher and Demi Moore used to have sharing an irreverent glimpse into their personal lives in happier times), and they have breakdowns (too sad to name names; we just hope that the public nature of these breakdowns mean the celebrities got help faster than they might have otherwise). We'd like to point out a few examples, mainly to teach a few hard lessons about Twitter that are nonetheless important to consider:

✔ **To lie:** For a while, cyclist Lance Armstrong used Twitter to make very strong accusations against anti-doping investigations against him. This did not end well. It would be impossible to list or even tally the number of assertions by politicians on Twitter that did not hold up to even cursory fact-checking. Lesson: Don't believe everything you read on Twitter.

✔ **To cheat:** Unfortunately, the dark underbelly of Twitter includes quite a lot of inappropriate activities and ways to connect with people in ways that hurt other people. Politician Anthony Wiener famously tweeted an extremely inappropriate photo to an equally inappropriate woman because he thought he was only sharing a private message via direct message. Lesson: The best advice we can give you is to work very hard to maintain open and honest communication with your loved ones, especially your partners and children, so that everyone makes good choices.

Twitter functions as a sort of impromptu fan club for tech-savvy celebs, both renowned and up-and-coming. Here are a few more Twitter accounts you may want to take a peek at:

- ✔ The Dalai Lama (@DalaiLama)
- ✔ Stephen Colbert (@StephenatHome)
- ✔ Jimmy Fallon (@jimmyfallon)
- ✔ Rainn Wilson (@rainnwilson)
- ✔ 50 Cent (@50cent)
- ✔ John Mayer (@JohnMayer)
- ✔ Wil Wheaton (@wilw)
- ✔ Soleil Moon Frye (@moonfrye)
- ✔ John Cleese (@JohnCleese)

People do start Twitter accounts using celebrities' names, and they often get a slew of followers who have no idea that they're not following the "real" celebrity — the person they think they're following. Impersonating someone on Twitter without very clearly disclosing that it is a parody account violates Twitter's terms of service. Twitter has, and will continue to, shut down accounts by impersonators or require that the account name be changed to disclose that it's not the real person. In addition to looking for the blue verified-account icon, you can check whether the person is legit by looking at the number of followers relative to comparable celebrities and by checking the star's official web properties for a link to their Twitter account.

Twitter Directories

To be honest, the *Twitter For Dummies* team simply can't compete with timeliness or thoroughness of some online websites when it comes to finding the buzzworthy people to follow for you. Fortunately, Twitter.com and several other sites have made finding popular users even easier.

Twitter.com has a list of popular accounts sorted by topics of interest. We mention a few earlier in this chapter. The main page is at `https://twitter.com/who_to_follow/interests`.

In the top-left navigation bar, click #Discover. You get five discovery options in the current interface: Tweets, Activity, Who to Follow, Find Friends, and Popular Accounts.

As mentioned at the beginning of this chapter, you can browse Popular Accounts by topic to find popular and prolific users who match the kind of Twitter stream you want to cultivate. Many people find it inspiring to follow Twitter accounts engaged in changing the world in positive ways. You might want to take a look at the social good Popular accounts (see Figure 6-5) and choose some of your favorites.

Figure 6-5: Social Good is another great Popular Accounts list to browse.

Additionally, blogging about the top Twitter accounts for any given interest, category, profession, or hobby has remained very popular. Sometimes, the best way to find new people to follow is to leave Twitter altogether and run some Google searches. Look for recent blog posts suggesting topical people on Twitter.

Signing Up for Automated Material

Not every Twitter account is written. Quite a few really useful Twitter accounts are automated *bots* (short for robots) that publish Tweets that have never touched human hands. At first, this sounds kind of awful, but there are some great reasons for doing this.

Want to be among the very first to know when there is earthquake activity near San Francisco, California? Follow SF Quakebot (@EarthquakesSF) to receive Tweets based on real-time seismographic information from the USGS. Want a funny way to explain McCarthyism to a friend? Go look at

Robot J. McCarthy (@RedScareBot) which scans Twitter for Tweets containing words like "communist" and automatically shares them with ironic commentary as if they were written during the height of anticommunist witch hunts. Concerned about government accountability? Congress-edits (@CongressEdits) automagically tweets whenever wikipedia.org is anonymously edited by someone whose IP address shows they are accessing the site from within the US Congress.

Some Twitter accounts simply syndicate material from online outlets: event listings, blogs, newspapers' websites, and so on. Done well, accounts like these are quite welcome in Twitter's community. Accounts like the *New York Times* (@NYTimes) and CNN (@CNN), while no longer just the bots they originally were (see Figure 6-6) make up some of Twitter's most-followed media accounts because even when they were 100% automated, they were still tremendously useful.

Figure 6-6: From humble bot beginnings, @NYTimes has grown to millions of followers.

Other popular forms of automated accounts can be worthwhile. Companies don't need a human being to type great quotes or famous lines from movies and click Post when it's time to publish them. If set up mindfully and including great sharing copy and articles, an automated Twitter account that helps people follow a blog with automated Tweets can be a great idea. Or, automated Tweets can be a good addition to otherwise manually composed Twitter accounts.

Many, if not all, business users employ some degree of automation to ensure that their account is sharing useful, engaging, relevant content throughout the week at the times their audiences are more likely to want to engage with it. They do this by scouring for great stuff to share and then composing Tweets in advance, using a scheduler such as Buffer, HubSpot's Social Tools, or HootSuite.

It's also not uncommon, especially among business users, to allow certain apps to make automated posts to your otherwise handwritten account on your behalf. Use these apps with care. Laura allows @Jobvite to post up to four @HubSpot marketing and engineering job openings a week on her @Pistachio account. She likes that these posts might turn into employee referral bonuses, but she also does it because people generally react very well. Each time, several people actively engage by asking questions, retweeting the posts, or marking them as favorites.

Part III
Twittering in High Gear

Need a little inspiration to help you get started? Check out this list of people who are rocking Twitter with visual content at www.dummies.com/extras/twitter.

In this part . . .

- ✔ Improve your Twitteracy with etiquette, linking, shorthand, and exploration.

- ✔ Find out about tools and tricks that make your Twitter experience more efficient, more rewarding, and more accessible.

- ✔ Understand hashtags and use them like a pro.

- ✔ Add photos, videos, and other visual media to your Tweets.

Chapter 7

How to Tweet Like Tweeps Do

You've signed up for Twitter, you're discovering your flock, and now it's time to accept that you're a *tweep*: a Twitter person or, more accurately, a Twitter "peep."

Along with tweep comes various Twitter vernacular, which is why this chapter is dedicated to increasing your Twitter fluency, understanding when and how to craft your Tweets, and using text messages to update or interact on Twitter.

Following Twitter Protocol

Many Twitter neophytes want to know what the rules are or whether Twitter has standard protocol and etiquette. Like many other social media sites, Twitter sprang from a close-knit group of early adopters who set the rhythm. Because Twitter was a favorite of Silicon Valley's new-media elite long before it broke into the mainstream, some insider jokes and conventions used can be confusing, but they've since become part of the lexicon.

Longtime users have certainly fallen into certain habits or sets of rules. But remember that Twitter is what you make of it, and you're free to do your own thing.

Like any other social media company, Twitter has a terms of service (TOS) agreement that all members must adhere to or risk having their accounts suspended or deleted. You can access Twitter's terms at `https://twitter.com/tos`. Think of them as a baseline of Twitter etiquette. You won't find anything particularly surprising in them: You must be at least 13 years old to create an account and use the service, you can't engage in abuse or harassment, you can't spam other members or participate in activities that break any laws, and so on. The terms are actually more liberal than most web services' regulations; pornography and explicit language, for example, aren't banned.

Beyond the terms of service, Twitter etiquette is simple: Be genuine and non-deceptive, and provide value. Other than that, just use Twitter how it suits you. Consider this to be an unofficial code of conduct (although it's more like a guideline).

If you're wondering if you can get by with deceptive behavior, think twice. Twitter keeps tabs on deceptive activity; it can and will ban accounts that impersonate celebrities or companies if those accounts don't make it clear that they're unofficial or parody accounts. This policy is a contentious point in the Twitter community. Many members were upset when the @cwalken account, belonging to an aspiring comedian pretending to be actor Christopher Walken, was deleted from the system.

Beyond the simple regulations, you can't really use Twitter in a right or wrong way, because no two people use it for exactly the same reasons. But some members certainly have their opinions:

- ✔ Some users complain when others tweet too often, whereas others complain that their contacts don't tweet enough. This complaint is a little silly. Don't like the contents? Turn the dial. Use a third-party tool. Unsubscribe. You don't have to follow a user whom you think tweets too often or not enough.

- ✔ Some users take issue with strings of @replies and wonder why those conversations weren't conducted in a private forum. But again, you always have the choice to control who you follow and whom you engage with.

- ✔ You may encounter confusing, even conflicting, advice and back-seat tweeting from the handful of people on Twitter who aren't comfortable without rules. Don't take them too seriously. Twitter itself just isn't that rigid. Your Twitter community will help define your standard.

Be polite on Twitter, for the most part, but no more or less so than you're expected to be in the real world. Just keep in mind that Twitter is a public forum. Twitter posts and feeds get exported outside Twitter and embedded in websites, blogs, other social media sites, and aggregator sites.

Although users love Twitter's largely rule-free nature, some generally accepted behaviors have evolved over time. You can ease your transition into the culture of Twitter by getting familiar with these behaviors and speech tendencies before you start. Establish dedication and credibility early, in part by knowing your way around the following Twitter customs.

Language and abbreviations

Over time, any group of people that interacts regularly falls into its own way of talking. Twitter is no exception to that rule; in fact, it may be even more subject to it because of the 140-character limit. Twitter's lexicon has evolved to include unique words, phrases, and abbreviations that most active users understand and recognize. But you may find these references confusing.

Right off the bat, you see a lot of puns involving the word *Twitter,* with the prefix *tw* or *twi: tweet, tweeple, tweetup,* and so on. At first, it looks like baby talk — and indeed, it can get a bit over the twop. (See our point?) Not all members are fans of corny terms such as *tweeple.* Others think that the Twitter-specific language is fun or an easy and obvious way to delineate something as being Twitter-specific. Either way, whether you plan to use Twitterspeak or not, it does help to know what this stuff means.

Plenty of eccentric people use Twitter, not to mention loads of subcultures and subcommunities. Just because you see an unfamiliar term doesn't mean that it's part of the Twitter vernacular. For Twitter terms you should be familiar with, check out the glossary at the back of this book.

In our glossary, we purposely didn't include some of the nonsense words with the *tw* prefix. Twitterers don't widely use them, many avid users find them rather annoying, and beginning to use them more often may be the first sign that you're a twitterholic!

Engaging others on Twitter

On Twitter, the name of the game is engagement. Whether you use Twitter for business or fun, you don't just want to sit back and watch the stream flow by — you want to genuinely interact with people. You have to know how to listen as much as know how to converse (this goes twice for businesses) — but it always boils down to engagement. Don't ever feel shy about finding and following interesting folks on Twitter. That's really what it's all about.

While you sift through the Twitter conversation, don't be shy about clicking the usernames that you see (as in @replies) to view the profiles of the people who sent or received the Tweets you find. You'll be amazed how good an idea you get of someone just by glancing at his last 20 Tweets. Interested? Follow him. It's not like other social networks where you're really only expected to connect to folks you already know.

Now, click away from the profile and back to the Tweets that first caught your eye. You can click reply and try writing to these strangers and offering your own opinion. You may have to try this through several conversations before strangers start writing back, but if you're adding to the conversation, they will.

But even if you don't @reply, your Tweets still appear in Search, and other Twitter users can spot them. If you have something interesting to say, people start to reply to your Tweets. If you seek out and use relevant keywords and #hashtags, you will start to connect with others who share your interests. Your early days on Twitter will probably be pretty quiet when it comes to replies and conversation. All those twitterers are just getting to know you, after all. Don't worry; the more you engage, the more great stuff you share, and the more good contacts you add to your network, the more people will begin to notice you.

Tweeting frequency

Twitter users tend to settle into a rhythm of tweeting frequency, often unconsciously, over time. Some Twitter users are considered to be noisy because they tweet so much, whereas others can come across as standoffish because they don't tweet frequently. So how much is too much or too little? How often should you tweet?

A good rule when you're starting is to post at least four to five Tweets per day. We find that tweeting four to five times a day leads to the most engagement and retweets from other users.

You most likely find yourself tweeting much more often than that — our friend Dan Zarrella, a social media scientist at HubSpot, found that an average user tweets 22 times a day — but if you aren't fully comfortable with Twitter yet, four or five Tweets per day should get you going at a solid, unobtrusive, and value-adding pace for personal and business use.

It's also worth thinking about who you want to reach. People who are new to Twitter and following only a few people get bowled over by frequent tweeters simply because those people's Tweets are all they see in their stream. Some people use Twitter like texting — having back-and-forth conversations with their friends. This is a fine use, but would likely involve many more Tweets a day than, say, a business user or someone just figuring out what they want to do with the platform.

Inserting Links into Your Tweets

Virtually all Twitter users incorporate links into their Tweets on a regular basis. We've seen that roughly 23 percent of Tweets contain links. You can insert links to web pages, blog entries, or even other Tweets. The toughest part of including these links is getting them to fit in the 140-character limit while leaving yourself room to say something about why you're sending the link out in the first place.

The *URL shortener* is a tool designed to manage exceptionally long URLs so that they won't break over lines in emails and so that they're easier to copy and paste. Twitter and services like it have heightened the need to save space when linking. Sites such as Bitly (`https://bit.ly`) can convert a link to a shorter set of numbers and letters that forwards to the original link and can cut the link's length by as much as 70 or 80 percent.

It's important to note that shortening your Tweet doesn't give you more space to tweet. Twitter is smart enough to recognize a URL and give that URL 22 to 23 characters of its 140-character allowance. The benefit of using a shortened link is in presentation of your Tweet. Whether you use a full link or a shortened link, you have 118 characters left to compose your message. A short URL is more attractive than a long URL; the longer Tweet (Figure 7-1) includes an ellipsis that makes it visually unappealing. Figure 7-2 shows a Tweet that includes a URL shortened by a service such as Bitly. As you can see, the Tweet is much more welcoming.

Figure 7-1:
A Tweet with a long URL.

Long URL

Link shortening has become so common that many mainstream websites offer their own short URLs to make it easier for people to refer to their sites. *The New York Times,* for example, uses `http://nyti.ms`, and Flickr, the photo-sharing website, uses `https://flic.kr`. These brands have set up their own unique URL shorteners so that any time someone tweets a shortened URL from one of these sites, it's clear that that link is from the brand's website.

Figure 7-2:
A Tweet
with a
shortened
URL.

Shortened URL

You can create your own shortened URL in a few simple steps. Take any URL, visit `https://bit.ly`, and copy your URL into the text box, and you get something like `https://bitly.com/1i1WpXi` that you can use in place of the long URL.

It's important to include a short reason for the link, such as a headline or a hook, that tells people why they may want to click it. Refer to Figure 7-2 for a Tweet that the accompanying message gives followers a glimpse of the content they can find through the URL.

Believe it or not, crafting your Tweets is a real art. Some of the most popular tweeters have large followings because they're good at writing attention-grabbing Tweets. It's also nice to give credit to a fellow tweeter by typing @ username if you're sharing someone else's Tweets or links. Typing @ followed by a Twitter username automatically links to that Twitter account's profile page so that you can see more about who that person is. It's context. In the example in Figure 7-2, you'll notice how we included @LinkedIn, that way the organization is aware I'm further spreading their content.

Short-URL analytics

Shorteners such as Bitly also track how your link performs, showing you how many people clicked or, in some cases, retweeted your link. The number of clicks your shortened links receive can be critical in understanding whether or not people are responding to the content you're sharing, which can help adjust what you push to your network over time.

One nice thing about using Bitly as your URL shortener is its built-in analytics. If you want to see how a link is doing and how many clicks it's getting, add a plus sign (+) after it. Bitly takes you to an analytics dashboard, giving you a history of who's clicking that link, when they clicked it and who's currently talking about it.

To access analytics on your Tweets, you have to sign up for Bitly. Don't worry; you don't need a new username or password. Simply click Sign In in the top-right corner of the Bitly home page and then click Sign In with Twitter. The site creates an account for you with your existing Twitter account, allowing you to create endless links and see the analytics for them.

Add the + sign to the end of any Bitly link to review analytics for that URL. Try it by clicking `https://bitly.com/1i1WpXi+`.

Adding Your Location

If you like, you can include your location in your Tweets. Although it's not terribly exciting to do so while you're sitting at your desk, you may want to share your location when you're tweeting at a conference or visiting a new city or a popular location.

If you're tweeting your location from your phone, you need to give your Twitter application permission to detect your location. If you have an iPhone running iOS 7, for example, tap Settings > Privacy > Location Services and turn on location detection for Twitter.

Alternatively, third-party applications such as Foursquare (`https://foursquare.com`) use the Twitter application programming interface (API) to report on location information. Foursquare lets you tell both Foursquare friends and Twitter followers where you are at any time. When Foursquare forwards that information to Twitter, the location information is embedded in the tweet data, like a time stamp.

If you find yourself needing to get rid of your location information for whatever reason, Twitter can strip the location information out of all your Tweets.

To wipe all location data from your Tweets, follow these steps:

1. **Click the gear icon in the top navigation bar of the Twitter home page.**

2. **From the drop-down menu that appears, click Settings.**

3. **Select Security and Privacy on the left side of the page.**

4. **Click the Delete All Location Information button.**

It may take up to 30 minutes for Twitter to delete all location history from your past Tweets. You always have the option to turn location information on and off for every Tweet you publish.

Subscribing to Text-Message Notifications

Receiving Twitter updates as Short Message Service (SMS) messages right on your phone has its advantages and disadvantages. For one thing, it lets you choose to remain much more closely up to date on a small subset of your Twitter connections, which can be cool. Web celebrity iJustine (`@iJustine`) does this to find her real friends among the people she follows.

To subscribe to text-message notifications, you need to activate your phone within Twitter. To do so, follow these steps:

1. **Navigate to your Twitter settings, and click the Mobile tab.**

2. **Choose your country from the initial drop-down menu, and enter your mobile number.**

3. **Click Activate Phone.**

   Twitter prompts you to text GO to a country-specific short code.

4. **Select the text notifications you'd like to receive (see Figure 7-3).**

   You can even enable sleep settings to keep these messages from blasting when you're snoozing.

As you see in Figure 7-3, you have many options for text notifications. Many users prefer simply to use the Twitter mobile application, but text notifications are a great way for nonsmartphone users to stay updated with their Twitter activity — you can find out who is favoriting your content, retweeting your content, and so on.

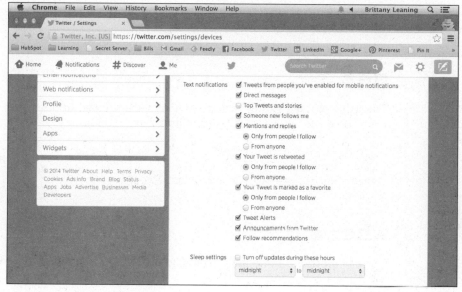

Figure 7-3:
Twitter has various settings for your text-message notifications.

If you're following a large number of people who update frequently, your mobile phone may never stop beeping, vibrating, or doing whatever it does when it receives a text message. You may want to be wary of how many text-message notifications you sign up for, particularly if you have a monthly text-messaging limit.

To perform Twitter actions through text messages, you need to use the following text short codes.

fav

If someone's most recent Tweet made you laugh (say, one in our @dummies account), you can favorite that Tweet by sending an update to Twitter, as follows:

```
fav @dummies
```

If you're receiving updates on your cellphone, sending `fav` by itself adds the last update you received to the Favorites tab on your home screen.

stats

If you ever want to know how many followers you have and how many users you're following, text the update `stats` followed by your username.

```
stats @anum
```

You can also text someone else's username if you're interested in seeing that person's account stats.

get

The `get` command allows you to quickly view the last update from a user. Want to see @anum's latest Tweet? Simply use

```
get @anum
```

Twitter reports back with @anum's last Tweet.

whois

If you want to get someone's profile information quickly (say, Laura's), use the `whois` command

```
whois @pistachio
```

Twitter sends you a message that contains the user's proper name (Laura Fitton), how long she's been on Twitter (since April 2007), and her current bio from her profile page (@Pistachio).

See Figure 7-4 for examples of the `stats`, `get`, and `whois` commands.

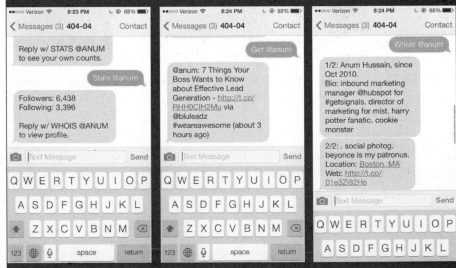

Figure 7-4: Text-message notifications on an iPhone.

follow

```
follow @bleaning
```

Using the `follow` command allows you to begin following a user from your phone. Although you may already be following her on your Twitter account, following her from your phone will send you live text messages every time that user is tweeting. So if you text `follow @bleaning`, you'll begin receiving texts every time Brittany tweets.

leave

```
leave @bleaning
```

The `leave` command seems that it would be the opposite of `follow`, but it's not — at least, not quite. The command `leave username` simply blocks the individual's Twitter updates from coming to your phone; it doesn't unfollow that person on Twitter.

on/off username

```
on @bleaning
```

The `on/off username` command turns device updates on and off for individual users. Like `follow`, `on username` connects you to people on Twitter so that you're following their updates. Like `leave`, the `off username` command stops device updates but doesn't unfollow the username account.

In other words, `on/off username` has no unique functionality that's different from `follow` or `leave`.

invite

Do you want to invite someone to Twitter? Send the `invite` command followed by her email address or mobile phone number, as follows:

```
invite friend@example.com
invite 212 555 1212
```

Twitter sends either an email or SMS to that person to let her know that you've invited her to use Twitter.

Codes may come, and codes may go . . .

Because Twitter is a living application, its commands come and go. In fact, our list is only a small portion of the full list of Twitter text short codes.

For a recent list of Twitter commands, browse to Twitter's Help forums by clicking the help link at the top of every Twitter page. As we were writing this edition, `https://support.twitter.com//forums/10711/entries/14020` had the most accurate list of Twitter commands.

---

quit and stop

```
stop @pistachio
```

The `quit and stop` command discontinues all service between Twitter and your cellphone, taking your cellphone number out of Twitter altogether. If you use this command, you have to log in to your Twitter account and redo the steps to add your cellphone back to your account.

Chapter 8

Improving Your Twitteracy

In This Chapter

▶ Using tools to enrich your Twitter experience

▶ Understanding the infamous hashtag

▶ Finding programs that make using Twitter easy

Twitter is a useful tool on its own, but by design, it remains extremely simple, even stark, in its functionality. The folks who created it wanted to make Twitter a platform for users to build on, improve, and enhance, so they opened Twitter's API (application programming interface, or code) to the public. As a result, enterprising and creative software developers can create applications that work with Twitter to offer even more compelling features and ways to use the dynamic system.

Twitter itself is constantly evolving and changing — from design facelifts to new features to changes in how the back-end technology works. The Twitter team pays close attention to how people interact with the system and what those users want to do with it. Because the long-term success of Twitter depends completely on a healthy base of users generating a regular stream of content, management obviously wants to do its best to keep Twitter on its toes.

As a result, Twitter is a living application and community, extending far beyond what Twitter itself controls. Conventions and third-party tools have popped up to fill in functionality that Twitter may have missed, chosen not to implement, or intentionally left for other developers to handle.

You can find a rich tool set online to enhance and personalize your own Twitter experience. In this chapter, we introduce many of the third-party tools that enrich the service.

By the time you read this book, dozens, if not hundreds, of new mashups, services, applications, and other tools and products may be built out into the Twitter ecosystem. The ones listed here are a few of the big players that we predict will last through it all.

Finding Interesting Twitter Talk with Search Tools

With so many conversations going on every day on Twitter, how can you find the ones that are relevant to you?

You can use search applications, track people and topics, find data about what's trendy and buzzworthy up to the second, and more.

You can search Twitter many, many ways, but here are two noteworthy ways:

✔ Twitter Search (integrated into all pages of Twitter.com)

✔ Topsy

Twitter Search

Summize, a powerful search engine that trawls through the enormous volume of public Tweets in real time, emerged in 2008 and soon became the go-to tool for searching Twitter. The powers that be at Twitter noticed. Seeing the value in Summize's application, Twitter acquired Summize and began a slow process of incorporating it into Twitter itself, renaming it Twitter Search (`https://twitter.com/search-home`). So although the Summize name is a thing of the past, Twitter Search is a powerful and important part of the Twitter experience. An advanced search tool is available at its own web address, `https://twitter.com/search-advanced`, as shown in Figure 8-1, or you can run a basic search by using the search box at the top right of your Twitter home screen.

Twitter Search isn't static: It keeps searching for your query even after you click the Search button. When Twitter Search finds a new search result, a link appears at the top of your Twitter Search results, telling you how many new matches for your search term have appeared since you last clicked the Refresh button in your browser. This may not seem like a big deal, but it's extremely useful when news is breaking or you're following a live event. Just click a trending topic to see what we mean. You'll notice that with more popular topics, Twitter lets you know that more Tweets with the relevant trending topic have come up since you first ran the search. Click the notification, and the new Tweets load.

Something else that makes Twitter Search so useful is how specific you can get with Advanced Search. You can fine-tune searches by usernames, locations, or keywords. Keep in mind that you're better off using only a couple of advanced search settings at a time; otherwise, you may find no results at all!

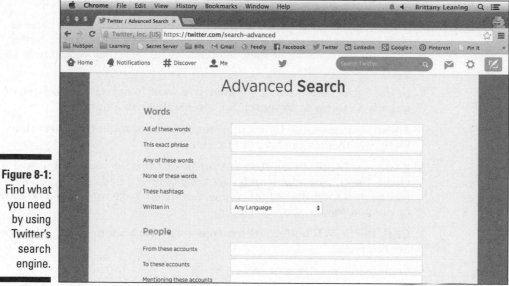

To use Advanced Search, follow these steps:

1. **On the Twitter Search page, click the Advanced Search link located below the text box.**

   A new page appears, containing a fill-in-the-blank interface to help you search for the information and people you want to find.

2. **In the Words panel, fine-tune your search by word.**

   You can specify that a search match all or none of the words in your query, the exact phrase you input, Twitter hashtags (which we talk about in the section "Joining the Hashtag Revolution," later in this chapter), or even set your Advanced Search defaults to all or one of 51 languages. (Under the Words section of advanced search, you see a Written In field with a drop-down menu to select any of the 51 languages.)

3. **In the People panel, specify whether you want to search by user.**

   You can search Tweets that come from, are sent to, or reference a certain username.

4. **In the Places panel, enter information if you want to search by location.**

   You'll notice that next to the Near This Place text, Twitter already populates a location near you, but you can adjust it to what you'd like (or not use a location at all).

   You might search for only Tweets of users who enter their location as a given city, for example.

5. **In the Dates panel, select a specific date range for your Tweets.**

   If you're looking for a specific time in a particular period, this panel is your place to do it. If you're looking for a specific Tweet from a conference, for example, input the conference dates, and that should help you narrow your results.

6. **In the Other panel, select whether you want to search for positive or negative Tweets or to search for Tweets that ask a question.**

   These options search for natural-language clues about the Tweet that imply whether it's positive or negative.

   If you use Twitter to improve customer relations for your business or a client, the Other panel search can really help you find certain types of feedback. It's not perfect, of course, but it can make rooting out negative or positive feedback much easier.

7. **Click the Search button, which appears at the bottom of the Advanced Search page.**

   Your search results appear.

Here are a few things to keep in mind about Search:

- ✔ Search is a living thing. Having fine-tuned a useful search, many times you'll want to do something with it, such as watching it over time, subscribing to it, or sharing it with others.

- ✔ Keep the Search window open to watch as new results come in, or subscribe to the RSS feed for the search to monitor it longer term.

- ✔ You don't need to fill in every field in the search tool. Just share what you'd like to try to get the results you desire.

Topsy

Topsy (http://topsy.com) is a search engine that stores a comprehensive index of Tweets — as its site says, "all Tweets since 2006." A Twitter certified partner, Topsy behaves a lot like Google Search for Twitter. Using the tool is quite simple. Follow these steps:

1. **Type a keyword query in the search bar.**

   Topsy swiftly gives you the results. You can drill further down into the search results through a few options.

2. **In the Latest Results panel, select the time frame for your search.**

   You have the option to see Tweets from the past hour, past day, past seven days, past 30 days, all time, or a specific range.

3. **In the Everything panel, select Tweet types to narrow your search.**

   You can drill down on search results based on whether they include links, Tweets, photos, or videos. You can also drill down by influencers; Topsy searches for people it considers to be relevant as influencers. If you're searching for Tweets from the Inbound conference, for example, @HubSpot appears as an influencer. This makes sense, because HubSpot hosts the Inbound conference.

4. **In the All Languages panel, select a language for your search.**

   This setting displays only Tweets published in that language.

Figure 8-2 shows the results of searching for @anum. The results for the options Past 9 Days, Everything, and English provide a mix of the latest 213 Tweets, including links, photos, and general Tweets.

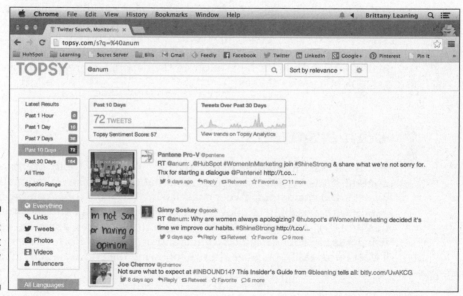

Figure 8-2:
Find what you need by using Topsy.

Topsy also provides a sentiment score to show how positive the Tweets are, as well as an option to view the trends for this search query with Topsy Analytics. A sentiment report essentially shows you how positively or negatively people resonated with the Tweets. This can roughly indicate to you how happy or upset people are about the topic being searched.

Joining the Hashtag Revolution

Hashtags have become part of the core culture of Twitter for many avid users. Basically, *hashtags* are a way to delineate a keyword that people can use to organize discussions about specific topics and events. (You may sometimes hear them called *meta tags* or *meta hashtags*.) Originally, the website Hashtags (`www.hashtags.org`) automatically tracked and displayed these hashtags. But Twitter occasionally turns off the portion of its API that the Hashtags site uses, so you can't always search it reliably.

Not all Twitter users like hashtags: Some users think that hashtags make the Twitter stream clunky. Admittedly, seeing Tweet after Tweet go by containing hashtags such as `#GNO`, `#journchat`, `#justsayin`, and `#sxsw` can seem noisy and disjointed if you don't follow or understand those hashtags. You can always unfollow a heavy hashtag user if the hashtags really bother you, but don't pull the trigger too quickly: You can probably get used to hashtags, along with the rest of Twitter's quirks, before too long. The ability to tag Tweets is extremely powerful. People are just starting to figure out hashtags, which have a very interesting future. Even social sites such as Facebook, Instagram, and Tumblr have adopted the hashtag approach. In this section, we look at a few use cases.

Conversations

Hashtags make it possible to quickly filter Tweets by topic, event, or other content by using an easy abbreviation that doesn't take up too many of a Tweet's 140 characters. Tweeps discussing the same topic can tag a conversation with a hashtag to allow others to discover that content through the hashtag. Perhaps you're an avid Harry Potter fan, like `@anum`. In that case, using `#HarryPotter` allows `@anum` and other Harry Potter fans to spot your Tweet more easily, because they're following the conversation out of their own interest.

Live events

People at the same event or meeting can use the same hashtag. Later on, if you want to review the information related to that event or conference, you can simply search for the hashtag on Twitter Search to find all Tweets that reference it. Figure 8-3 shows the results of a search for `#MISTBoston14`, for example. Sure, you can search by keyword, but the # in a hashtag is a signal to others that the hashtag is *the* keyword to use to easily find, read, and share all Tweets on a certain topic or event. At the MIST Boston event, the organization made it clear in its promotional materials that `#MISTBoston14` was the hashtag to use to tag conversations.

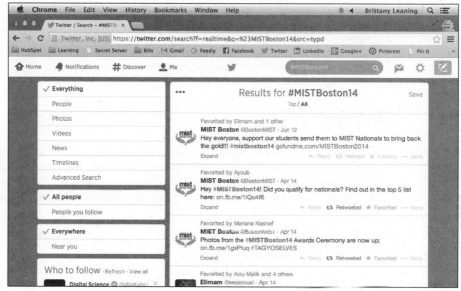

Figure 8-3:
Tweets with
the #MIST
Boston14
hashtag
appear in a
search.

A hashtag that catches on forms an instant digital community. Most of these communities are short-lived. #MISTBoston14 is likely to fade out but rise in a new form as #MISTBoston15. Other communities have ongoing conversations, recurring real-time events, or even entire online movement.

Hashtags are handy for taking notes and having conversations during events, especially if the organizers say something like "Include #ourevent in all your Tweets" (where ourevent is a unique label for that event). People tweeting about it just type the #ourevent tag in each Tweet to contribute to the combined flow of Tweets that everyone can watch and respond to. More and more, talks and conference panels in the tech and media industries display the search results for the official hashtag, creating a shared billboard of ideas, notes, questions, and other information. People who aren't present at the event can participate in the discussion by searching the hashtag stream and following along with the presentation or speaker, just as though they were there. From the way that the hashtag is included in Tweets, you can often discover other attendees at the conference that you may want to meet or talk to (although sometimes, the people tweeting from offsite are so engaged that you might think they were in the room with you).

Although hashtags can help your Tweets get spread and noticed by other users using that same hashtag, it's important to keep your Tweets from looking spammy. We find that more than three hashtags look like spam and keep people from reading your Tweets.

Beyond the number of hashtags you use, also carefully consider which ones you use. For example, using `#MISTBoston14` along with `#conference` or `#Boston` further emphasizes where you are and what you're doing. But simply putting hashtags such as `#fun`, `#lolz`, or `#speakers` wouldn't necessarily add any additional value to your Tweet.

Twitter chats

Suppose that you want to start a discussion or debate on Twitter, and you want to establish a hashtag for that conversation. All it takes to start a hashtag is use it in a Tweet. When you do, you start a Twitter chat. A *Twitter chat* (also called a *Tweet chat*) is a virtual meeting or gathering of people to discuss a common topic.

Trending hashtags

Near the bottom of the left column of your Twitter home page, you see the Trending Topics section. As millions of people tweet away, Twitter keeps track of the hot topics and displays and ranks them in Trending Topics. When you use Twitter, you can see topics and hashtags trending (becoming popular) in real time.

If you click or tap any of the trending hashtags, Twitter pulls up real-time search results for that topic. (Go ahead and try!) You can use these results to gauge the popularity or success of anything from a person to a political theme to a marketing campaign. The results can also help you figure out what the global Twitter population finds newsworthy. Often, when you see a celebrity's name trending on Twitter, that person had a big news day or recently passed away. (In the latter case, you usually see `#RIP` trending along with that celebrity's name.)

Trending hashtags give you real-time statistics on public appeal and can be a great resource for worldwide events, such as tsunamis and earthquakes. They can also be effective for finding announcements, such as Apple product releases and *House of Cards* season releases. By the same token, Trending Topics often picks up a lot of nonsense and off-target information, such as `#NoDisrespectBut` or `#DontYouHateWhen`, so take trending hashtags with a grain of salt.

Trending Topics defaults to global reach — meaning you'll see topics being discussed by any Twitter user in the world — but you can customize yours for any geographical location or to reflect what's trending for your Twitter network (following and followers) rather than for the world or a specific area.

To adjust the scope of Trending Topics, click the Change button in that section. A dialog box appears, allowing you to home in on what's most interesting to you.

Using hashtags effectively

Here are some tips for using hashtags effectively:

✔ If you want to avoid confusion, check Twitter Search for the hashtag that you want to use to make sure that someone else hasn't already claimed it. People use the popular `#wishlist` hashtag, for example, for everything from software feature wish lists to requests for birthday presents, so searching for it brings up a fairly cluttered stream.

✔ Make sure that everyone attending your event or discussing your topic is aware of the proper hashtag in advance. For example, for the annual INBOUND conference, the team always uses the conference name plus the year. So `#INBOUND13`, `#INBOUND14`, `#INBOUND15`, and so on.

✔ After you choose your hashtag, make a note of it on your event page or blog post — or, of course, tweet it — so that other people can use the same hashtag.

Expanding Your Twitter World by Using Clients

With an understanding of search and hashtags under your belt, let's discuss using Twitter across different useful clients.

Twitter's open API allows software developers to create applications, mashups, and services that feed off the Twitter platform. Figure 8-4 shows the desktop client TweetDeck.

Many of these third-party applications are *Twitter clients* — programs designed to let you update Twitter on your mobile phone instead of having to use the web interface or text messaging. Many of these applications automatically load Tweets from your Twitter followers. This feature is nice, because on the website, you have to click the blue bar showing how many new Tweets have arrived every few minutes to see what's going on.

Each of these applications has a different way of letting you display, organize, search, and interact with Tweets, which makes these applications a very diverse crop. A competition is afoot to become the preferred way for most twitterers to engage with Twitter. Whether a few clear leaders emerge or whether people continue to interact with Twitter in dozens of ways remains to be seen.

Figure 8-4:
Put Twitter
on your
desktop
with a client
such as
TweetDeck.

Desktop clients

Many Twitter clients for your Mac or PC take the form of a web application. These web apps operate just like any website you use — such as Facebook, Google+, or the like. Meaning, you simply navigate to the site through your browser to use them. Some involve a software download that you install and run from the desktop.

Here are a few desktop clients that stand out from the crowd because they're easy to use and offer the features that most Twitter users want:

- ✔ **HootSuite** (www.hootsuite.com): The free, easy-to-install web application was launched on the premise of helping businesses and organizations collaborate on social media campaigns. The tool can be used for free so you have an easy-to-use program for monitoring your Twitter activity. It's particularly helpful if you're monitoring and engaging on Twitter through multiple accounts — perhaps one that's personal and one that's for an organization. At this writing, Twitter's web application doesn't have any option for multiple-account sign-in.

- ✔ **TweetDeck** (www.tweetdeck.com): This free Twitter client, also available as a web application, is compatible with Mac and Windows. TweetDeck is for power Twitter users. Its main selling points are the ability to form specific groups of your contacts, integrated Twitter search, and multiple-column interface. You also find many of the same features as in HootSuite, including the ability to get content from more than one social network. TweetDeck is almost too functional for some casual Twitter users, but if you use Twitter frequently, you can't easily beat seeing trending topics in a column or performing a detailed Twitter search right from your desktop.

Mobile clients

The most basic way to use Twitter on a mobile phone, smartphone, or personal digital assistant (PDA) is through the mobile website (mobile.twitter. com) (discussed in Chapter 4). If you don't have a smartphone, another option is text messaging (discussed in Chapter 7).

Most people will choose to download one of the following mobile applications to their device. Trust us, Twitter can be incredibly helpful when you take it on the road, so it's worth the effort of downloading and setting up a mobile client.

Twitter themselves maintain a variety of "native" apps for various mobile phone and tablet platforms. As of this writing, that includes iPhone, iPad, Android, Windows Phone, Nokia, and Blackberry. You can find all of them listed at `https://about.twitter.com/products/list`. Below, we list some additional third party options for the most popular current platforms.

- ✔ **For an iOS Product:** You can use Tweetbot (`http://tapbots.com/software/tweetbot`), Twitterrific (`www.twitterrific.com`), as well as other apps found by searching in Apple's iOS App Store.

- ✔ **For a BlackBerry:** Your third party choices are limited. Check Blackberry's website (`www.blackberry.com/twitter`) to see current options and what other users think of them.

- ✔ **For an Android-based phone:** If you're not happy with Twitter's own Android app try TweetCaster, which can be found on Google Play (`https://play.google.com`).

- ✔ **For Windows Mobile-based smartphones and PDAs:** Your best bet is to check their app store for current options (`www.windowsphone.com/en-us/store/search?q=twitter`).

Tag clouds

Tweet Cloud (`http://tweetcloud.icodeforlove.com`) and TagCrowd (`http://tagcrowd.com`), Trending Topics, and hashtags have something in common: They can generate a Twitter *tag cloud,* a visual display of words in which the relative size of the word corresponds to how many times it has been mentioned. Tag clouds provide an easy visualization of what's going on in the Twitterverse in real time. Words that twitterers use a lot appear in the tag cloud, and the more mentions a word gets, the larger, darker, and bolder its display is. Tag clouds represent another, often quite visually appealing way to see what's going on.

Monitoring beyond Twitter.com

Sure, building connections and influence on Twitter is a great objective, but there's even more value in the Twitter experience when you take the opportunity to tune in to what people are saying about you, your company, and your favorite topics. A finely attuned listening program greatly enhances your ability to build connections and influence on Twitter.

You can find plenty of tools that let you track your social media presence. Many of these tools are free, though you can pay for some tools that come with additional business features, such as analytics and better organization of search results.

In the following sections, we skim the surface of what's possible. But no matter which service you use, make listening a priority on Twitter. Listening to the tremendous firehose of information about consumer sentiment and world events can bear fruit and help you make effective use of the time you've invested in social media engagement.

Google Alerts

Setting up some basic Google Alerts, although they're not Twitter-specific listening tools, is something that every person and company should do as a minimum social media listening program. The Google Alerts tool trawls the web, looking for new blog posts, Tweets, and news stories that mention whatever keywords you want to follow; then it delivers those posts, Tweets, and stories to your Gmail inbox, as shown in Figure 8-5.

To set up a Google Alert, follow these steps:

1. **Log in to your Gmail account.**

2. **Navigate to** `www.google.com/alerts`**.**

    A drop-down menu appears.

3. **In the Search Terms field, enter the topic, keyword, name, business name, or phrase that you want to monitor.**

Doing a Boolean search, such as putting quotes around two words to keep them together, can help you fine-tune your Google Alerts results.

4. **Click the blue Create Alert button.**

   The alert will automatically be created.

5. **Click the pencil icon next to the new alert, and choose how often you want to receive them, what languages they should capture, and what regions they should come from.**

   You can create as many as you need.

Figure 8-5:
You can have Google Alerts delivered directly to your Gmail inbox.

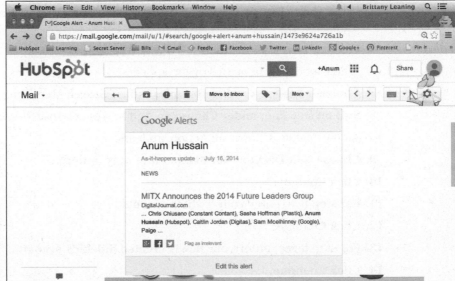

Sidekick plus Zapier

Sidekick (www.getsidekick.com) is a free Chrome extension and iOS application that provides instant notifications when someone opens or clicks an email you sent. If you combine Sidekick with Zapier (https://zapier.com), a free tool that allows you to connect various web applications, you can connect Sidekick to Twitter to receive instant "zaps" when someone on Twitter mentions you, your brand, or important keywords that you'd like to keep track of.

For example, you could do the following.

1. **Go to www.getsidekick.com to download the free email tracking tool.**

   In addition to using it with Twitter, you can use it to see who is opening your emails.

2. **Follow the signup module to get set up.**

3. **Once Sidekick is downloaded, go to https://zapier.com and click the orange Try It Free Today button.**

4. **Follow the steps to start your Zapier account.**

5. **Once you're in your Zapier account, click the orange Make a New Zap button.**

6. **For step one, under Choose a Trigger App, select Twitter.**

   A new module, Choose a Trigger, appears.

7. **Choose a trigger; for this example, choose Search Mention.**

8. **Still on step one, under Choose an Action App, choose Sidekick.**

   A new module, Choose an Action, appears.

9. **Choose New Desktop Notification (the only option).**

10. **Click Continue.**

11. **For step two, enter your Twitter account.**

12. **Click Continue.**

13. **For step three, enter your newly created Sidekick account.**

14. **Click Continue.**

15. **For step four, add any keywords to get your alerts for those searches.**

    For example, if you're working on a conference like INBOUND, you can enter #INBOUND15 to get alerts anytime anyone mentions that hashtag.

16. **Click Continue.**

    Options to customize how the desktop notifications look appear.

17. **Customize the desktop notifications.**

    For example, you can change what title appears; for example, maybe you want the notification to read "New INBOUND mention." Think of this like an email subject line — it's simply the first words to appear to let you know what you're about to read.

18. **Click Continue.**

    You notifications are all set up!

Social Inbox

For businesses or organizations (or individuals with a budget working on their own brand), HubSpot's Social Inbox (`www.hubspot.com/products/social-inbox`) is likely the most personalized tool for monitoring your social media activity. Like the other tools, it allows you to receive notifications for custom search queries so you don't have to be glued to your Twitter stream. Unlike the other tools, Social Inbox allows you to see the relationship someone has with your business or organization by labeling each Tweet with a color that identifies a visitor, lead, or customer.

If you'd like this tool for yourself, you can try it for free with a free trial of HubSpot's marketing suite.

1. **Navigate to** `http://offers.hubspot.com/free-trial` **to start a trial.**

2. **Create a password for your account.**

3. **The HubSpot trial will now walk you through a series of steps. For example, if it first asks you what your website is, feel free to skip and click the gray Continue button. You can keep continuing through the user setup until you get to the dashboard.**

4. **On the dashboard of your trial, click the Social tab in the top navigation.**

5. **From the drop-down menu that appears, click Monitoring.**

6. **A green Get Started with Social Inbox button appears. Click it and follow the steps to set up your account and start checking out the tool.**

Knowing Your Network: Follower and Following Tools

While your Twitter universe grows and grows, you probably want to find the best way possible to keep up with your followers and the people you're following. Twitter itself falls short in this area. For some reason, Twitter doesn't offer a way to search your follower or following lists. It also doesn't offer a way to sort your followers alphabetically or navigate in any way more efficient than a slow page-by-page scan.

You can quickly find out whether someone is following you back by trying to send that user a direct message (DM). If you're on the Twitter web interface's DM update screen, that twitterer's username appears on the drop-down menu only if he follows you back. If you're on a desktop client, you can try to DM that user; if he doesn't follow you, you get a message telling you so.

Networking is by far one of the most powerful uses that anyone can make of Twitter. But finding interesting people, maintaining your network, and digging in to really understand who you're connected to aren't always straightforward. Here are some tools that can improve your networking experience on Twitter:

✔ **Find your followers.** You can use sites such as Your Tweeter Karma and Friend or Follow to check who follows you and whom you follow, and to keep up with the people you want to add to your follow list. You can use these services to check out your followers and to double-check that you're following the people who are important to you:

You can take it with you

Depending on how you use Twitter, having your own copy of your Tweets, relationships, and conversations may be a mere nicety, or it may have some very real economic and or emotional value to you. Laura, for example, frequently mentions her children's milestones or captures meaningful moments in her life through her Tweets.

One of the areas of likely innovation in the Twitter ecosystem is better publishing tools. You can take your unwieldy stream of Tweets and extract a few key moments, perhaps embellishing them with the videos and photos you linked to or visual displays of the conversations you were having at the time. Personal scrapbooks or annual reports could be really nice things to have. A great example is Nicholas Feltron's work. Nicholas is an infographic designer and former member of the product design team at Facebook, who annually publishes "Personal Annual Reports," which measures a year's activities with graphs, maps, and statistics. You can see his work at `http://feltron.com`.

For a business, this kind of recordkeeping has even more obvious value. Having the data in a format that you can search, parse, and analyze will come to be a business necessity as more and more types of business interactions take place on Twitter. We become what we measure, and measuring effectiveness will be a crucial reason to get a copy of your Twitter data. You can get your archived Tweets by following these steps:

1. **Click the gear icon in your top right navigation.**

2. **In the drop-down menu that appears, click Settings.**

   Twitter should automatically land you on the Account tab of your settings.

3. **On the last module, you should see the Your Twitter Archive option. Click the Request Your Archive option.**

   Shortly after, Twitter should automatically email you with a file you can download of all your Tweets.

- *Friend or Follow* (`https://friendorfollow.com`): This site came onto the Twitter scene more recently than Your Tweeter Karma did, and its interface is a little bit easier to understand. The interface tells you who your mutual follows are, who you follow without being followed back, and who follows you without your following them back. Then you can pick and choose who to follow and who to stop following. Friend or Follow connections don't automatically opt you into people's device updates, so it's okay to use the tool to connect to many people, even if you have device updates turned on for your account.

- *Your Tweeter Karma* (`www.dossy.org/twitter/karma`): This site offers you a way to see who you follow, who follows you, and which users both follow you and are followed by you. You can also use the site to add followers, as well as remove users whom you no longer want to follow. Your Tweeter Karma tends to select Notifications On as the default setting when you add a new follower from its interface, so be sure to double- check that user's profile if you don't want to receive her notifications by text message.

✔ **Find new people to follow.** The resources below help you find some interesting people to follow. Following great accounts is the absolute best way to get value out of Twitter. For even more about how to find and follow amazing people who will improve your Twitter experience, see Chapter 6.

- *WeFollow* (`http://wefollow.com`): This user-generated Twitter directory was launched by Digg founder Kevin Rose at South by Southwest (SXSW) in April 2009. It associates up to three hashtags with each twitterer who lists herself in the directory and then presents the most-followed people and accounts. Because the results are searched by follower numbers, it's a particularly good way to find the top celebrities, musicians, journalists, politicians, and others who are using Twitter at any given time.

- *Twellow* (`www.twellow.com`): Structured like a Yellow Pages for Twitter, this site allows you to find new followers based on category, name, location, or Trending Topics. If a Twitter user has been active long enough to have a few Tweets on record, as well as a bio, you can find him on Twellow. If you search for yourself on Twellow, you can claim your profile, meaning that you contact Twellow and prove that you are you to get editing privileges for it, and then tweak it to categorize yourself so that others can find you based on your interests, services, or professional categories.

- *Twitter* (`https://twitter.com/search-home` *or your home screen*): We'd be remiss not to remind you that you can find new people to follow on Twitter itself in three useful ways. Twitter's people search function is, ironically, the weakest. To find a specific person whom you know to be on Twitter, you're better off searching Google for his first and last names and the word *Twitter*. Twitter also offers a list of suggested users, and while there has been some controversy about who gets to be in that list and who doesn't, it includes some pretty interesting accounts and is worth browsing. But to really fine-tune your interests, periodically search Twitter for Tweets about topics close to your heart and your unique interests. You never know who you might find. Click a user's name in any Tweet he's written, and peruse his last page or so of Tweets. You get a surprisingly good feel for who he is as a person that way.

✔ **Find users by location.** TwitterLocal (`www.twitterlocal.net`) used to use Twitter's XMPP feed to show what users were in certain locations. Because Twitter has its XMPP feed switched off for the time being, TwitterLocal is offered only as a downloadable Adobe Air application that you can use to view Tweets by location. You can also try several other good sites for finding local twitterers:

- Twellowhood (`www.twellow.com/twellowhood`) lets you find twitterers by city, using a zoomable map.

- Justunfollow (`www.justunfollow.com`) is an easy tool that shows who you are following but isn't following you back. That way, you can easily clear your stream by finding any users whose content you don't care to see anymore, particularly if they haven't reciprocated the love.

Chapter 9

Flaunt Your Feathers with Photos and Videos

In This Chapter

▶ Uploading photos to Twitter in different ways

▶ Exploring your video sharing options on Twitter

▶ Uncovering other media you can share on Twitter

*W*e all love taking pictures — of food, family, and more food. In 2013, more than 500 million photos were uploaded to the Internet *daily*. Although traditionally these photos have gone to sites like Facebook and Instagram, Twitter is growing as its own unique photo sharing destination.

But rather than displaying just the typical family photos you see on Facebook or the food photos you see on Instagram, Twitter also highlights photos of news stories, industry facts and quotes, interesting events or conferences, and photos that are slightly less personal (which makes sense, given that most people use Twitter publicly). That's why this chapter is dedicated entirely to what you can do visually on Twitter.

Exploring Your Uploading Options

When you upload photos to Twitter, you have a few options. You can attach an image while tweeting from your desktop or mobile phone, but you can edit that image only through the Twitter mobile app (see the sidebar "Enhance your photos with the Twitter mobile app," later in this chapter).

These tweeted photos are given their own home in your Twitter profile. You'll notice that Twitter groups all of your media uploads on their own tab — conveniently called Photos/Videos — so you can scan them when desired.

Whenever you're conducting a general search on Twitter, you'll notice that photo Tweets are categorized on their own tab. This tab allows you to review all photo search results separately from all search results. This separation allows users to understand quickly what a particular search may be about.

When searching for Tweets on #BringBackOurGirls, a hashtag campaign focused on returning girls abducted from the Kummabza village in Nigeria, for example, you can see that celebrities such as Emma Watson and Michelle Obama were among the top-tweeted photos in the campaign.

Before we dive deeper into the uploading options you have on Twitter, we'll review how to upload your photos. Follow these steps:

1. **Below your profile info in your home feed, click the white Compose New Tweet box to start crafting a Tweet.**

    As you begin typing, a camera icon appears below the compose module (see Figure 9-1).

2. **Click the camera icon.**

3. **Select an image from your saved images to attach it to your Tweet.**

Figure 9-1:
A new com-
posed Tweet
before
typing any
text or
attaching a
photo.

Attaching photos to your Tweets

Most simply, you can directly upload any photo to Twitter by using Twitter. com or the Twitter mobile app. You can use the mobile app to crop and enhance the image before it publishes on Twitter — more on this later in this chapter.

Uploading a photo to Twitter consumes 23 characters of your 140-character limit, which leaves you with 117 characters to add your own caption for the image you're attaching. The image will be uploaded as a link as well as displayed inside your Tweet. The link is automatically added to the end of your Tweet copy, and you can't customize where this image URL is placed in your Tweet. This link will look something like this: pic.twitter.com/ rqgnvQw19q.

Making collages in your Tweets

Suppose that you'd like to share multiple photos in your Tweet. That's where collages come in. Twitter allows you to upload up to four photos at a time and then automatically makes a four-piece collage for a single Tweet. This is a great way to highlight an experience you had, an event you went to, or the stages of a meal you're cooking — whatever floats your boat!

As Figure 9-2 shows, after you attach an image to your Tweet, Twitter displays an Add More option. The resulting Tweet has a four-image collage alongside it.

Figure 9-2:
After uploading a photo, you can easily attach three more images and make a mini photo collage.

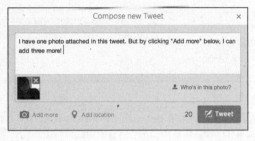

Tagging users in your tweeted photos

Previously, if you wanted to tweet a photo that showed multiple people, you had to sacrifice characters from your limited 140-character limit to include the Twitter handles of the people in your photo. Your Tweet may have looked something like this:

"Loved this outing with @Pistachio, @anum, and @bleaning, the *Twitter For Dummies* co-authors!"

But then Twitter responded to user frustration and made it possible for you to tag up to ten people in your photos.

After you attach a photo (refer to Figure 9-2), to the right of your compose window Twitter will ask "Who's in this photo?" If you click that link that appears, you'll be able to type in up to ten usernames. These can be individual accounts (like @anum) or business accounts (like @HubSpot). So now your Tweet will just appear as:

"Loved this outing with the *Twitter For Dummies* co-authors!"

Enhance your photos with the Twitter mobile app

If you use a smartphone, you can use the Twitter mobile app to enhance your photos before uploading them to the network. Many people prefer tweeting their photos from their mobile devices for this very reason.

When you tap the icon to compose a new Tweet in the mobile app, you should see a white text box containing the words *What's happening?* to type your Tweet into. You also see an icon that looks like a photo of a mountain and moon. Tap that icon to go into your smartphone's photo library and select a photo.

When the photo is attached, it may seem like that's all you can do. If you tap the image, however, Twitter's mobile app directs you to a new destination where you can edit your photo. You'll notice three icons on the bottom navigation bar:

- **A magic-wand icon:** Tap this icon to automatically brighten and enhance your image.

- **An overlapping-circles icon:** Tap this icon to select one of nine colored filters to alter your image's appearance.

- **A square icon:** Tap this icon to crop your image in any way you want. We recommend selecting the Wide option to give your photo the rectangular presentation that appears best in Twitter's news feed.

When you're tagged in an image, you'll get a notification that, for example, @anum has tagged you in a Tweet. If you have a public Twitter profile, anyone can automatically tag you in Tweets. Similarly, you have the ability to tag any public Twitter account in your Tweets.

Don't want to be tagged in any photos on Twitter? Click the gear icon in the upper right corner of your Twitter page. Choose Settings from the drop-down menu. Then select the Security and Privacy tab on the left to select who can tag you in photos. You can choose one of three options:

- Allow Anyone to Tag Me in Photos
- Only Allow People I Follow to Tag Me in Photos
- Do Not Allow Anyone to Tag Me in Photos

Sizing Images for Twitter

Like every social network, Twitter has its own set of optimal dimensions, so not every photo you upload to Twitter will appear properly in your friends' feeds.

Although networks such as Facebook and Instagram currently thrive on perfect square photos, at this writing, Twitter's perfect photo is more horizontal.

By uploading your photos through the Twitter mobile app, you'll be able to crop your photo to the horizontal frame that works best in a user's feed, as you see in Figure 9-3.

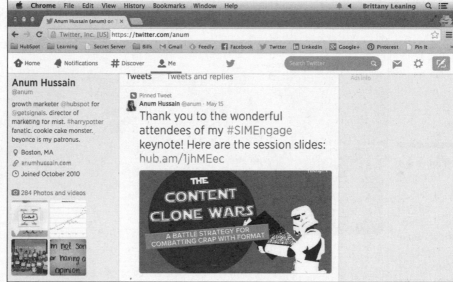

Figure 9-3: A horizontal photo displays clearly and cleanly in Twitter feeds.

In the following sections, we review every photo type on Twitter and its proper dimensions. Twitter, like all social platforms, is constantly changing. But at this writing, these dimensions are correct and — from what we hear — here to stay for a bit.

Adding flavor with a header photo

The *header photo* is the equivalent of a Facebook cover photo. This photo is a representation of your personality in your Twitter profile. As you can see in Figure 9-4, Brittany has a cover photo that she made with `Canva.com`, a free online tool. She added her own Instagram photos to the template Canva provided, and Canva did the rest.

As of this writing, the ideal header size for these images is 1500 x 1500 pixels. If you upload any horizontal photo, you should be able to move it around and make it look decent enough. But if you'd like to ensure that your Twitter header photo fits the exact header size, here are some free resources:

✔ **HubSpot's header photo templates:** HubSpot has premade Microsoft PowerPoint templates that you can use to create and adjust your Twitter header photo. Grab it here: `http://offers.hubspot.com/social-media-cover-photos`.

✔ **Canva's free Twitter templates:** Canva is a free tool for nondesigners that provides free, easy-to-use templates that you can customize for your own background. Check it out here: www.canva.com.

Figure 9-4:
Brittany's Twitter header photo shows some "natural" personality.

Identifying yourself with a profile photo

Your *profile photo* is the square image that appears next to each of your Tweets. It's your main form of identification on Twitter and also appears in your profile. At this writing, the ideal size is 400 x 400 pixels, but uploading any square image should suffice.

Although you can use many tools and programs (such as Photoshop and PowerPoint) to crop a photo, we've used mypictr (http://mypictr.com), a free site that allows you to quickly upload a photo and select a network for which you'd like to crop a profile photo (in this case, Twitter). The site returns a Twitter-ready photo for you to upload and use as your profile photo.

Uploading photos with your Tweets

Although ideally you have to worry about your header photo and profile photo only once, you'll likely get into the habit of posting photos in your individual Tweets much more often.

New user capitalizes on photo capabilities

Even if you're just getting started on Twitter, you can quickly understand what works best for this platform and tailor your content appropriately. Just don't be afraid to jump in and experiment!

Take user Nabeel U. Ali (@NabeelUAli), for example. At this writing, Nabeel is a medical student at Albany Medical College and a researcher at Harvard University. Folks in the medical field aren't traditionally known as being the first to jump onto platforms like Twitter and begin using it for personal use or branding. But in early 2014, Nabeel decided to join Twitter and give it a try.

Without investing too much time in Twitter, he experimented with hashtag tagging, link sharing, and photo uploading to see what worked best. To his surprise, he quickly saw images help him interact with other users in the health-care community very well. So he began to use them more and more in his strategy.

For Nabeel, sharing photos on Twitter was as simple as taking horizontal screen shots of images in the articles he was reading and uploading those images as the main feature of his Tweets. If you go to his media stream (https://twitter.com/NabeelUAli/media) you'll see this strategy in action.

"In the medical research field, we typically share our ideas in academic journals," he said. "Twitter has proven to be a great way to share ideas with different audiences for a more global perspective." Nabeel quickly made use of his Twitter real estate with proper visuals. He has three key visual components on his page:

- A simple blue header photo (his favorite color) for personality.
- A profile photo wearing Google Glass and a white coat (representative of his work).
- A pinned Tweet to an article with an appealing horizontal photo as the main content in the Tweet.

Nabeel accomplished all this within just a few months of being on Twitter. Once a "Twitter dummy," he's now in control of his network and using a visual strategy to stay engaged with the health-care community on Twitter.

To be clear, you can upload any photo of any size and orientation to Twitter. Users will be able to click your Tweet and see the photo. If you want photos in your Tweets to display well, go with a landscape (horizontal) oriented photo that is (at this writing) 880 x 440 pixels (refer to Figure 9-3).

Here are some resources to help you upload the right-size photo (unfortunately, most of them are mobile-only):

- **Native Twitter app:** The Twitter mobile application allows you to upload and crop your attached image for the ideal Twitter size. When you upload your photo with the app, tap the crop button, and you'll see a horizontal frame to work with.

- **Aviary mobile app:** The Aviary mobile app allows you to easily crop your images to the proper Twitter size. Aviary is a photo-editing app, so you can also improve the quality of your image with it or add fun stickers over the image.

- **HubSpot's Social Inbox:** If you're already paying to use HubSpot's Social Inbox, the marketing software also provides an easy-to-use image editing service that allows you to crop your image to the right size for Twitter. This feature works through integration with Aviary, but the benefit is that you can use it on your laptop.

Uploading Videos to Twitter

Twitter isn't just a network for photo uploads. It's a media site that's capable of much more, such as video. As of 2012, an estimated 700 million YouTube videos were being shared on Twitter every minute, an astonishing rate which has dramatically increased since. On top of that you will see Vines, Facebook videos, Instagram and other kinds of videos, and now Hyperlapses, and you can see that video sharing is an incredibly popular use of Twitter.

Videos appear in Tweets similar to the way that photos appear. They're given their own links in your Tweets and placed right below your Tweet copy so users can play the videos directly from the Tweet. Unlike photo links, which are automatically added to the end of a Tweet, video links can be placed anywhere in the Tweet copy (although most people just place it at the end anyway).

The following sections look at your video options on Twitter.

Vine

Vine (`https://vine.co`) is a mobile application, owned by Twitter itself, for creating 6-second video clips. These clips are uploaded to the Vine network and can be shared automatically through your Twitter account. Your Vine videos can be about anything. Many people have begun using it for comical videos.

One of the most famous users of Vine is user BatDad (`https://vine.co/BatDad`), a father who impersonates Batman in various situations while being a typical father. His simple concept, which started just as light amusement and fun with his kids, lead to a popular channel with more than 2 million followers. On top of that, his videos have been shared over 100 million times.

YouTube

Although Vine is a Twitter-owned and -run app, you can still use video sites such as YouTube (`www.youtube.com`). Simply by using a YouTube video link in your Tweet, you can easily share videos longer than 6 seconds with your Twitter followers.

YouTube videos are most often tweeted when users are sharing a funny video they just discovered. Many people tweet videos as a part of a campaign, such as a company's new product launch or a nonprofit's new initiative.

GIFs

GIF stands for *Graphics Interchange Format*. In simple terms, a GIF is an animated image. In Anum terms, it's like one of those cool moving family photos in the Harry Potter movies.

The popular content site BuzzFeed (`www.buzzfeed.com`) is known for its use of GIFs. These animated images can add personality, flair, and color. Many users on the social platform Tumblr have Tumblr blogs dedicated to uploading GIFs alongside brief captions (such as `http://coldcallmemaybe.tumblr.com`).

Figure 9-5 shows what your Twitter profile looks like when you tweet a GIF.

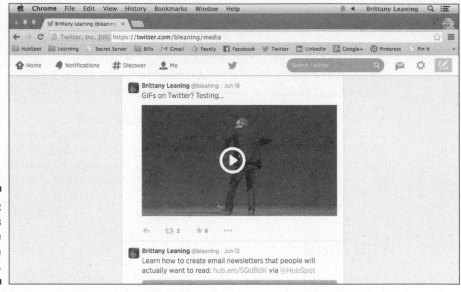

Figure 9-5:
Brittany's
profile page
contains a
GIF.

Uploading Other Visuals on Twitter

Beyond photos and videos, you have a few other options for sharing visual media on Twitter. Some work well and some don't.

Instagram

Although Instagram (`http://instagram.com`) isn't directly related to Twitter (it's owned by Facebook), the image-sharing network allows you to share photos to Twitter.

Unlike photos shared directly on Twitter, Instagram photos appear in your Tweets as long URLs. Rather than being able to see the photos right within your Twitter stream, you must click the link to view the media on the Instagram site. For this reason, Instagram photos don't engage as many of your followers and isn't our recommended method of uploading photos or videos to Twitter.

SlideShare

SlideShare (`www.slideshare.net`) is a social network that focuses on sharing presentations. Although links to this type of media don't populate in the photo and video sections of your profile, SlideShare presentations still appear like photos and videos within your tweeted content, as you see in Figure 9-6. SlideShare presentations appear in the Tweet, allowing users to view them without having to leave Twitter.

Figure 9-6: Anum tweets a link to her SlideShare presentation.

People use SlideShare to present content in a highly visual form. SlideShare is similar to video presentation, but rather than listen to a voice over, you click through slides (typically made in PowerPoint) to walk through a story. You can share a link to this content through Twitter, giving your profile unique visual content to share.

Part IV
What's the Point? Using Twitter to Your Advantage

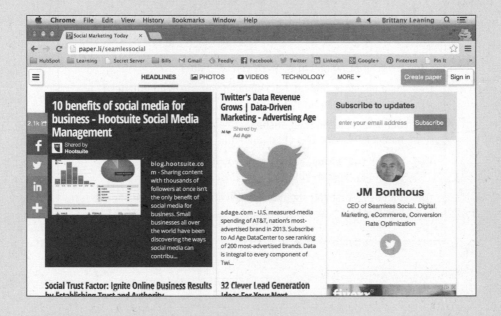

Want to really wield Twitter like a conversational master? Check out www.dummies.com/extras/twitter to learn the difference between the @mention and the @reply, how they work, and when to use each.

In this part . . .

- ✔ Give some thought to why are you on Twitter.

- ✔ As a business, find out how you can you use Twitter to build and stabilize your brand.

- ✔ Consider how the relationship between Twitter and the global media landscape has changed both.

- ✔ As a not-for-profit, find out what you can you do to make people evangelize your cause.

- ✔ Discover what you should say on Twitter and who you should you talk to.

Chapter 10

Finding Your Tweet Voice

In This Chapter

▶ Diving into Twitter

▶ Deciding whether to tweet for work or fun

▶ Figuring out who you're tweeting to

▶ Measuring your reach

▶ Knowing what to keep personal and private

*I*f you let it, Twitter can conveniently become an integral part of your day-to-day life. As we've learned, Twitter is available almost everywhere through many platforms. Wherever you have Internet or cellular coverage, you can more or less use Twitter.

But as you get up to speed and even "embrace the twecosystem," writing and sharing in only 140 characters at a time definitely takes some getting used to. It may seem a bit limiting at first, but over time that limitation changes the way you write and communicate. If you plan to use the service with some regularity, you'll probably want to think at least a little bit about how your updates compare with the image you want to convey.

In this chapter, we explore different approaches to using Twitter and finding your own unique voice.

Finding Your Voice

When you first sign up for a Twitter account, you don't follow anyone yet, and nobody follows you. Updating your feed may seem a bit awkward. You're tweeting into the void, you have no idea who's really listening (if anyone), and you're almost certainly wondering what the heck the point of tweeting even is. Don't feel bad — most everyone's first Tweet (see Figure 10-1) is a little awkward. But if you follow our advice, you should be able to get the hang of Twitter in no time!

Figure 10-1:
Anum's first
Tweet.

When you start following users and other users start following you, you may want to think about what sort of things you want to share with your following. For many new users, one of the great debates is whether to use Twitter for business or pleasure, so we address that a lot in this chapter. You might have joined Twitter for either reason (or both). As you come to embrace the medium to its fullest, you'll find yourself figuring out what kind of voice you want to use on Twitter. The answer, as with so many answers about Twitter, depends entirely on what you want to get out of the Twitter experience.

Part of determining your identity on Twitter involves choosing your username (which we cover in Chapter 2). If you choose a nickname or pseudonym for your username, you probably aim to employ Twitter for personal use. If you use your business name as your Twitter handle, you likely intend to create a presence for your company. But if you use your real name as your username (which is probably the best way to go), you simply imply that you are who you say you are, and you can take your account in the direction that makes the most sense to you as you evolve. That's one reason why you probably want to use your real name or some variation of it.

Whatever name you pick, you can change it at any time on your Twitter account's Settings page. We explain how to make this change in Chapter 2.

No matter what you name your Twitter presence, you need a voice and personality that's uniquely yours. We go over some tips and thoughts on how to make your Twitter voice your own in the section "Individuals on Twitter," later in this chapter.

Individuals on Twitter

Twitter was originally popular for helping individuals keep in touch with their friends and acquaintances through mini updates. Many personal Twitterers still tend to use Twitter in this manner, updating a close circle of friends about thoughts and happenings in their lives. Over time, you can keep up with people you otherwise might not contact often and even make new friends. Twitter removes many communication barriers.

A few things to consider for your personal Twitter presence:

- ✔ **Keeping your Tweets private:** If it helps you feel more comfortable with your personal use of Twitter, you can set your updates to Private. Enabling the privacy feature ensures that no one, other than the users you authorize, has access to your updates. Note: If your friends choose to retweet something pithy you said, that Tweet they share isn't private. However, setting your updates to Private also prevents Twitter Search from picking up your Tweets; it's a minor inconvenience that you may be willing to accept if you feel strongly about protecting your personal updates from the world.

- ✔ **Introducing your business:** Regardless of whether you plan to build your business by using Twitter "just as a person," you might want to include some information about your occupation and company in your Twitter profile, and perhaps add a link back to your company's online presence. The *social capital* (trust, thought leadership, and more) that you earn within the Twitter community may lead to new opportunities for you and for your business. Also, your opinions and statements may be biased because of your job, so in the interests of transparency, disclosure is a good idea.

- ✔ **Making it personal:** You don't have to include any business information on Twitter if you don't want to. Twitter was built with personal connections in mind. Twitter is personal, so dress up your profile and adjust your settings in a way that makes sense to you and reflects what you want to get out of your Twitter experience.

Businesses on Twitter

Can you use something as simple as Twitter for business? Absolutely! However, you can't exactly adopt the usual salesperson "Sell! Sell! Sell!" mentality on Twitter. To operate as a successful business presence on Twitter:

- ✔ Master the art of give and take.

- ✔ Figure out how to engage your Twitter base in conversation.

- ✔ Give your audience, clients, and customers a reason to read your Tweets.

Twitter is a conversational medium, and for businesses to mesh well with user expectations, companies and businesses need to understand how to navigate the landscape as a brand. You can read about strategies and case studies in Chapter 11 (bankruptcy pun intended).

If you're representing a large company (such as @JetBlue or @Starbucks), your Twitter presence might be a little more complicated because you're not representing just yourself, but also your business — and for some companies, that may mean tens of thousands of people. That's a lot of responsibility!

If you're managing a Twitter presence on behalf of your company, we highly encourage you to start a separate account for yourself so that you can get used to the service. Before you start tweeting on behalf of your business, know what users expect from brands and businesses, and how customers like to be approached. Getting used to how businesses operate on Twitter can prevent you from making a serious faux pas down the road. That said, a lot of what makes the best business accounts great is their personality and humanity, so the case can also be made for not always having two different (business and personal) accounts.

In Chapter 11, we go over how businesses can best take advantage of Twitter.

Mixing business with pleasure

Some of the most successful Twitter personalities have embraced Twitter by transparently sharing personal, professional, family, and other aspects of themselves all rolled together. This is nothing wildly new. We've always spent time with colleagues, clients, and our professional network at the golf course, dinner, charity events, and the like. Most networking events have a highly social component to them. It's simple: People like to do business with people they like.

Some find balancing your personal life and your professional life on Twitter tricky at first, but you can definitely do it. Give yourself time to discover what you're comfortable doing. We don't really know anyone who completely stops talking about work when out with friends — or vice versa — because work (whether we like it or not) is a big part of who we all are. Because Twitter is built for human communications, it can handle many facets of your life; you just have to find your own balance.

It's all about balance

Balance is important on Twitter, as in life, if you want to connect with people in a genuine, mutually beneficial way. Twitter is a pretty "what you give is what you get" kind of a place. Your true voice is often the best bet unless you're really constrained for business reasons and need to rein it in. Accounts that are nothing but business (or, worse, strictly business-promotional) all the time may have a pretty hard time growing much of an engaged base.

Want to be über-personal all the time? There is absolutely nothing wrong with that, but it will influence the size and shape of your network. Don't be offended if it's not everybody's cup of tea. Present yourself the way you feel most comfortable.

If you cover both business and personal stuff on your account but aren't an official "for the business" twitterer, it can be good to go easy on how frequently you tweet about business-only stuff. We get asked for a specific ratio all the time, and it's really hard to say. As car ads say, "Your mileage may vary." (On Twitter, #ymmv.) Try a mix that's comfortable to you and then just see whether you're getting the results you hoped for. Also, please remember, the number of followers is much less important than the quality of the conversations. For long-term sustainable value, true engagement beats tonnage any day.

If you're updating under your business handle (for us, it's @dummies), followers probably expect that nearly all Tweets from that account will relate to that business. After all, they're following that account for business info! If you're really inconsistent, off-topic, or overboard personally all the time, and violate your followers' expectations too much, you may find your audience shrinking. Everyone needs to strike a balance, but most successful brand accounts stay relatively on topic. If you're an individual twitterer, followers probably want to hear about you and how you're going about your business. It's a subtle difference but an important point to establish yourself as genuine, and not a selfish peddler of goods.

Your goal should be to permit your followers to get a good understanding of what your business offers and come to trust you as who you are. Make the bulk of the content that you add to Twitter about you and the value that you provide (as a person and through your work). Think of some updates as "give" and other updates as "take": When you share or talk about things that are genuinely useful and helpful to customers, you're providing something they want. That sets the stage for occasionally promoting the goods or services that you sell, because you've earned the trust and attention of your readers. Just remember that promotional Tweets that aren't framed from the perspective of your customer's needs too often come across as a "take" because you're asking followers to buy what you're selling.

Want to know if the balance you strike is effective? Reread your Tweets at the end of the day or the end of the week and keep an eye on replies, retweets, the numbers of people clicking links you share, and, yes, follower growth. If you feel that your update stream comes off as too sales-y, then back off on the selling and stick to providing value. Twitter's about being a genuine individual. Over time, Twitter gives your followers a lot of information about you, who you are, and what you represent. That builds trust, confidence, and interest in you. Be real.

Be yourself

As with the individual and business-only accounts, be sure to give your name in your bio. Transparency about who you are and what you do can go a long way toward growing your Twitter foundation. And a good Twitter foundation is key to establishing a stable and growing Twitter network. Using your real name adds to your value as an individual.

Just as in other business interactions, you need to be genuine on Twitter and establish yourself as a trustworthy, multidimensional person.

At the same time, think carefully about how much of your private matters you want to share. Occasional mention of your love life, health, and other more personal stuff can be very funny, very humanizing, and very honest, but being really negative, self-indulgent, or tedious about the same will put people off. When you really need to talk about those things, it's very possible you'll find supportive people on Twitter. Having found something in common or someone who wants to help, you may even get into a more in-depth conversation with a twitterer via direct message (DM) or leave Twitter altogether via email, instant message (IM), or over your favorite beverage. You can also definitely connect with people on more public personal topics like sports, TV, books, movies, or politics without revealing all your deepest secrets.

As a person on Twitter, you might find value in talking about your business problems in the open. Many fellow twitterers are willing to give you advice about how to overcome a business challenge or situation. If you've spent time cultivating a network that works for you, you have many resources at your fingertips. Ask them!

Understanding Your Audience

Whether you're a business or an individual on Twitter, if you want to grow your Twitter network, it's helpful to think about your audience. If you haven't transplanted your existing social networks onto Twitter, it may be a good time to do that and to put a bit of time and effort into expanding your network.

Think about the kinds of people you'd like to talk to or the subjects you'd like to discuss through Twitter. Trying to build up business? Target your customers. Want to communicate with other avid cyclists on Twitter? Search keywords and look to see who tweets about major cycling events.

Send updates that are relevant to whomever you'd like to reach or about the topics that interest you and engage yourself in that conversation. Yes, it's that easy.

When you start using Twitter, it's pretty hard to determine who your audience will be — your followers grow based on what value you can provide for other users. So if you're trying to reach other cyclists to talk about racing, the Tour de France, or the latest in derailleur technology, start talking about it and search for other users already chatting about the subject. (You can find out about searching for users and topics in Part II.)

And don't be shy about finding people who share your interests, even if you don't know them yet. You can use Twitter search (`https://twitter.com/search-advanced`) to look for Tweets related to your work, hobbies, or passions. Then click through to the profiles of the people who published the Tweets you find. You can also click their profiles to see their most recent Tweets before following to ensure their interests align with yours.

You don't have to be one-dimensional in your Twitter chat. If you want to engage cyclists, you don't always and only have to talk about cycling. People understand that you have more to you than a single activity or idea (unless you're a company or targeted Twitter account, for which the implicit rules are a little different; see "Businesses on Twitter," earlier in this chapter), so don't feel that you need to talk about only one thing to be of value to your target audience. Be yourself and talk about the things you like, but if you want to engage other cyclists, just talk a bit more about cycling than anything else. That's all. Over time, your cycling network will grow.

Who's following you?

Although you have little direct control over who follows you, you can easily see what type of user you're attracting. Browse through your list of Followers and click through to open some of their profiles to get a general idea of who's following you. (On any Twitter screen, click the Followers link under your profile.)

You do have some control over who follows you in the sense that you can block an account. Click through to the user's profile page and then click the gear icon that is to the left of the Follow/Following button. Select Block or Report and then click the red Block button. If you want to be a bit more subtle about removing someone from being amongst your followers for whatever reason, block him, as above, and then immediately unblock him. This will break his subscription to your account without his being actually blocked.

When you look into who's following you, you might realize that you're drawing unexpected people as followers. Reaching people and businesses you never expected to reach is most likely not a bad thing. If you're a business, unpredicted followers could show that you're increasing your business's social reach, meaning a sign of successful Twitter use. If you're twittering as an individual, you're broadening your horizons, and other users are considering you and your Tweets to be interesting.

Diversifying your network

You can help guide who tends to follow you by talking about a myriad of topics. People aren't one-dimensional, and no one really expects you to be on point all the time. Although you may have interests that you talk about more than others, getting a sense of what you're talking about and whom you're talking to can come in handy; it enables you to target your Tweets to topics that are most interesting to your followers.

One of our favorite tools for understanding how often and what you're updating is TweetStats (www.tweetstats.com). This tool enables you to see who you're talking to, when you're talking, and what you're talking about — all in graph form.

Targeting specific networks

If you're targeting specific people with whom you want to interact more regularly, find a way to add value to the interactions for them. You can target these types of people by searching keywords and hashtags for that topic and seeing who uses them and who the real leaders appear to be. Once you're following a few key people within that interest area, look for whom they talk to, listen to, and value. For example, if you're a gardener, check to see who Martha Stewart (@MarthaStewart) follows and talks to about gardening topics. Click through any appealing @replies and consider following those people. You can also use this information to get a sense of what's important to any given twitterer and what types of information they like to receive. With Twitter, you can essentially browse not only the connections between people, but also topics of interest. You can also easily drop into active ongoing conversations about specific themes. One or two key people can lead you to an entire subject-matter landscape on Twitter.

In a very real sense, an individual or Twitter account that represents something can become the foundation for a community. Likewise, if you're trying to target a specific type of individual, go to the Twitter streams of those individuals and see what they're tweeting about. Join the conversation that they're having with other people and engage those other people, as well. Over time, if you're adding value to that conversation, then other people look to you as a person who's involved and relevant in that community, whether it's computer programming, baking cupcakes, or cancer research.

Measuring your influence

While you start to gain a foothold within communities on Twitter, you might want to get a sense of what your network looks like and how far your updates travel.

As you read, please bear in mind that some of the less measurable results are the most important. The most important thing to measure is the thing you're actually trying to accomplish, not just numbers for numbers' sake. Are you meeting new friends? Finding new business leads? Sharing information widely about issues important to you?

Do your messages spread? In her keynote presentations at business conferences like the Inc 500|5000, Laura argues that messages can be much more important influencers within Twitter than influential accounts and individuals, because good messages get repeated. A truly great message, even if it starts in quiet little corners of Twitter among people with small following networks, will echo and get repeated until eventually it reaches much of the network.

Measuring your overall presence

Twitter itself has a few ways to measure your Tweets. You have following and followers counts. Although those numbers would seem to provide a good baseline for understanding how far your updates go and to whom, they don't say much about what types of people follow you and how influential those followers are. It also doesn't show how many people your followers follow; if one of your followers is following 1,000 people, it's unlikely he will see all of your Tweets in the activity stream.

Less ethical people aggressively boost their follower numbers, sometimes through questionable habits like following people just until they follow back and then dropping them to go follow someone else. Important lessons? Don't automatically trust an account with a really high number of followers. Don't build your network around high numbers at the cost of high relevance and high engagement.

For all intents and purposes, these follower numbers don't really measure influence or reach. First and foremost, use Twitter to communicate; and, although high follower counts may indicate genuine popularity, they can be gamed and don't necessarily indicate importance or quality. Laura goes so far as to say "The most important, influential person in your Twitter stream is you; be proactive about your life."

Think of your follower counts as a measurement of the type of Twitterer you are. Here are three types of users that we see often:

1. **Conversationalists:** These users typically have an even number of people following them and people who they follow. They enjoy participating in all Twitter chatter and consistently spark conversations based on Tweets they see.

2. **Broadcasters:** These are users who typically have more followers than people they follow. They're focused more on sharing valuable information, such as links to articles, motivational quotes, or interesting facts. They seek to share knowledge across the network rather than consuming it.

3. **Listeners:** These users typically follow more people than the number of people who follow them. They use Twitter to consume as much information as possible. Some may even use Twitter as their own personal news source to stay up-to-date with the latest world happenings (more on this is in Chapter 12).

Measuring the reach of your Tweets

Beyond follower and following count, you can look at which of your Tweets interest the most people through Twitter's built-in analytics. To access, sign into your Twitter account in your web browser and navigate to `https://analytics.twitter.com`.

In these analytics, Twitter shares a variety of interesting metrics.

- **Tweet Impressions:** As shown in Figure 10-2, Twitter shows all your recent Tweets and their specific number of impressions, engagements, and overall engagement rate. The graph above that chart presents the overall impressions you garnered across all the Tweets shared per day. It's possible that one of your Tweets on a specific day reached far more people because it received a high number of retweets. It's also possible that you simply published more Tweets on one day than the next, increasing your overall impressions for that day.

- **Engagements:** Figure 10-2 also shows various graphs of Engagements on the right side of the screen. Here you can see your daily engagement rate, daily number of link clicks, daily retweets, daily favorites, and daily replies. Each of these specific Twitter actions is discussed in detail in Chapter 3 and the glossary, but think of them as measurements of how people are interacting with what you're sharing on Twitter.

- **Follower Growth:** You can get deeper insight into your followers in the Followers tab, as shown in Figure 10-3. Here, Twitter shows your overall follower growth, what your followers' top interests are, what their most unique interests are, and where they are located. It also highlights their gender.

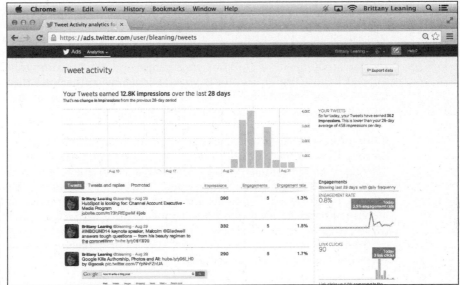

Figure 10-2:
Analytics for Brittany's Tweets.

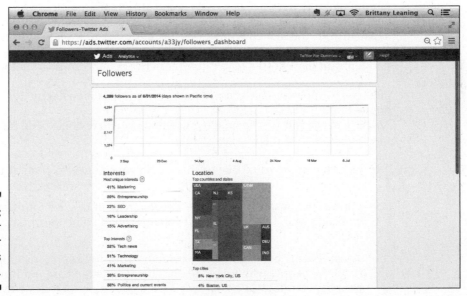

Figure 10-3:
Follower analytics for Brittany's Tweets.

Understanding your extended network

Twitter, by itself, can tell you only the number of people you follow and the number of people who follow you. As described in the previous sections, those numbers give you just part of the story.

If 100 people follow you and communicate with you, then your actual extended network is much larger than 100 people because conversations relay messages and connect new people on Twitter. Say that Follower 86 has 1,000 followers. Whenever Follower 86 mentions your name, 1,000 people receive an update that contains your name. And you may find that kind of exposure quite useful. Twitter is an excellent way to "harness the power of loose ties" or benefit from friends of friends of friends who are more likely to know about things nobody in your social group knows.

If Boston-based Laura was trying to locate a venue in Nashville, Tennessee, to hold a Twitter marketing seminar, she might send an update that reads, "Trying to locate a good 700-person venue in Nashville to give a talk. A place to stay would be nice, too. Suggestions?" Because thousands of people read Laura's Twitter stream, chances are good a handful of them live in Nashville. If some of those handful wanted to connect Laura with a local business owner, they might ask their own networks, who may have an answer based on their own geography. In this sense, Laura's primary network gives her secondary access to all her followers' networks as well.

It's pretty cool how friends of friends can end up becoming your direct friends, too. Say you're following five friends, and two of them are constantly communicating (via @replies) with some other person whom you don't know. Out of curiosity, you may start following that other person just to make sense of your friends' conversations. Because you're friends with two people that the other person talks to frequently, he follows you back. Now, all of a sudden, you have both a larger Twitter network and extended network.

Figure 10-4 shows a page out of Anum's e-book about social media management (`http://offers.hubspot.com/the-future-of-social-media-lead-management`). The image presented visualizes this social media machine to highlight a few key points:

- ✔ Establish what you'd like to share with your network, such as links, quotes, stats, or random updates.

- ✔ Publish various Tweets. These Tweets are sent to your followers, who can click your Tweet and may even download some information if included.

- ✔ These Tweets can also be retweeted by your followers, pushing them to all the people who follow them. This results in those additional 1,000 people potentially clicking your Tweet, sharing it further, or even following you too.

Although finding new and interesting people in your Twitter network happens organically, the Twitter community has come up with a couple of tools to help grow your network in a way that's relevant to you. You can browse interesting tags for people in the Twitter directory `http://wefollow.com` that North Technologies co-founder and former Digg CEO Kevin Rose (`@kevinrose`) started in spring 2009.

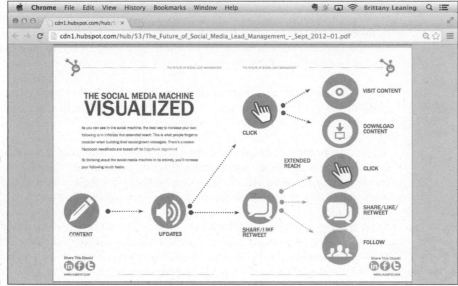

Figure 10-4:
A visualization of how Twitter's engagement machine works.

Keeping Your Tweets Authentic

Because of the frequency and personal nature of what people share on Twitter, any twitterer absolutely must be genuine and real, whether she's representing a business or tweeting as an individual. Joining Twitter as a private citizen is the route many users take, even if they have business to promote. Twitter is ideally suited for personal connection, and you can often more easily make yourself accessible and personable when you use Twitter as a person, not as your business.

Being genuine

Authentic people and businesses, using Twitter in real and interactive ways, can experience tremendous growth and return on investment from Twitter because they make real contributions and build up a rich base of trust, influence, and social capital. People respond much better to an authentic, human voice. They engage more closely because they feel comfortable responding, retweeting, and otherwise paying attention to the genuine voice. Bring some value to the Twitterverse by adding your authentic contributions, whatever those may be.

For example, if you're tweeting about politics, whether you're a conservative, moderate, liberal, apathetic, or whatever, feel free to agree or disagree with someone. Twitter is, after all, a digital extension of real life, so if you want to engage in that type of dialog, be yourself. Don't try to come off as something you're not just to appeal to people.

If you're representing a business or tweeting on behalf of your company, you probably want to avoid politics, religion, sex, and other hot-button topics, so as not to offend your potential customers.

Your update stream speaks volumes about you. Twitter is a network built on trust and relationships, and being insincere jeopardizes the quality and effectiveness of your network, both on- and offline. You lose some of that hard-won trust that you've been building since you joined Twitter.

Even though you want to be genuine and real at all times, remember that you can easily forget to be nice to people behind the safety of a monitor and keyboard thousands of miles away. Treat others with respect, as you hope to be treated, and you can have a positive online experience. Try not to engage in arguments over petty things; this behavior gets you branded as a troll, and people start to avoid you and stop taking you seriously. (Get the scoop on trolls in the sidebar "Don't feed the trolls," later in this chapter.)

Evangelizing your causes

When you're on Twitter as an individual, if you share a favorite cause or a local event in a way that makes it interesting to others, you'll attract those with common interests. They may get involved and show support, and the more fellow twitterers know about you and about the things you have in common, the more connections and ideas will flow in your network.

Don't be afraid to voice your support for social causes and charities that are important to you. By tweeting about your cause, you both spread awareness about what's important to you (which may lead to more contributions for that cause or charity) and give your audience a better idea of who you are as a person.

In just its first four days, the grassroots Twitter movement #YesAllWomen produced over one million Tweets, most of which were women sharing their personal stories of everyday sexism and misogyny. The hashtag arose after a 22-year-old male shot six people and himself because he wanted to punish women for not being attracted to him. The news was so troubling, and yet so resonant to so many women, that the movement arose spontaneously. Other times, efforts like this are more pointedly organized.

Don't feed the trolls

In Internet parlance, a troll is someone who intentionally posts messages to upset people — for example, making rude and insulting comments on someone's blog or replying to someone's Tweets with personal attacks.

Because so many conversations happen so quickly on Twitter, sometimes about touchy subjects, users need to be on the lookout for others who insist on asking inappropriately-charged questions, saying questionable things to users, and otherwise being a poor citizen of the Internet. Because Twitter's a network based on trust, you can often easily identify trolls and block them.

You feed the trolls by acknowledging their existence and allowing them to take control of the dialog. Just ignore them, and they eventually get bored and go away. (If you block them, you may reduce your chances of having to hear from them again, but that's a pretty aggressive move if

they're simply annoying. They can still view your public profile — assuming you haven't protected your Tweets — and they can even still reply to you if they want, which will show up on your Mentions tab, but they have to make a real effort to do that, because your Tweets won't show up in their timeline if you block them.)

On the other side of the coin, some people get a little intimidated by the thought of tweeting about something serious. Some people actually decide to not even try Twitter because they worry that they don't have anything interesting to say! We promise, whatever you feel like tweeting about, someone, somewhere on Twitter, is into that subject, too. You might have to tweet for a few days or weeks before you connect with them, but after you find one person who "gets" you, the floodgates open; hundreds more twitterers start to hear what you have to say and want to share with you.

For example, Stephanie Germanotta, more famously known as @LadyGaga, famously mobilized her following to advocate for the legalization of same sex marriage in New York in 2011. She shared phone numbers, websites, and other resources that her fans — The Little Monsters — could use to directly impact the government vote.

So, if you're passionate about cancer research, domestic violence, or another cause and want to have a fundraiser for it, a Twitter update that you send about the fundraiser might get repeated and reach 50, 500, 5,000, or 50,000 people (or more) who are directly and indirectly connected to you. Spread the love!

Many have raised money for worthy causes right on Twitter. One of the first was Beth Kanter (@kanter), whose network sent a Cambodian woman to college in a matter of a few hours of Twitter conversation about it and links to a donation site. For more about Twitter and charity, see Chapter 14.

Keeping Twitter Personal . . . but Not Too Personal

Above all else, remember that Twitter is a public forum. Even when you're talking to your trusted Twitter network, your Tweets are very much public; Google and other search engines still index them, and anyone on the web can link to them.

You can adjust your settings to prevent search engines and the occasional passerby from viewing your updates by protecting your account.

All the public exposure that Twitter offers can really help promote you and your business, but that exposure also comes with some responsibilities:

- **Use common sense.** Don't publicly tweet or @reply someone your address, phone number, or other personal details that you should keep private. Send that kind of information via DM or, even better, via email, IM, or phone. Keeping your personal details private protects both you and anyone in your care, such as your kids.

- **Use DMs cautiously.** Typing d `username` and then your message does send a private direct message from any Twitter interface. But trust us, if you made a typo or wrote `dm username`, you would not be the first person to accidentally post a private DM publicly. In fact, the problem was so rampant that you can use the `dm` short code to DM someone. But in our opinion, that doubles your chances for a typo. The best way to direct message a user is to simply go to their profile and message them with full confidence.

To avoid accidental updates, make it a habit to use the Message button on a user's page, double-check your d `username` Tweets before posting, or use `https://twitter.com/direct_messages` to send DMs. Note that you have to be logged into your account to use that link. You want to be extremely careful if you decide to send sensitive information by DM. Better yet, use an even more secure medium like email or even encryption. *Never* send passwords, credit card numbers, Social Security numbers, or other valuable private data by Twitter (or even email, for data that secure).

- **Maintain boundaries.** Try to be aware of how you are (or aren't) maintaining boundaries with the people you interact with frequently on Twitter. Especially before you agree to meet someone in person, take a look at how you've interacted in the past and make sure that you've kept your relationship clear from the start, whether it's for business or friendship.

Things you probably shouldn't say on Twitter

You definitely want to keep some information to yourself when you're tweeting away:

- Your home address
- Your home or cellphone number
- Your kids' real names
- Your financial information (such as credit card numbers, your yearly income, and anything else you wouldn't want the whole world to know)

- Vital health details (such as diseases you have or a diagnosis you just received — unless you're comfortable with the world knowing about it)
- Details about schools and other locations where you or people you know spend time — you never know who might drop in after seeing your Tweet on a Google search

Protecting personal details

Many people opt to not even use the real names of family members or children who don't use Twitter. Twitterers commonly refer to relatives, friends, and kids by nicknames or initials, just to give those loved ones a layer of protection. Use a bit of caution and ask permission before tweeting someone's real name (or any other information that we mention). Laura, for example, uses her daughters' initials S and Z, as shown in Figure 10-5. Twitter is a powerful influence on search engines, so casual mentions of unique names remain findable for a long time. If Laura used even their first names on her Tweets (which all also contain her last name), they'd appear in Google search results for their *firstname lastname*.

The same words of caution go for any number of personal details. Dive into information about your health or your private life in private conversation. Although being authentic and a little bit personal goes a long way on Twitter, everyone understands that you need a layer of privacy to keep you, your loved ones, and the details about them safe.

Maximizing privacy and safety

After you Twitter for a while, you've given away a lot of information about yourself. If you mention who you spend time with or that you always hang out at a certain cafe, someone can start tracking where you've been and what you're doing. We don't want to scare you, but whenever you post in a public medium, anyone could go through the information you've published and start piecing things together. Laura loves the unique charms of her neighborhood and street, but she keeps the details as fuzzy as possible, preferring Boston as specific enough. She also favors livestock guardian dogs weighing over 100 pounds, in case anyone wondered.

Figure 10-5: Laura (@Pistachio) referencing her kids in a Tweet.

Chapter 11

Twitter for Business

• •

In This Chapter

▶ Putting your business on Twitter

▶ Using Twitter to make your business look good

▶ Creating a network on Twitter and communicating with it

▶ Getting and giving useful information on Twitter

• •

Perhaps you want to find out more about what Twitter can do for your business. In this chapter, we cover some of the essentials, explain what some other businesses have tried, and point you in the right direction to get started yourself.

Understanding the Business of Twitter

In the earlier days people were constantly asking Laura, "What's the business use of Twitter?" She frequently answered with a different question, "What's the business use of email?" This still holds true today. It's not that the technologies are similar or play the same role; it's that Twitter has the potential to filter into every possible aspect of business as a versatile communications platform and problem-solving tool. Both technologies are extremely open communication platforms that have uses way beyond the marketing and customer-engagement layer. Twitter can affect pretty much everything, from the way enterprise software works to how project status is shared. It can fundamentally change communication and problem-solving, as well as match resources, accommodate human-resources challenges, and lower expenses.

Twitter can have powerful effects on personal and professional networks. Sales professionals can use it to generate leads, journalists can locate sources, publishers can discover new content, and any business can create better relationships with customers. You can listen to and harness the massive flow of ideas and information passing through Twitter so that you can advance your business objectives.

You can use Twitter to create ad-hoc communities, organize and publicize live events, or extend an experience to a remote audience. You can sell directly — if you do it right — or you can just develop an inexpensive listening and conversation post among the very people whose problems your business solves. You can use Twitter to generate traffic to your business's website. You can use it to solicit feedback. It can even make your company and brands easier for users to find on search engines such as Google.

To get started, let's take a look at some ways Twitter might fit with your brand.

Putting Your Best Face Forward

Businesses can use Twitter to talk to their customers and potential customers, and generally increase brand recognition. Given that Twitter has so many potential uses that are so diverse, how can you get started?

You can probably guess that your profile is your business's face on Twitter. Even though many people use Twitter through a service on their phone or desktop, rather than through the web page itself, assume that most everyone will at least look at your profile page — if not the web URL that you provide within that profile — before deciding whether or not to follow what you're doing on Twitter.

Dress nicely on Twitter: Fill out the whole profile page when you set up your business's Twitter account, and upload an avatar. (In most cases, your company logo is appropriate, but in others, a photo of your team or customers could be better.) Link back to your main website, and link to your Twitter account from your website. You need to verify that the business account is actually yours and promote the availability of the Twitter stream to all your customers. With a Twitter stream widget embedded on your site, you can even tweet to your customers (keeping freshly updated content front and center) without their even logging into Twitter.

Make sure that the Twitter bio section, short though it may be, tells Twitter users about your business. Also, the content of your business's Tweets needs to honestly, transparently show what you're doing on Twitter. Perhaps you'd like to introduce the people behind your business's Twitter account; they're the people your Twitter readers and connections actually talk to, so you could let the individuals behind the keyboard shine through. (For more on polishing your profile, see Chapter 2.)

After you create a great profile page, what do you do? Here are a few simple ways to get out of the Twitter background and into public awareness:

- ✔ **Listen.** Pay attention to what's going on around you on Twitter. Twitter users have fascinating things to say about pretty much everything, but more important for you, they may already be talking about you and your business. You're going to want to find as many ways as you can to tune in. You can get useful information from Twitter in many ways, from Twitter Search to sophisticated social media listening tools (see Chapter 17). If you think of Twitter as a giant consumer sentiment engine, you can start to understand its potential. You can learn a lot by listening.

- ✔ **Balance.** For the average business Twitter account, you need to have a good ratio of personal (or conversational) Tweets to business (or promotional) ones. This ratio depends, in part, on how much you interact on Twitter and what you hope to accomplish — not to mention the nature of your business and your target audience or customer base.

  You may want to come up with an approximate numerical ratio that accomplishes your balance goals. You could decide, for example, that you want to make only one or two of every ten Tweets personal. Alternatively, you can opt to put a particularly personal or original slant on promotional Tweets, making them notably funny, valuable, or interesting to your readers.

  If you have a more conversational Twitter account that you still want to connect to your professional life, make about half your Tweets personal, fun, or off-topic, and the other half about your business. If you prefer to deliver business value all the time, set up your account to curate and cultivate links about events, blog posts, news, and ideas that are relevant to your field. You can also sprinkle in some self-promotional Tweets, but make sure it's not the only thing you do. Even when you share things about your company, make an effort to show how what you're sharing relates to your readers. Whatever you do, be useful. Offer value. You want to keep people engaged, which is what Twitter is all about.

- ✔ **Engage.** While you listen and talk on Twitter, be sure to interact with other Twitter users. Twitter is a communications tool, and although it's based on a one-to-many concept, it works best when you make friends and have real conversations right in the Twitter stream. Sometimes when you find people talking about subjects relevant to your business, you can offer helpful contributions to their conversations! When it comes to business, public relations, and customer service (which we talk about in the following sections), you absolutely need to engage other people on Twitter.

- ✔ **Connect.** Use the ability to take conversations offline and into the real world via tweetups, events, and meetings to your business's advantage. Twitter makes finding ways to meet and engage with customers in real life easy, and therein lies its largest business value. Take your business's conversations and connections beyond the 140-character limit.

Public relations

You can use Twitter as a fantastic public relations (PR) channel, whatever kind of business you work for. It offers global reach, endless connections, networking opportunities, a promotion platform, and immediate event planning and feedback. Best of all, if you float your ideas out there in genuine, valid, and interesting ways, others can pick them up and spread them around. Many Twitter users — from individuals to large corporations — report scoring numerous press opportunities as a result of engaging other Twitter users and sharing on the Twitter platform.

Some traditional public relations firms may be intimidated by Twitter's potential to connect stories, sources, and journalists. Many of them don't yet see the opportunity, or they're thinking about it too narrowly. Twitter is just one more tool — albeit a powerful and efficient one — to add to your arsenal if public relations is important to your business. Twitter simply gives you a way to make what you do more accessible to people who might otherwise not hear your message.

Twitter has introduced a revolutionary new way that journalists can report on the news in real-time. One New York City-based startup called Muck Rack (http://muckrack.com) realized this early and jumped on the Twitter bandwagon, taking real-time news and allowing you to filter and analyze that news. The platform includes a tracking tool that emails you when a journalist tweets about a specific or relevant term. This means that instead of your searching the Internet to find a specific story, that story now comes to you.

It's possible that you heard about Twitter in the first place in the context of a mainstream news story about an event of global importance that was first reported via citizen journalism on Twitter. One of the most famous examples of this occurred in January 2009 after the emergency landing of a commercial airplane in the Hudson River (https://twitter.com/jkrums/status/1121915133). Indeed, Twitter is an exceedingly powerful tool for detecting breaking events. You don't always get in-depth analysis (at least, not until links to longer writings about the story begin to spread), but you do frequently find yourself way ahead of the game when a story breaks if you're on Twitter.

Another noteworthy example of news breaking on Twitter was during the Boston Marathon bombings in April 2013 (see Figure 11-1). The *Boston Globe* (@BostonGlobe) was the first to tweet an accurate update about the news (https://twitter.com/BostonGlobe/status/323873235949207552). Then, several other marathon attendees and participants followed by tweeting images of the mass chaos that broke out, including photos and videos of police helping wounded victims. It wasn't before long that the Boston Police Department (@bostonpolice) tweeted a picture of the bombing suspects from their own account (https://twitter.com/bostonpolice/status/325002310369542144) and asked for help with identifying them. All this real-time tweeting and live footage actually led to successfully identifying and capturing the suspects.

Figure 11-1:
The Boston
Globe
breaking
news about
the Boston
Marathon
bombings
over Twitter.

It's not every day that you see news stories such as the airplane in the Hudson River or the Boston Marathon bombings. However, even on a regular day, journalists and PR practitioners are among some of Twitter's most avid users, and they do some pretty interesting things with it. On Monday nights, professionals from both fields gather to talk about current stories, their professions, and the future of media simply by tagging their Tweets with the word #journchat. Because #journchat is an agreed-on tag and a longstanding event, people know to point their search tools (or https://twitter.com/search-home) to that word and watch the conversation scroll by.

It was Twitter innovator @prsarahevans who came up with the idea for #journchat, and the community she built catapulted her from obscure community-college public relations practitioner to an extremely well-known social media innovator. National Public Radio (@NPR) implemented a similar standing event that used #NPRWIT to extend its voice beyond radio broadcasts.

Because Twitter usernames are short and frequently easy to remember, they can be a powerful way to introduce people and pass along contact information. In an interview, a reporter was surprised how easily Laura could rattle off half a dozen sources that the reporter might like to talk to. Armed with these Twitter handles, the journalist used the profiles behind those usernames to get a quick snapshot of those users' interests, abilities, and points of view, plus links to further detailed information about them and easy ways to make contact.

Here are some tips to make your Twitter-based public relations more user-friendly and successful:

- ✔ **Keep it real!** The "Be genuine" Twitter rule applies at all times, even when you're embarking on a publicity campaign (often *especially* when you're attempting to drive sales or awareness to your product, service, or site). Twitter's users can be very turned off by empty marketing banter.

- ✔ **Remember your balance.** Just because you want to see fast results doesn't mean that you should bombard your Twitter followers with *link spam* (numerous Tweets that contain links to your business) or constant nagging about whatever you're trying to promote. Remember to space it out. On Twitter, overly aggressive promotions can slow your progress and reduce your audience. Tread with respect.

- ✔ **Give your idea wings.** Come up with a pithy or witty statement about your promotion that inspires people in your network to share and pass it along (to *retweet* the statement, or *RT*) to their own networks. Getting your message retweeted is much more effective than hammering your point home on your own.

- ✔ **Be genuinely helpful.** Watch for conversations about topics relevant to your company or product, and provide unselfish solutions, ideas, and help to those conversations.

- ✔ **Listen to feedback.** If someone asks you a question, answer it in your own public feed so that you can continue to generate organic interest in your promotion. Answer others who happen to tweet related questions, but make sure that your answers aren't selfish or too pushy. How can you tell? Pay attention to how effective your efforts are.

- ✔ **Measure effectiveness.** Do people click your links? Do they retweet your messages without your having to ask? Do they complain that you're being promotional — or, worse, do they not say much at all? Use trackable link shorteners such as Bitly so that you can see which of your Tweets people are bothering to click or retweet (passing your messages along for you). Sometimes, you may need to tweet a little less frequently to avoid letting spamminess make you less effective. Want to really dig into some data about your effectiveness? Cruise on over to `https://analytics.twitter.com` and have a look around. By exporting your data, you can even see in great detail which Tweets get the most impressions, engagement, favorites, retweets, click throughs, and more.

- ✔ **Offer incentives.** By *incentives,* we don't mean giveaways or money, but value. Give people an unselfish reason to pay attention to you. It takes more than just promotions. Followers listen to you for the value you add, and if you consistently add insightful and worthwhile thoughts to their Twitter streams, they'll be there for you when the roles reverse and you need them.

Twitter provides all users access to influential journalists, bloggers, writers, and people from all walks of life. If you use it consistently and well, you can find powerful, inexpensive ways to share messages that help solve people's problems and gain visibility for your work.

Customer service

Big-name companies such as Comcast, Nike, and JetBlue use Twitter as part of an overall strategy to reinvent their reputations for poor customer service and turn things around for their brands.

How did they do it? More important, how can *you* do it? Comcast has a few Twitter accounts that are specifically designed to receive customer service inquiries: `@comcastcares` and `@ComcastWill` are both run by Will Osborne and `@ComcastBill` is run by Bill Gerth, both Comcast employees specializing in customer service. Although these accounts don't schedule or tweet any broadcast messages, all three are very active in the Tweets & Replies section of their accounts, where they have many 1-1 conversations going on with frustrated or confused customers.

Another example of a brand that has a separate Twitter handle for support-related inquiries is Nike at `@NikeSupport`. In the Twitter bio you'll see that this Nike account supports seven different languages (English, Spanish, French, Dutch, Italian, German, and Japanese), which truly makes this account a global source of help for anyone having trouble with a Nike device or product.

Although many brands create separate Twitter accounts for support-related matters, JetBlue has chosen to use their main account for both marketing and support. They simply vow to always respond quickly and use humor when it's appropriate (see Figure 11-2 as an example). The benefit of using your main account is that customers won't get confused as to which Twitter handle they should be tweeting to when a question or issue comes up. This also means that any praise or positive messages will come directly to the `@JetBlue` account instead of only negative problems.

All three of these brands got in the trenches of social media through Twitter and engaged their customer bases, facing criticisms and complaints head-on, and showing a desire to help and respond quickly without making excuses or shifting blame. Twitter users around the world can witness this transformation and watch the companies respond to others' complaints, which improves the companies' images for even more people.

By listening diligently for mentions of their companies and quickly extending a helping hand, Comcast, Nike, and JetBlue have generated substantial goodwill (not to mention press coverage). Even when the products and services sold under those brands elicit unpleasant reactions from the public, having a real person reach out to help in a public forum can do a lot to prevent or dissipate consumer anger. Used artfully, one-to-one contact via Twitter instills a sense of hope that the people behind the company walls aren't leaving customers hanging. A presence and timely responses on Twitter can make the difference between a firestorm of complaints and a quickly managed situation.

Figure 11-2: JetBlue using humor to engage and appeal to its audience.

Customer service on Twitter allows businesses to catch consumers in their moments of frustration and help them right away. But Twitter alone can't fix back-end customer-service infrastructure problems such as overloaded call centers or poorly trained representatives who have no real power to help.

You don't need to be a huge company (and you certainly don't need to be suffering from a bad reputation) to create an effective business presence on Twitter. Twitter provides a great customer-service channel for small and medium-size businesses, too. If you're at a small company, Twitter can broaden your ability to reach out widely and listen carefully at almost no expense (only some time and possibly tools) while saving you the cost of having an entire customer-service department. Having a Twitter account for your business can make your business more accessible, not to mention let you help people who have real problems in real time, and see instant improvement in how consumers perceive your business.

When you first dive into Twitter for customer service, you may see negativity about your company, particularly at first. Keep going. The best part about Twitter as a customer-service channel is how you get feedback when a customer leaves satisfied. Many satisfied customers send out thank-you Tweets that all their contacts see, which gives you instant good public

---

"Command and control" is dead.
Long live conversation!

Many companies struggle to come to terms with how they might use social media because they are reluctant to let go of their old "command and control" models of corporate communications. What they need to realize is that they no longer have control of the message, because anyone can publish — by commenting, posting on a message board, blogging, or tweeting — complaints about the company in places that anyone can find them.

Twitter's content is very search-engine-friendly. When a static web page, a blog post, and an active Twitter account all contain the same keywords, the Tweets will probably appear above the web page or blog post in the search results for that keyword. Don't believe us? Try searching for the word *pistachio* on Google on your computer right now. Chances are good you're going to find Laura's Twitter profile (`@Pistachio`) pretty close to the top of that search.

---

relations buzz — and that kind of buzz is priceless. Letting go of control (you don't necessarily have control anymore anyhow) of your brand and engaging publicly with dissatisfied customers can really get that goodwill going.

Networking on Twitter

Whether you do it via Twitter or an old-fashioned card file, your business, personal, and career success depends heavily on a little thing called your network. If you're looking for ways to network more effectively — or you want to find interesting, valuable people efficiently — Twitter can help you build up a genuinely interesting, astonishingly relevant, and powerful network. Entire new horizons of opportunity can open up when you finally connect with the people who are right for you. Building a network comes naturally on Twitter. The platform makes it easy to interact and connect with people and businesses that share your interests and goals, and because of @replies and other links between Twitter networks and Twitter users, to randomly interact with and discover interesting new people along the way.

The more you interact on Twitter, the more your network increases. You can build almost any specific type of network on Twitter, too. Twitter offers access to all levels of people and businesses, from those seeking work or a better social life to CEOs and national politicians. It even offers a level of transparency that erases normal boundaries and rivalries.

Twitter can also help business networking in the employment sector. It's a fantastic way to meet and evaluate new employees, and also to find new work. This Twitter job-hunting movement creates a more open and flexible hiring environment for all kinds of companies. You can observe potential employees while they talk about what they know, get referrals from people who know them, and introduce yourself — all in real time. Twitter also efficiently harnesses networks of loose ties — the friends of friends who are more likely to know about job opportunities and job candidates.

Freelancers who network and collaborate on projects can use Twitter to find former colleagues from past companies with whom they lost touch, and to get to know their existing employees and customers. We really can't overstate how versatile a networking tool Twitter can be. In so many ways, Twitter acts as a portable business networking event that you can pop into when the time and availability suit you. Bonus: You don't have to talk to anyone whom you don't want to.

Building Brand Awareness

If you're planning on using Twitter to help grow your business, one of your goals might be to simply increase awareness of your brand's existence. By building up your brand's reputation on Twitter, you're fostering a space for your followers to find entertainment or helpful information. It's important to give folks passing by a reason to actually click Follow, so they come back and keep reading, and eventually might want to pass a mention of your brand along to their friends.

Three examples of consumer products making waves on Twitter are `@OldSpice`, `@Charmin`, and `@Skittles`. These three brands tend to take a more humorous and likeable approach in order to build brand awareness and grow their following. These brands are constantly getting retweeted due to their non sales-oriented tweets that include hilarious pop culture references, clever use of trending hashtags, or seemingly risqué interactions with other brands.

Take Figure 11-3 as an example of two brands interacting with each other on Twitter. Here, you'll see that Old Spice tweeted a funny thought that their target audience would enjoy. Notice that this Tweet is just for fun and doesn't include a 140-character sales pitch. Taco Bell comes back with an equally humorous thought to keep the conversation going, and Old Spice follows up once more. This quick exchange on Twitter, although seemingly "just for fun," helped both brands gain visibility, new followers, and generally become more loveable due to the high number of times the thread was retweeted and the fact that the interaction became "news" that was picked up by blogs and other publications.

Similar to the Old Spice and Taco Bell example in Figure 11-3, Old Spice was involved in another brand-on-brand Twitter interaction with Oreo in December 2013 — just in time for the holidays (`https://twitter.com/Oreo/status/413852283651510272`). This interaction helped show product function and versatility in a humorous way.

Building up a reputation and a following like @OldSpice, @Charmin, and @Skittles might take some time, but with the right strategy in place you could certainly get there. Remember that you don't need to build a giant audience; you just need to build a well-targeted and engaged one. A smaller scale example of using humor to build a following is @CrapTaxidermy, an account that started by posting pictures of taxidermy gone wrong. People thought this account was so funny that the person who created the account compiled his Tweets into a book: *Much Ado About Stuffing: The Best and Worst of @CrapTaxidermy.*

Figure 11-3:
Old Spice and Taco Bell communicating for visibility on Twitter.

Offering Promotions and Generating Leads

If you represent a company that has something to sell, you can find a unique home on Twitter. You may need to adjust your messages a bit so that you can shift from a hard-sell philosophy to an attitude of interaction and engagement that doesn't necessarily follow a direct path to a sale. But after you find and flip that switch from "talking at" to "talking with" potential customers, people on Twitter can interact with and respond to your company's information ideas and products in ways that often lead to benefits for both sides.

You can sell-without-selling just about anything on Twitter. Whether you want to sell something large (such as used cars) or something small (such as shoes), you can probably find people on Twitter who need and want them. These potential customers have questions for you about your item, your company, your staff, and *you,* and you can let them talk to you on Twitter about their concerns. You're in business because you solve problems and fulfill needs for people. Spend your time on Twitter being useful and informative about the types of problems you solve, and the rest really does follow.

Some brands "sell-without-selling" by using Twitter as a point of entry to a long buyer's journey, rather than trying to earn immediate action. One example of this is @Lowes on the business-to-consumer (B2C) side. Of course Lowes tweets last-minute deals such as "Get $100 off a Dyson vacuum — today only!" but they also post creative photos and Vine videos that lead users to helpful blog articles for home remodeling or even the Kitchen Planner Guide. If you're looking to turn your Twitter account into a return on investment (ROI) engine, take a page from Lowes' book.

On the business-to-business (B2B) side, a great example of entering a long buyer's journey through Twitter is @HubSpot. Because this is a B2B company, the term generally used here is "lead generation." Let's walk through an example of how HubSpot might generate leads using Twitter. First, the account tweets a helpful blog post, possibly including an eye-catching photo or additional media. Once a Twitter user clicks the link in the Tweet, she's led to a helpful blog post such as "How to Use Twitter for Business." When the reader scrolls through the post, she sees a call-to-action (CTA) to download a free e-book. This e-book generally expands on the blog post topic. When the reader clicks the CTA and reaches the landing page for the free e-book, she sees a form to enter her contact information in exchange for free information. From here, HubSpot follows up with relevant emails and other forms of helpful communication in hopes of "nurturing" her as a lead and building a relationship until she is closer to being ready to buy.

If you'd prefer to stick to Twitter-only promotions, take a page from the @DunkinDonuts book. This account hosts endless contests and sweepstakes, including #DunkinAppSweeps, #PumpkinatDunkinSweeps, and #DDCaptionThis. Often, these contests are quite simple: unscramble a phrase, caption a photo, and tweet your answer to the hashtag. Prizes include gift packs, free food products, or even cash. What Dunkin' Donuts gets out of these contests are new followers, awareness to the company's Twitter account and hashtags, loads of engagement, devoted fans, and ultimately more sales.

Running a contest isn't the only way to offer promotions on Twitter. @JetBlueCheeps is an account dedicated to posting limited-time deals for last-minute flights. Because Twitter is such a fast-moving, real-time network, this is the perfect place to post deals on the fly for avid and spontaneous travelers. Suddenly, this Twitter account feels like an exclusive all access ticket to peek at JetBlue's best-kept secret. People following this account can even receive SMS text updates to their phones whenever JetBlue posts a new deal (see Chapter 4 for details on how to do this).

You can replicate these companies' successes by keeping these tips in mind:

- ✔ Be interesting.
- ✔ Be accessible.
- ✔ Be genuine (mean what you say).
- ✔ Be yourself.
- ✔ Don't hard-sell.
- ✔ Don't link spam.
- ✔ Follow the 90/10 rule: 90 percent unselfish Tweets to 10 percent promotional Tweets.

Promoting Bands and Artists

If you're in any way in the business of creating, whether it's art, music, film, photography, or what-have-you, Twitter can become a home away from home. Twitter users are incredibly receptive to creative people who tweet. Just ask Miley Cyrus (@MileyCyrus). The former teen idol turned racy pop singer had a childish image. She'd been the star of *Hannah Montana* on the Disney Channel, and nobody was taking her seriously as a young adult. But she joined Twitter around the same time that she drastically changed her look and dropped her album and tour called Bangerz. Throughout this transformation, she shared updates (bizarre photos included) with her followers on Twitter to let the world see another side of her.

Cyrus is a pretty drastic example of how you can use Twitter for rebranding, marketing, and self-promotion as an artist, but Twitter can also help relatively unknown people make it to the top for the first time.

Twitter also helps artists such as Natasha Wescoat (@natasha) increase their prominence in the art world. Wescoat's work is finding a home in art galleries, movies, and more, and she can attribute some of that increasing reach to contacts that she made on Twitter.

How can you (as an aspiring musician, artist, photographer, or other person who makes a living in the creative industries) find success on Twitter if you aren't already on the level of Miley Cyrus (@MileyCyrus), MC Hammer (@MCHammer), Taylor Swift (@taylorswift13), Lady Gaga (@LadyGaga), and Justin Timberlake (@jtimberlake)? Here are some simple tips that you can follow:

- ✔ **Surround yourself with successful people.** We don't mean just others in your profession or field who are more successful than you! We also mean people in other fields or areas of creativity that inspire you. You can start to find them by finding out which of your real-world contacts in the industry are on Twitter or by doing a few Twitter searches to find like-minded people while you build your network.

✔ **Take it offline.** Take the connections that you make on Twitter and organize events and get-togethers that bring the experience offline. You can also find out about other members' tweetups that are relevant to your business. In creative industries, the talent is what counts, and so real-world connections can really lead to new opportunities, fan segments, and opportunities to build your loyal fan base.

✔ **Share your content.** You don't have to give away all your hard work, but put your music, art, videos, or other work out there for people to sample and play with. Start a SoundCloud (`https://soundcloud.com`) channel, upload a short video to YouTube, offer free MP3s on your website, or set up a page that features a few Creative Commons–licensed photos. Whatever you do, give people a way to take a look or have a listen so that they can get to know you and what you make.

Creative Commons (`http://creativecommons.org`) is an organization that makes it easy for people to license their work so that they retain their copyright but allow it to be shared. For more information on how Creative Commons works, go to `http://creativecommons.org/about`.

✔ **Tweet on the go.** Give your fans and potential fans a look backstage, in the van, behind the canvas, on tour, or behind the lens. Take them with you by tweeting while you travel with your music, art, film, or other creative medium. Also, let them know where you are! Many fellow Twitter users would love to hang out with you if you happen to be in town.

✔ **Engage your fan base.** Don't just post static links to content or schedule changes! Talk to your fans and respond to them through Twitter. They probably want to ask you about the thoughts behind your work, your experiences, and you. Let them. Answer them. Engage them in good conversation, and watch as they spread the word about your work to their friends and followers.

✔ **Be yourself.** Put a good face forward, yes, but don't try too hard to project a persona that really isn't authentically you. Twitter is a medium that rewards authenticity, candor, and transparency. Try too hard to put your best face forward, and you may lose yourself and stop being genuine. Twitter people notice if you aren't being real. Don't worry about impressing people. Just do what you do and be yourself, and the fans will follow.

Check out some of the most-followed people in each category on user-generated Twitter directory Wefollow (`http://wefollow.com`). Categories include musicians (`http://wefollow.com/interest/music`), TV personalities (`http://wefollow.com/interest/tv`), actors (`http://wefollow.com/interest/actor`), comedians (`http://wefollow.com/interest/comedy`), and other celebrities (`http://wefollow.com/interest/celebrity`).

Sharing Company Updates

If you have a new or growing company that you want to introduce to the world through Twitter, start a separate account for the company. You may find balancing traditional corporate professionalism with the level of transparency that Twitter users have come to expect to be a little tricky sometimes, so keep these guidelines in mind when you start your new account:

- ✔ **Provide value to the Twitter community.** Your company account can become a source of news, solutions, ideas, entertainment, or information that's more than just a series of links to products and services. Educate your Twitter followers. Reach out to people whom you can genuinely and unselfishly help. You can even offer sales incentives for products, in the way that @DellOutlet does, as long as what you offer has genuine value. Establish your company's leadership in providing ideas, solutions, and innovation.

- ✔ **Be human.** Most brands use their company logo as their Twitter avatar to keep things official, but they'll add a little personality to their header photo or individual Tweets. A commonly favored approach is to let your followers become familiar with who's behind the company voice; it makes them feel more engaged. Take photos of your company during team outings to show off the culture, or tweet a dorky industry joke here and there. Humans like to talk to other humans, so make sure your brand doesn't feel robotic.

- ✔ **Don't spam.** Don't flood the Twitter feed with self-promotional links or product information that don't deliver genuine value to readers. Whether self-promotional or not, you never want to clog up people's Twitter streams with irrelevant information. You might not talk about your cat or your marriage on a company account, but you can still make it personal. Profile an employee, talk about milestones for employees, or talk about what's going on in your office. You can even hold tweetups at your office and invite your followers to stop by, as Boston's NPR news station WBUR (@WBUR) does. This approach gives people a peek at what makes your company run.

Before tweeting in earnest for your company, it's a good idea to openly discuss your plans to demonstrate that you're taking a productive, innovative approach and to prevent any misguided fears that joining Twitter means you will somehow suddenly start to leak sensitive company information or otherwise break reasonable corporate policies. As with any public communications platform, you do need to consider just how much you can say about what goes on inside your business. Transparency is key, but you don't want to disclose industry secrets in a public forum. Every company has a different style. It helps to have a good plan in place and make sure that the employees assigned to the company Twitter account are trustworthy and have solid judgment.

Building Community

Community-building sometimes suffers from a "Kumbaya" perception that devalues the importance of using tools such as Twitter to connect with people. But building a truly engaged community is extremely valuable.

Apple is an example of a company that benefits tremendously from its engaged community in terms of promotion, sales, and even customer support administered from one Apple fan directly to others. Apple built its community by building great products people get passionate about, not by worrying about any particular tools. So as you approach the Twitter opportunity, remember how powerful and engaged community can be and remember what people actually engage around — the things they really and truly care about.

At its best, the community concept of sharing and connecting can help you spread a positive image and good comments about your company; done wrong, it can veer into feel-good, self-help banter that's ultimately empty. Again, don't fuss too much about Twitter as a tool. Think more strategically about the community and what they care about and engage them with substance and real contributions.

Building a community is not necessarily the same as building a network:

✓ **Network:** Your network is there for you and your business, a kind of foundation for concrete professional growth.

✓ **Community:** Building a community means inspiring the people who follow you on Twitter to embrace your brand and create a feeling of solidarity around your business, service, staff, or product.

With a community, you can build a loyal corps of evangelists: people who are passionate about your brand, even though they have no professional or financial stake in the company. If you can engender the community feeling through your use of Twitter and how you interact with your customers, your customers begin to feel emotionally invested in your success online.

You can see this community feeling with JetBlue. The Twitter users who follow the airline are so dedicated that they act like they're legitimately invested in the brand's success. JetBlue fosters this effect by staying on top of what people on Twitter are saying about them, or about flights and traveling in general, through the use of monitoring tools. Then they jump in with help, as needed. If you tweet about having trouble finding a flight, for example, you can expect a JetBlue employee to send you a direct message (DM) or @reply in less than a day that includes links to the proper pages on the JetBlue site. Plus, JetBlue has spent so much time building a strong community that Twitter members who don't even work for JetBlue will routinely pass along information they see or hear and will even reach out on behalf of the company and connect potential customers with JetBlue.com.

@TheEllenShow's #Oscars Selfie

Talk about a brand leveraging Twitter to build a community! Samsung may have pulled off the most remarkable Twitter marketing stunt of all time. During the 2014 Academy Awards, host Ellen DeGeneres (@TheEllenShow) was running around the event with her Samsung smartphone, taking hilarious selfies (a self-portrait photograph taken with a smartphone or digital camera) as she navigated the televised event.

The reason DeGeneres was doing this was not for comedic relief alone, but also because Samsung had sponsored the entire event and needed a representative. The #Oscars hashtag already had a significant amount of user-generated buzz coming from the live television event, but Samsung wanted to make it epic.

Samsung gave DeGeneres a Galaxy Note 3, which she connected to Twitter's mobile app. She then proceeded to run into the celebrity audience and announce that she was attempting to break the record for most retweeted Tweet ever while being on live television. Until that point, the winner was President Barack Obama's "Four more years" Tweet (`https://twitter.com/BarackObama/status/266031293945503744`), with more than 770,000 retweets.

Gathering stars such as Bradley Cooper, Jennifer Lawrence, Meryl Streep, Julia Roberts, Brad Pitt, Angelina Jolie, and Kevin Spacey, DeGeneres took a selfie that will go down in the history books (`https://twitter.com/TheEllenShow/status/440322224407314432`). With more than 3.4 million retweets, this Tweet will be a difficult one to surpass.

Community is also a huge aspect of the Twitter experiences of many musicians and artists, such as Imogen Heap (@ImogenHeap) and John Mayer (@JohnMayer). Heap uses Twitter to interact more directly with her fan base, which increases the loyalty of her listeners, who have come to see a more human side of her and feel like they've even come to know her. If someone tweets something about Heap that her Twitter followers don't like, you can watch the community leap to her defense. At the same time, Tweets from her Twitter community usually reflect the tone of her own calm Tweets, remaining mellow and not shrill.

Musicians, actors, and other celebrities are really personality-based businesses, and bringing forth those personalities on Twitter by asking questions and sharing parts of their lives cements a valuable engagement between the artist and fans.

You can build community through

- ✔ Offering genuine interaction
- ✔ Asking questions
- ✔ Being honest and transparent
- ✔ Following people back who follow you
- ✔ Not overautomating
- ✔ Being more than a link list
- ✔ Providing value

Conducting Research

Twitter is an excellent tool for crowdsourcing and focus-group research. You can easily get the answers you seek after you establish a relationship with your followers that encourages participation, conversation, and sharing. Larger corporations are continually diving in to conduct their own research and build their own tools that can make sense of the tremendous amount of data being generated on Twitter all the time.

If you're willing to experiment with different ways to watch the Twitter stream, you can collect *passive data* (what people happen to be mentioning), do *active research* (asking questions and conducting polls), and even engage actual focus groups and ad-hoc communities in live events.

Growing your numbers naturally

Although effective questions and good tagging can help your research spread beyond your direct network, to do most kinds of research on Twitter, you need a healthy following first. This network will have much more value in the long run if you grow your numbers through natural conversational methods and organic back-and-forth follows. (Note: Don't post "Please follow this account," the way that actor Ashton Kutcher did when he was trying to race CNN to 1 million Twitter followers.) When you know that you have a diverse crowd of intelligent people following you on Twitter, including those who are both fans and critics of your brand, you can feel relatively comfortable starting to ask them for feedback and insight.

Take it slow, and wait for a solid, engaged, relevant network to build up. Your business and you can begin to thrive on the real-time feedback about your products, services, and staff. Twitter can, among other things, help you find out before it's too late that a new flagship product is flawed, spread the word about your excellent customer service directly from the customers that were involved, and invite interested customers to come to real-life tweetups to find out more about your brand. Any forward-thinking business that has transparency on the mind or wants to remain on top of brand perception at all times has started to use Twitter.

As you build your network and start gaining more followers on Twitter, it becomes a very useful tool for informal conversational research. If you ask a really good question and send it into the world with a #hashtag to make the answers easier to find, you can even do research with a very small following, because the tag attracts curious bystanders who may later become new followers. As you ask questions, you can use any number of polling tools or even a simple manually generated tracking system (such as a Microsoft Excel spreadsheet) to collect the answers and data that you receive.

Twitter can be thought of as a global, human-powered, mobile phone–enabled sensing and signaling network. What Twitter knows about the world is pretty incredible, and when businesses understand how to work with that information, the combination can contribute toward closing some pretty important gaps in our economy between supply and demand.

Going Transparent

Transparency is a crucial marketing buzzword for some businesses and a scary reality for others. Lest you think we're asking you to live out that unpleasant dream in which you forget to wear your pants to school, relax. Transparency doesn't require exposing company data to corporate spies or baring your soul for the Internet. More than anything else, it simply means being honest, disclosing your biases, admitting to mistakes, and not trying to force your message and spin on everyone all the time.

Although many Twitter users find themselves becoming more casual in their use of the service over time, you need to find your own personal comfort level between acting like a real person and oversharing. After you find that line for yourself, your business, and your employees, being genuine and transparent on Twitter becomes second nature. Transparency fosters trust and relationships. It's no secret that people like to work with people they like.

Here's how to achieve transparency:

✔ **Release control.** Stop worrying about what might happen to your brand. Instead, listen to what your customers are trying to tell you and respond to that feedback. The truth is, you haven't been able to control your message for a while now; you just may not have known it.

Look at the hashtags #McDStories and #AmazonFail. In the former example, McDonald's attempted to start a cute hashtag sharing warm and fuzzy stories about the brand; it failed spectacularly when stories about poor restaurant conditions and pictures of questionable food started surfacing. McDonald's customers used Twitter to express their anger and ultimately got the campaign suspended. The Amazon Fail incident happened when books pertaining to gay and lesbian themes were suddenly pulled from the online retailer's bestseller lists. Again, Twitter users smelled something fishy and instantly started spreading the word. Both companies learned from going through this process that a better Twitter listening practice would have helped them address concerns early and prevent a conflagration.

✔ **Admit to problems.** When you acknowledge that your business and you occasionally have rough patches, you can form stronger, more genuine connections with your community. That kind of open disclosure has limits when it comes to some professions. Obviously, people in the legal and medical professions, as well as government agencies, have to restrict and curtail their Twitter use because of privacy issues. But for most businesses, honesty is the best policy.

✔ **Reach out continually.** Don't stop seeking out the customers who are talking about you and reaching out to them. That personal touch goes very far in establishing and maintaining a positive perception of your business or brand.

✔ **Be proactive.** If you're engaged with the community in a genuine way, people forgive most mistakes. Twitter's community is pretty cooperative, and if you embrace it, you can be rewarded with unexpected benefits such as loyalty; advocacy; and even organic, voluntary promotion of you and your work.

Advising Employees on Tweeting

Business owners often feel some uncertainty and concern about how to manage employees so that they don't waste time or make costly mistakes when using Twitter. Remember to apply common sense and manage based on behavior and results, not just specific tools. Your existing guidelines about email, blogs, commenting on message boards and forums, and even conversations with outside individuals cover any concerns that you have about your employees' use of Twitter.

That said, it's important to remember that information spreads fast on Twitter, and that Twitter is a very open and searchable public forum. Errors can — and will — go farther, faster, so the exercise of common sense is in order.

Before you start using Twitter for your business, provide staff guidance on how to use it and what to be cautious about. Twitter is extremely new to many people, and they may not be familiar with just how public and open it is. Definitely set a few ground rules to help prevent common mistakes. You can simply write a one- or two-page set of reminders or direct employees' attention to the parts of your existing human-resources policy that cover public communications.

Make the guidelines basic, clear, and easy to follow. Here are some thoughts to get you started:

- ✔ If you wouldn't say it in front of your parents, kids, or boss, perhaps you shouldn't say it on Twitter.

- ✔ If you do something confidential at a company, keep private information under wraps. Respect clients' privacy as well as your company's.

- ✔ Respect the company brand when you're out at *tweetups* (Twitter-based meetups) and events. Anyone can get quoted at any time.

- ✔ Perception is reality. Even if the complaint you tweet right after a client phone call wasn't about the client, it can be misconstrued that way.

- ✔ Manage your time on Twitter well so that it doesn't interfere with your workload.

Unless your business has other issues that come into play (if you work for a law firm or government agency, for example), these basic rules should be enough to keep people from abusing their time on Twitter. Customize them however you want.

Twitter can be an extremely valuable tool for building your professional team and bringing them together. You can set up meetings, tweet notes, meet customers, and more, and your staff can connect more easily by using Twitter as well. The more of a team you can build, the better you can weather any economic buffering.

Sharing Knowledge

You can use Twitter to share knowledge, collaborate inside the company and out, and gather business information and research. After you start to build a healthy network, you need to send out only a few Tweets about your project, problem, or issue before people come out of the woodwork to try to help your business and you. If you haven't been building your Twitter network, you may have to wait a while for this aspect of Twitter to become useful for you.

Suppose that you come up with a major presentation about what your company does or sells, but you need something to complete it, such as a chart or a link to a relevant study. Twitter can probably help you find that missing piece. People on Twitter usually offer a helping hand when it comes to knowledge sharing, collaboration, and information gathering, especially if you spend time interacting on Twitter and building your network. Avid Twitter users are all aware of the same thing: By helping others, they can get a hand when they need it.

The very existence of this book is an example of Twitter bringing people together for knowledge sharing and collaboration. Laura got to know two Wiley employees on Twitter and in person at conferences, which led to a conversation about Laura's writing *Twitter For Dummies*. Laura in turn had met Brittany and Anum via Twitter-related conversations and events, and they built trusting relationships over time. We also reached out via our personal Twitter accounts and @dummies on Twitter to ask the broader Twitter community what they thought belonged in a book about Twitter. Moving forward, we'll continue to listen and interact via the @dummies account, so feel free to ask us questions and engage with us there.

Chapter 12

Twitter and the Evolving Media Landscape

*Y*ou may have first been turned onto Twitter by hearing about it in the mainstream media. News outlets such as CNN (@CNN, @cnnbrk) and popular shows such as *Ellen, The View,* and *Oprah* have all begun to incorporate Twitter and the global, real-time conversations it fosters into their onscreen time.

Twitter is cropping up in print media, too. Celebrities are adopting it as a way to beat the paparazzi at their own game and give their fans a more direct voice to listen to. Musicians are tweeting to bypass regular radio and sell more music, as well as interact with more fans. Twitter has even made it into nontechnical print publications such as *The New York Times.*

And even before its exposure on mainstream media, Twitter had already become a natural outlet for the phenomenon known as *citizen journalism.* Thanks to service technologies like mobile phones and portable video cameras, real people can report on real events as they're unfolding.

In this chapter, we dive into all this further.

Tweedia: Understanding Twitter and the Media

We used to read news at breakfast, with a physical newspaper in hand, and updates only as recent as whatever was researched and printed the night before.

But now we don't have to rely on yesterday's news. We can get news the instant it happens. We can get news from media companies using Twitter, or we can get news from everyday citizens reporting what they see. We can get news about the latest iPhone launch as the official announcement is streamed online, or news about the latest weather storm and what areas we should avoid to stay safe, or even about who is winning the latest sports game.

All of this information can come from any user and almost instantly catches on to a unique hashtag that connects all the news in one destination for people to read.

An annual report on the state of news media from the Pew Research Journalism Project (http://www.journalism.org/packages/state-of-the-news-media-2014) even shows how people are receiving over a third of their news from Twitter. And as Twitter continues to be a quick and easy destination to share quick updates, this will continue to grow.

One of the reasons Twitter is seeing such success in the news space is likely due to its 140-character limit. Unlike other social platforms, Twitter's limiting character count helps people be incredibly concise in their updates. It's easier for a Twitter user to read a 140-character update on a news event than to sit and read a few paragraphs or even an entire article. But if that brief Tweet is interesting enough, users will search for the full story.

The Egyptian Revolution

The Egyptian Revolution of 2011 is one of the earliest instances of Twitter becoming among the primary source of news as it happened. During an intense political time for a country with very different rights, such as the absence of the free press, most traditional news publications in the country were either controlled by the government or in far too much fear to be sharing what was actually happening in the country.

But that didn't stop millions of protestors from various backgrounds to demand the overthrow of their president, Hosni Mubarak. And with major news sources neglecting them, their uprising was sparked and driven through Twitter. Like many news events, the Twitter voices of this revolution were connected through the hashtag #Jan25.

At the time, a 21-year-old Egyptian woman was the first to use #Jan25 through her now-deleted account, @alya1989262. This hashtag was then picked up by all participants — other Egyptians, American media, and other Twitter community members. She was quoted as saying "Hashtags allow us to share on the ground info like police brutality, things to watch our [sic] for, activists getting arrested, etc."

You'll notice her Tweet is informal and even has a typo, but all this is accepted in the Twitterverse. It's a less formal network.

In the end, the president was overthrown. And due to all the social activity driving the revolution, an entire book was written, called *Tweets from Tahrir* (OR Books, 2011).

A true example of news not only being discussed on Twitter, but also helping benefit the world, is the 2011 Egyptian Revolution. The sidebar earlier in this chapter dives deeper into what happened.

Breaking News through Tweets

Now that you've learned how to be a citizen journalist, you may have never thought you'd be using it to break news. The sidebar on #Syria later in this chapter is one example of news breaking through Tweets from a reporter. But any individual user can be responsible.

Breaking news from individual users

Twitter user David Eun (@Eunner) was onboard the Asiana Airlines flight that crash landed at San Francisco International Airport in July 2013. Once he was safely off the plane, he took a photo of the plane with his phone and tweeted about the event (see Figure 12-1).

Figure 12-1: @Eunner breaks the news of Asiana plane crash.

Although David isn't a journalist, he was affected by the tragic event and was equipped with his journalistic tools to tweet out a breaking news piece. No journalist could get to this story faster than someone who lives it and shares it.

When it comes to breaking news on Twitter, most of the time this news is unfortunately tragic. That's not to say positive news isn't broken through Twitter — such as Twitter itself announcing it was going public as a business in 2013 — but in general breaking news on Twitter highlights major weather or shocking events. However sad the events may be, they do alert the world of what it needs to know. Here are some more examples of individuals breaking news through Twitter:

✔ **Miracle on the Hudson, January 2009:** Let's start with a historical example. When a US Airways plane hit a flock of geese, its engine stalled and the pilot had to glide the airbus to a stop. With 155 passengers, the plane stopped right in Manhattan's Hudson River, crash landing but with few injuries.

While passengers were busy getting to safety, an onlooker broke the news of the event through his Twitter account. Janis Krums (@jkrums) tweeted, "I just watched a plane crash in the Hudson."

✔ **Whitney Houston's death, February 2012:** While the exact Tweet that broke the news is not known, the death of American singer, actress, and model Whitney Houston was first shared on Twitter. Among them was a Tweet from Big Chorizo (@chilemasgrande) reading, "My sources say Whitney Houston found dead in Beverly hills hotel. Not in the news yet!!"

Furthermore, the news broke on Twitter 27 minutes before any actual news article on the unfortunate passing was released. The Tweet came from the Associated Press, and was tweeted more than 10,000 times just that day.

✔ **Boston Marathon bombing, April 2013:** News of this tragic event cut close to the hearts of our three Boston-based authors, and broke rapidly on Twitter. The *Boston Globe* was among the first, tweeting "BREAKING NEWS: Two powerful explosions detonated in quick succession right next to the Boston Marathon finish line this afternoon."

You'll notice this Tweet, unlike full reports, lacks details of specific location, specific time, and specific explosion cause. But media outlets like the *Globe* have come to recognize the importance of breaking accurate news, and following up with details after the general public is alerted.

Breaking news from brands or organizations

Although individual users play a large role in breaking news through the network, Twitter accounts representing various organizations and institutions have also employed Twitter as their news breaking source. Any organization that needs to make an announcement could either work on a formal release and hope media picks up on it fast enough, or they could simply send out a Tweet and let their users know right away. As users engage with that Tweet, the media follows with more information. Here is a timeline of a few breaking news Tweets known for being heard on Twitter first.

✔ **Royal Engagement, November 2010:** The British monarchy used a Tweet (`https://twitter.com/ClarenceHouse/status/4489951894835200`) to announce the engagement of Prince William and Kate Middleton, as shown in Figure 12-2.

Figure 12-2: @Clarence House tweets the royal engagement.

✔ **Newt Gingrich Presidential Campaign, May 2011:** Newt Gingrich announced his desire to be a Republican nominee for the 2012 U.S. presidential race. He shared the update right before an interview that detailed his plans in order to alert fans to tune in for more.

✔ **Twitter IPO, September 2013:** Unsurprisingly, Twitter itself knows the value of using its own network to announce breaking news. When submitting their S-1 to the SEC with the intention of going public, Twitter simply published a Tweet with the update. They avoided a traditional press release and used their own platform to release the exciting business news.

Using Twitter as Your News Source

In the summer of 2013, *The Guardian*'s News & Media CEO Andrew Miller said 10 percent of the newspaper's traffic came from social media, with Twitter as the central driver.

"Twitter has really helped *The Guardian*," he said. "We're at the heart of us breaking news. Twitter is the fastest way to break news now. So core to what we do and core to what we do on a daily basis."

Most news organizations now have over hundreds of thousands of followers to distribute their content, and Twitter's growth as a news source is highly influenced by everyday users like us. As people read news, they share it with the easily located share buttons right on the articles. This helps distribute more news articles to the Twitter sphere through individual users — in addition to official news accounts — making Twitter an ever growing source of news.

Integrating Twitter into your news experience

Twitter has fundamentally changed the way news is experienced. Navigate to just about any media website — the New York Times, CNN, Al Jazeera America — and you'll find social media icons clearly on their homepage. Every article published has an easy-to-use social share button to quickly tweet out the article to your followers.

Once upon a time, news was consumed at your desk and then discussed when people got together. Now, not only are you reading news, but you're using Twitter to share it instantly. No need to wait for the next dinner party; you can begin sharing your thoughts the second you begin reading.

When studying broadcast journalism, Anum was contributing to a show on the 2012 political campaign by WEBN-TV, Emerson College's broadcast television station. This was the first time in the station's campaign production history that one segment of the entire show was solely focused on social media chatter. A reporter was seated at a desk with the screen of all Twitter activity as a backdrop. She spent the evening going through Twitter commentary and questions and presenting it live on the news show. This was a major development in the news experience.

That said, Twitter wasn't readily adopted or easily accepted by all journalists. More traditional journalists heavily criticized the credibility of Twitter for use in journalism. The traditional reporters complained that when these digital journalists tweeted links to articles, they were compromising their journalistic objectivity and showing favoritism for their own work.

Building your newspaper

If you're the kind of news reader who cares most about what the latest news is — instant and in real time — Twitter may be a valuable platform to create your own newspaper. Here are some ways you could make Twitter your official news source:

- ✔ **Twitter Lists:** The simplest way to build a Twitter stream of news sources is to use the Lists tabs (see Chapter 4). To start, click the Me tab in the main navigation to go to your profile, and then choose More ⇨ Lists. On the screen that appears, you should see the Create a List option. If you're in the marketing field and interested in marketing news, for example, you could call your list "Marketing News."

  Now that you have your list established, you can easily add Twitter users to that list. So if you're in marketing and interested in marketing news, you could go to @HubSpot profile page. Next to the Follow button, you'll see a gear icon. Click it, and in the drop-down menu that appears, click Add or Remove from Lists. Now you can continue to add other users to that list, whether it's marketing experts or news outlets, to have one little "newspaper" of news for marketing updates.

- ✔ **Paper.li:** Paper.li (http://paper.li) is a content curation service where you can create your own Twitter-driven newspaper. Paper.li puts these digital papers together based on certain criteria you set. For example, you could create a digital paper based off a Twitter List — like the marketing updates example from the previous bullet. You could also make your Paper.li based on a specific keyword you're tracking, such as Apple iOS Updates, or by specific users on Twitter. Figure 12-3 shows an example Paper.li about growth hacking.

- ✔ **Twitter News:** Twitter itself has launched an entire media site (https://media.twitter.com) focused on sharing best practices, success stories, and resources. Under eight categories, seen in Figure 12-4, Twitter focuses on providing destinations for all news subjects — TV, Government, Sports, News, Music, Nonprofits, and Faith. Each of these subjects even have their own Twitter accounts to keep you up-to-date with the latest information. These handles may be worth adding to your Twitter lists to have complete lists of news sources for the different categories you're interested in.

- ✔ **Feedly:** The Feedly (http://feedly.com/#discover) tagline itself says "your news, delivered." Feedly allows you to search for your favorite sites seamlessly and then add them to your own Feedly account by clicking the green +Feedly button. Once you add enough news resources, you'll find you have a lovely newspaper gathering articles from the various locations you requested. Now, instead of going to the *Boston Globe,* Gizmodo, and Gawker websites, you can simply have them all populate in one location for you to search and enjoy.

✔ **Dataminr:** Dataminr (`www.dataminr.com`) was created out of a partnership with Twitter and CNN in early 2014. Its goal is to transform your Twitter stream into actionable alerts that identify the most relevant information being tweeted from clients in finance, news, and the public sector. Dataminr uses its own algorithms to deliver the earliest announcements of breaking news, real-world events, off-the-radar content, and emerging trends.

Figure 12-3:
Growth hacking on Paper.li.

Figure 12-4:
Twitter's own media resources fall under eight categories.

#Syria

In September 2013, Sam Dagher (@samdagher), Middle East correspondent for *The Wall Street Journal,* was one of the few American journalists in Syria. During the turmoil about chemical weapons, he was live tweeting messages like "#Syria deputy foreign min. Told me regime not responsible for chem attack & he was pained by dead children images saying they're "horrible" (https://twitter.com/samdagher/status/374975515935125504).

As you can see, the use of proper spelling and grammar is not needed for this breaking-news Tweet. Dagher was trying to get the information people needed to hear in one Tweet and not split up the content in a way that could be taken out of context. Amid the stressful environment and turbulent events, he continued to post on Twitter regularly what he was hearing or links to other resources.

That same month, President Obama gave a speech on Syria that became a major news event. Tweeters from around the globe were publishing posts about it, fueling almost 12,000 Tweets per minute as his speech ended. This was more than double the Tweets for his own name or even Tweets mentioning Syrian President Bashar al-Assad.

But whether it was Obama addressing the nation, a journalist live updating, or individual users sharing their thoughts, the hashtag #Syria was a central identifier of all the news trends emerging on Syria during this time.

Following news-related trends

Now suppose that you want to follow trends related to the news. One tool that's incredibly helpful in showing what's relevant to you geographically is Trendsmap. Trendsmap (http://trendsmap.com) shows you which key terms, handles, or hashtags are most being discussed anywhere in the world. You can zoom out to scan popular trends chatted about across a country or zoom into a specific city to see what's being tweeted in a specific area.

Most major news events get tied to a hashtag that unifies all the discussion on that topic. See the "#Syria" sidebar earlier in this chapter for a specific example.

Being a Twitter Journalist

Although news outlets have always been the main, well, outlet, for disseminating news, Twitter is now giving rise to citizen journalism. *Citizen journalism* is the concept that any individual citizen can be a reporter with the use of her cellphone camera, video camera, or other mobile device.

Just think about the hashtag revolution discussed in Chapter 8. Many major news events take form on Twitter as a hashtag, making it even easier for every Twitter user to contribute a fact, stat, or evidence of a news event instantly.

Citizen journalists can do more than just observe. Twitter's immediacy and portability (because of its availability on mobile devices) makes it possible for people to report during the moment, not just afterward. During one of the first major world news events to break on Twitter, the November 2008 terrorist attacks in Mumbai, Twitter was used to pass word of a blood drive to help victims. Citizen journalism has played a major role in the tragedy and social uprising still going on in Ferguson, Missouri as we work to finish this book. Twitter user @TheePharaoh live-tweeted photos of a police officer killing unarmed teenager Michael Brown. Thousands of protestors and observers, including Twitter inventor and co-founder Jack Dorsey (@Jack), are sharing images, video footage, and reporting from the scenes of protracted rioting and protests using the hashtag #Ferguson. Photos of heavily militarized police and reports of journalists being arrested go explosively viral when they hit Twitter. The new police chief's efforts to communicate better and ease tensions have also been widely shared.

As a part of the citizen-journalism movement, Twitter does what it can to help make the world safer for children. For example, #AmberAlerts are very quickly received and relayed via Twitter, as well as updates when new information comes in, or in the happiest cases, when the children are found safely. For an area that depends on the observations of regular people who care and pay attention, getting information to more people faster can be the difference between a happy ending and a tragedy.

Twitter and other forms of citizen journalism are changing the world for the better, but users need to fact-check, credit the proper sources, and flag those twitterers who are inaccurate or worse, deliberately misleading. While Twitter and the rise of the citizen journalist both augment and replace mainstream news, you must be vigilant and ensure that the news you're spreading is true.

One best practice for this is to see if you can relay any more speculative observations privately to reliable journalists who are live-tweeting the event. Laura experienced this firsthand during the violent overnight events leading into the Boston Lockdown of April 19, 2013, when Boston residents were ordered to "shelter in place" as authorities searched for the Boston Marathon bombing suspects, Tamerlan and Dzhokhar Tsarnaev. She'd been listening to the police scanner to try to corroborate assertions made on Reddit when the call came in that an officer was down at MIT. As the night unfolded she interacted via email and via direct message (DM) with two journalists who were tweeting heavily, and let them assess how and what to share publicly.

Citizen journalism hits the mainstream

Mainstream media outlets have long since capitalized on the possibilities, but in many respects CNN stands out as having been early to get it. Their *iReport* initiative (`http://ireport.cnn.com`), shown in Figure 12-5, allows anyone to upload photos, videos, or stories to CNN's website, and CNN then features some of those iReports on TV. Twitter plays a big part in spreading these reports. We don't know whether CNN was the first national news outlet to embrace citizen journalism, but it was the first to embrace it so openly via Twitter. Now, thanks to Twitter, the CNN iReporter interface, and other technology, and better phones with Twitter-friendly services, person-on-the-street reporting has become a reality — and an important part of 21st-century journalism.

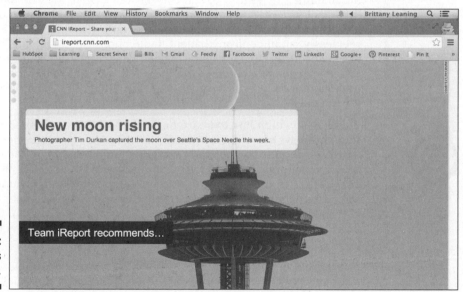

Figure 12-5:
CNN's
iReport.

That person on the street can be any person who has access to computers, phones, cameras, video cameras, or audio recorders. Now anyone can be the journalist, and Twitter brings that roving band of citizen reporters into sharp focus.

Twitter is the darling of the instant-gratification crowd, and it allows you to report events right away with no fact-checking at all, so do take everything you read with a grain of salt. If it's a story that's not being reported on by the major, respected media outlets, do a little fact-checking before you take it as the gospel truth.

Tweeting accurate info

How do you credit a source on Twitter or assure people that the news you tweet is accurate? As much as possible, offer proof that your news is valid. Here's how:

- ✔ **Include a link.** The most basic thing you can do is link to a reliable source or, if you can't verify, post the item as a question, asking others to share verification. The BBC learned this lesson the hard way when they posted an unverified rumor to BBC.com during one of the first major world news events to break on Twitter, the November 2008 Mumbai attacks. BBC's website said Twitter was the source but did not link to a Tweet that could be used to corroborate its validity. The rumor persisted because so many Tweets linked to the BBC story, making it much harder for Twitter to self correct. Once again in 2013, journalistic incompetence caused unfounded rumors about the identities of Boston Marathon bombing suspects to go crazy on Twitter. *The New York Post* recklessly put unconfirmed, identifiable photos of young men who were not suspects on their cover. Electronic versions of the image and the article had gone completely viral before it was uncovered that the *Post* had made such a serious error — see the sidebar later in this chapter for the full story.

  Torn about which link to share on Twitter when you post about a breaking news story? Laura prefers Wikipedia.org links because the entries are so thoroughly and rapidly fact-checked by myriad contributors and editors during the turbulent early hours of a story. Whatever site you prefer, look for one that frequently and thoroughly updates their stories with new information as it breaks. That way your Tweet is still useful if it's seen much later or if it gets repeated and shared over a long period of time. It also makes things a bit more self-correcting as the facts come in.

- ✔ **Author a blog post.** If you already have a blog, you might consider starting a new post to track and update the broader details of what you are sharing. In this post, you have more space to credit the sources of your news, and the ability to go back and update the information. To tweet about what you're observing, just link to that blog post. Make sure to keep your post updated with credit for each story and responsible updates wherever possible.

- ✔ **Build a network based on trust and continued reliable information.** Not only should you make sure that the people you follow and associate with are trustworthy, but you should also be certain that the people in your network feel the same about you.

✔ **Don't underestimate the power of the retweet.** The retweet (one of your followers repeats your Tweet for the benefit of her own followers) is critical to networking and viral spread. Retweets of your posts give them a level of validity because retweets prove what you say is worth repeating. Most third-party Twitter clients have built-in buttons next to each Tweet in your stream that let you easily set them up for a retweet, just like `Twitter.com` and its official mobile apps.

✔ **If you retweet, try to credit the original poster.** Breaking news is an excellent time to forgo the "manual" RT and just use that retweet button on every Tweet. Otherwise, the 140-character limit can mean you need to shorten the Tweet and also risk obscuring who the original author was. If you manually retweet, clearly include the name of the original author to acknowledge your source. Third party Twitter clients and the Twitter mobile app offer you a choice between the two retweeting methods, each of which have different applications depending on why you are sharing the other user's Tweet and what you may want to add to it.

The New York Post Mistake

After bombs exploded near the finish line of the 2013 Boston Marathon, not only was the city shaken, but the curiosity around who was behind the bombings heightened. Every journalist and reporter was working round-the-clock, desperate to be among the first to share who was behind the attacks. For some, this led to "shameless" reporting that not only was criticized by the media, but put innocent bystanders in danger.

On the cover of the April 18, 2013 edition of *The New York Post*, the publication printed an image of two young men with the giant tabloid headline text "BAG MEN. Feds seek these two pictured at Boston Marathon." The photo was tweeted, and then spread in their print version. (Given the libelous nature of the photo, we won't share an actual visual, but it's easily found online.)

Both young men photographed were innocent bystanders. The one most visible in the photo by face was a 17-year-old high school track star who came to the U.S. four years prior from Morocco with the dream of one day running in the Olympics.

In an interview with *The Daily Mail*, the innocent high school student reported that he'd had to go to police department to check whether he was actually wanted by the FBI. He went to clear his name, and all it took was a few calls before he was set free, indicating that his suspicion as a suspect was incredibly low.

However, *The New York Post* decided to publish the article after seeing an email sent among law enforcement authorities. As of March 2014, the photo subjects' libel lawsuit against the paper is moving forward. Word to the wise twitterer: Be extremely careful to avoid sharing this type of irresponsible journalism. Amplifying its effects can further destroy a person's reputation, and make you look really bad in the process.

Gathering your journalistic tools

You can use these tools to prepare for your Twitter-inspired citizen-journalist moment:

- ✔ **A mobile phone that has a camera and/or video camera:** Most cellphones have at least the former these days. And make sure that you have a cellular data plan so you can send your photos.

- ✔ **A cellphone with a video camera:** Your cellphone is likely with you at all times, and serves as a great tool for capturing videos. Videos made on mobile devices are typically the ones used in breaking news on Twitter.

- ✔ **An account on a free photo-sharing service:** These services include TwitPic and Flickr, which accept mobile uploads for sharing your still photos.

- ✔ **A Vine account:** If you want to simply use the video from your mobile phone, you can use Vine (see Chapter 9) to upload a 6-second clip and instantly post it to Twitter.

If you ever take live video or pictures of people, get their permission, or if circumstances don't require permission, at least warn them that you plan to broadcast the images or post them online. Depending on where you are, it may be illegal to post those images without the subjects' permission. If you intend to capture video or pictures for distribution online with regularity, consult a legal professional.

Using News to Grow Your Business

While Twitter is an effective community for breaking news and events, it's also a place to take advantage of breaking industry news that could benefit your business. Author David Meerman Scott calls this *newsjacking*, a way to inject your ideas into a breaking news story and garner business from it. He even wrote an entire book on it, *The New Rules of Marketing & PR,* 4th Edition (John Wiley & Sons, Inc., 2013).

According to Scott, there's a certain life span a news story takes on. It works on the following timeline:

1. News story breaks.

2. Journalists scramble for additional information.

3. Public excitement grows.

4. The story reaches its peak.

5. The story becomes old news.

6. The story is shared and done.

Scott believes that businesses should newsjack between life point one and two. While journalists need to discover more facts about the news to share it, as a business your opinions can be shared without that need for objectivity. You can take a unique angle on the piece and share it to capitalize on the increased searches that will be happening for the key terms of the announcement. Or you could use it as an opportunity to educate your audience or to simply be comical.

In fact, when the power went out into a complete blackout at the SuperDome in New Orleans during Super Bowl XLVII in 2013, various brands responded hilariously and gained tons of Twitter traffic:

- @Tide: "We can't get your #blackout, but we can get your stains out. #SuperBowl #TidePower"

- @Audi: "Sending some LEDs to the @MBUSA Superdome right now . . ."

- @Walgreens: "We do carry candles. #SuperBowl"

- @Walgreens: ". . . we also sell lights. #SuperBowl"

- @BestBuy: "Looks like #SB47 could use a visit from some @GeekSquad Agents with @Insignia LED light bulbs for the power outage."

- @Moz: "Oops, was I a bit too aggressive on crawling that server in New Orleans?"

- @TwitterAds: "It took just four mins after the lights went out for the first Twitter advertiser to bid on [power outage] as a search term. #SuperBowl47"

But despite all these examples, it was really Oreo who won the Internet with its timely blackout Tweet (https://twitter.com/Oreo/status/298246571718483968). This Tweet was sent just as the lights powered down throughout the entire stadium for seemingly unknown reasons. Of course, when the live event stopped showing up, everyone flocked to Twitter to see what was going on. It was here that Oreo totally prevailed. The image Oreo tweeted suggesting that "you can still dunk in the dark" was the most retweeted of the night. This was a huge moment for marketers all over the world, who wished they could do something equally strategic and high-impact.

Using tragic events or news to benefit your business is strongly discouraged and not the purpose of using news to grow your business. However, there are certain industry-specific and general business announcements that are appropriate for your business growth.

Fueling your efforts with advertising

We discuss Twitter for business in full in Chapter 11, but there are some specifics to the news world that are important to discuss here.

More and more businesses are using Twitter's own advertising tool to surface Tweets for certain searches and hashtags during major events. We should quickly note here that this practice is used for known events, such as the VMAs, the Super Bowl, or the elections. Any paid campaigns around a natural disaster is unadvised, unless focused on truly supplying those in need with resources and help.

That said, if there's an upcoming event that could help your business, it's not unwise to begin looking at hashtags. Or even as a user, to pay attention to what campaigns are springing up around subjects you care about.

We discussed the Super Bowl for newsjacking earlier, but let's continue with this example for its high media usage. In 2014, a new record was set as over half of all Super Bowl XLVIII ads mentioned a hashtag. Hashtags are used so often that Twitter even started @AdScrimmage, a program to feature the top ads from a big football game, usually the Super Bowl.

The third annual Ad Scrimmage in 2014 was won by @JaguarUSA for their #GoodToBeBad ad where they launched a new coupe (see Figure 12-6).

Figure 12-6:
@Jaguar USA shares a promoted Tweet with their Super Bowl 2014 campaign #Good ToBeBad.

Miley Cyrus, Robin Thicke, and the 2013 VMAs

The 2013 Video Music Awards, an annual awards show presented by cable channel MTV to honor the best in the music video industry, was viewed by an audience of 10.1 million people — over 60 percent more people than the previous year, making it the top-rated show in entertainment among the 12-34 age group.

How, you ask? A combination of Miley Cyrus, Robin Thicke, and Twitter.

Miley Cyrus, an American singer, actress, and songwriter (formerly known as the main star in Disney's *Hannah Montana),* was one of the shows performers. In hopes of shedding her previous "good girl image" as a Disney channel star, Miley saw the MTV VMAs as an opportunity to show just how much she had grown up. The provocative performance with Robin Thicke of his controversial song *"Blurred Lines"* shocked and disturbed audiences. Naturally, viewers went straight to Twitter, generating more than 120 national and world trending topics, a new Twitter record. You can learn more about trending topics in Chapter 5. For now, you just need to know that this underscores how wildly popular the subject became.

The performance drove over 300,000 Tweets per minute. To put that in context, the Super Bowl blackout we described earlier in this chapter generated a peak of 231,000 Tweets per minute. Although a record-breaking example, this event exemplifies Twitter's active presence in not only live programming, but television as a whole, connecting offline and online media for a truly all-encompassing media experience.

You'll notice that under the Tweet in the figure below, there's a section for "Related Headlines" which links to credible news sources covering the entire event. This is just another way Twitter and the media are connected to further your media experience both on and off Twitter.

Engaging with your favorite programming

Watching television has always been enjoyable. But with the introduction of Twitter, you can go beyond indulging in your favorite TV series and actually find others commenting on the show on Twitter.

Almost every TV show — new and old — has its own dedicated hashtag. Although the TV series *One Tree Hill* came to life in 2003 before the tweeting phenomenon began, many fans continue to use #OTH to tweet quotes and favorite moments, which Anum embarrassingly admits she does as well.

Meanwhile, *America's Next Top Model* (@CW_ANTM) uses Twitter to share behind-the-scenes footage and images not aired on the actual show. This gives fans a reason to engage with the show in addition to watching the actual show.

One of the greatest uses of Twitter for television, though, is its ability to allow users to live tweet their thoughts. Our sidebar on the 2013 VMAs describes how one event shattered records for live tweeting.

Chapter 13

The Social Side of Twitter

*J*ust as businesses can benefit from using Twitter to build goodwill, communicate with stakeholders, and establish personal relationships with customers (which we talk about in Chapter 11), individuals can use the service to maintain their networks of "weak ties" and even to build strong social connections. Through these connections, one can tap a wealth of resources that were heretofore unavailable due to limitations of time or distance. You may not know the answer to any given question, but with a healthy Twitter network, you can very easily get to the point where you always know someone who might know.

As we show in this chapter, your Twitter network can help in a myriad of ways that range from the prosaic (such as recommending a favorite pizza place in an unfamiliar town) to life-saving (coordinating disaster-relief efforts in real time). We also go into detail about the social benefits of strong Twitter connections, and provide tips for building and participating in a supportive Twitter community.

Using Twitter as a Support System

At its best, Twitter can do an incredible job as a support system for your support system. That is, by keeping you connected in real time with the people in your support system, you are better able to rely on them when you have a request for help or want to give back in appreciation.

Many users instinctively turn to their Twitter network when they need to commiserate over a loss by their favorite sports team, when they get a promotion or a new job, when they lose a loved one, or when anything else happens that they want to share with a supportive network of people.

Twitterers have used the service to help displaced families, victims of natural disasters, abuse victims, job-seekers, animals in need, and even researchers who need people to take part in focus groups. Twitter has also proved useful for couch-surfers, who have come to know interesting and accommodating people in different fields of expertise.

Because Twitter helps people get to know one another on a more personal level, new friends can meet online and eventually come to interact offline.

In case an alarm bell didn't just go off in your head, we're going to go ahead and state this very bluntly right here and right now: *Be careful.* As you would with any stranger, exercise caution when meeting people for the first time. Meet them in a public and visible place, like a cafe or restaurant, preferably during an organized public event with lots of other people around. Bring another friend with you, if possible, and stay in a public and highly visible location. Pay attention to your instincts; if something doesn't feel safe, it's just not worth testing whether it is. Finally, think carefully about how you model and explain this kind of meeting-up in front of your kids. You don't want to accidentally give them the impression that it's no big deal to meet "online friends" in real life. Talk about how you decide whom to meet, and share an age-appropriate version of the precautions you take when you do so.

For many, Twitter has replaced search-based electronic resources (such as Yahoo!, Bing, and Google) and become their go-to place for help and support. Depending on the nature and the strength of your network, asking your friends on Twitter (both the ones you now have and the ones you're making) for guidance or opinions can yield more detailed, varied advice and help than you might receive if you turned to only your offline network.

Twitter isn't meant to replace your offline network of lifelong friends and family of course. Quite the opposite. It's a technology designed to enrich that network. While connecting with your friends on Twitter, you may meet new friends and start to get a better feel for the people (both new and old) whom you can trust.

Just counting Laura's immediate social circle of friends (all four of whom she met via Twitter), there are already two marriages that started as long distance Twitter love stories. From a few random Tweets in February 2008, Canadian writer Meg (Fowler) Tripp and social media professional Gradon Tripp met in person for the first time in October 2008, got engaged in February 2011, and married in October 2011. Dating coaches Laurie Davis and Thomas Edwards started to interact online for professional reasons in 2009, but it turned personal pretty fast. Their Twitter-themed May 2014 wedding (hashtag #HappilyEverEdwards) was featured in both *The New York Times* and on People.com.

When you expand the circle to include Laura's online friends, countless additional relationships and marriages can be found (this sometimes makes her wonder when her Twitter Prince might come!), so keep a very open mind about the "strangers" you are getting to know as you dabble in this new-to-you medium.

Although Twitter is useful for supporting global causes and events, the most poignant uses of Twitter can just as easily be found in the simple ways in which users help each other, one at a time, all day, every day.

Twitterers reach out to one another through the trials and annoyances of everyday life (such as not having enough quarters at a laundromat) to crises of every size and measure. Twitterers have been support networks when loved ones are in the hospital, when couples divorce, when relationships break up, and more. When you use Twitter, your expressions of frustration and loss are often met by an immediate response. In its best moments, Twitter empowers humanity to act humanely.

Connecting with People

Because all Twitterers use the same basic tool set and (as far as Twitter is concerned) play on the same level, it's pretty easy to make new connections with most people on the service. The more people you connect with, the more your follower/following numbers go up, thereby increasing the breadth of your network. Take care to invest more time in the depth of your network, though. Never blindly chase after higher numbers at the expense of quality connections.

Many Twitter users are addicted to increasing their follower count and use tricks to artificially increase their number of followers. Some — if not all — of these tricks can affect your account negatively. For more information, check out the sidebar "Gaming for followers" in this chapter.

Are you feeling eager to have lots and lots of followers? First, a large following doesn't matter as much as you might think. Second, be patient, and build a network of actual, relevant, and engaged connections, not collections of usernames and large follower numbers. It takes time for people to notice you; you'll need to be posting interesting stuff and engaging with others at the very least. As you share posts that others find valuable (in other words, you write Tweets that people find interesting or informative), your follower count will grow organically. Getting more followers may take a while, especially if you have esoteric interests, but having a following of attentive and interested listeners trumps having a large number of followers any day.

Gaming for followers

Twitter networks are based on trust and reputation, and some of the first metrics that people tend to use when deciding whether to follow someone are how many followers that user already has and her ratio of following to followers.

Consequently, some Twitter users try to improve their follower/following reputation by collecting as many followers as possible. These individuals aggressively follow thousands of people with the hope that the followed users follow them back (and many do). Then these people unfollow the users who don't follow them back within a couple of days. The more aggressive "follow spammers" unfollow everyone to keep adding more and more and more. In fact, a couple of tools (which we won't name, and some of which Twitter has already suspended) automate this process. You can even buy "followers," which is even more detrimental to you because these followers consist of automatically generated zombie or even spam accounts that may lead to your account's getting flagged for violating Twitter's terms of service.

Does gaming for followers give you a really high number on your follower count? Yes. But this behavior is obnoxious, unethical, and strongly against the overall Twitter community spirit, and can lead to direct consequences for you. It's also obviously questionable how engaged those tens of thousands of "followers" actually are.

Twitter, in an effort to curb gaming for followers, has limited the number of people whom users can follow to 2,000 until the user is followed back, in turn, by a similar number of accounts. This is why the most ruthless gamers follow and then unfollow everyone they target to avoid hitting the "follow ceiling." If, for some reason, you hit that ceiling, you don't have to do anything but wait for your ratio to balance out; then, you'll automatically be permitted to follow more new people. If you're impatient, go back and prune your list of people you truly don't want to follow anymore or accounts that are no longer active.

You can help curb these gamers by not following back anyone you suspect is doing this and by reporting any obvious spam, zombie, or other follower-gaming account. Beware of #teamfollowback and related scam hashtags, and beware of @mention spammers — accounts that send nothing but "@username follow me please" tweets, most of which are insincere and verging on manipulative.

Do yourself a favor and don't be tempted to play any of these games. They're *not* good ways to quickly build a Twitter following. The network generated is random and low-value, and you run the risk of losing your account if other users block you or report you for abusing the system.

The single most important thing you can do to grow your following is be useful. Provide things that the kind of people you want to connect with will like: images, links to articles, quotes, data, entertaining content, smart tips, recognition and curation of other great accounts, probing questions, smart answers to others' questions, or maybe something you think up that others aren't offering.

You might even create a written mission statement for your account. Here is a template Laura recommends in her speeches and interviews:

_____ (your username) *is where* _____ (type of people) *can find* _____ (value offered on your account).

Now go into your settings and take a look at your Twitter bio. Rewrite it if necessary so that it reflects that mission statement and gives prospective new followers a sense of whether and why they should follow you. Periodically look back over a week's worth of Tweets to evaluate whether you're delivering on that promise and, if so, whether or not it's working well. Check whether people reply to, retweet, and favorite the types of content related to your "mission," and look to see when and where you're getting new followers. As with everything Twitter, a lot of success is in trying stuff and then circling back to evaluate whether it's working the way you want it to.

One extremely successful Twitter celebrity who personifies the mandate to be useful is entrepreneur and author Gary Vaynerchuk (@Garyvee). On a regular basis, Gary randomly tweets things like "Good morning everyone — need anything?" (https://twitter.com/garyvee/status/334663980624777216). At least one of his followers got a huge surprise May 15, 2013, when Gary sent that Tweet. The follower was out of eggs, and tweeted back to Gary about it. Gary followed up by asking for the address (https://twitter.com/garyvee/status/334664385115078656) and one hour later two cases of eggs were delivered to the man's apartment — enough to share with the entire building.

The first time you make a real, organic connection with a stranger on Twitter, it may feel a little weird, but it's also a bit thrilling. Whether you do something as simple as get (or give) a much-needed answer to a question, connect for business, or bond over something fun (such as music or sports), you've just made your first Twitter friend. Not sure how to start? See Chapter 15 for ten Tweets you can send right now that are likely to break the ice.

Twitter is based on people and their networks. These interpersonal networks are the most important aspect of this simple and (we admit) quirky service. Real connections power Twitter; those connections are the heartbeat of your Twitter community.

In its early stages, Twitter went through some serious technological growing pains while it got more popular, leading to significant site downtime and unacceptable levels of quality of service. But the power of the connections and the format of the service kept it going. Without that network of connectivity, no one who uses Twitter would have had the patience to not only stick around while the people behind the service worked out the kinks, but also embrace the problems and even help co-create solutions and new features.

Releasing the Fail Whale

When we wrote the second edition of this book in 2010, Twitter was still a young service, and although it had grown exponentially, it still had some growing pains. Most frequently, these growing pains revolved around service outages, which typically occurred when the servers became overloaded. For the most part, such outages have become extremely rare. Twitter has retired the beloved yet hated Fail Whale, but it's still an iconic story that you should know.

Twitter had a variety of kitschy graphics that appeared whenever the service went down. In May 2008 the service was down approximately 5% of the month. It was so bad that several of Laura's nascent Twitter for Business projects were delayed or called into question. Downtime in the first half of 2008 was bad enough to raise serious doubts about the future of the service. A now forgotten rival service named Plurk became almost as popular as Twitter during that awful month.

Of these early downtime graphics, by far the best known was the Fail Whale, who came out to play towed by seven Twitter-logo-like birds (four of them flying backward), each time the service went down. The Fail Whale started life as a birthday-card design called "Lifting the Dreamer," designed by Yiying Lu (@YiyingLu). There were other downtime graphics — cats with screwdrivers, the "unscheduled maintenance" caterpillar, the "just chill" ice cream cone, an owl, and a Fail robot, but none ever engendered the love and following of the dear Fail Whale.

Instead of becoming angry that their darling service was down, Twitterers reacted differently to the Fail Whale. The shared experience of losing access to the service fostered a sense of community so quickly among its users that they ended up adopting the Fail Whale as their mascot for banding together in tough times. They made T-shirts. They created a contest for designing a label for the Fail Whale Pale Ale, a mythical brew (see www.flickr.com/photos/7909366@N04/2879231531). You can still find Fail Whale plushies, and mugs, and more. Few companies are able to transform a potential disaster into a point of culture for its users, but Twitter pulled it off.

What makes that plot twist interesting is how emblematic it is of how users felt about the service as a whole. That sense of family and community transcends obstacles and gets things done. The adoption of the Fail Whale by the Twitterverse was a sign that Ev, Biz, Noah, and Jack, the Twitter founders, had indeed hit a home run.

One of the most common issues with Twitter during its early days was downtime. The server frequently became overloaded with too many users writing too many updates. Although users couldn't access their Twitter accounts, the development team was nice enough to let you know what was going on: In place of whatever screen you expected to see, Twitter returned a graphic of birds holding a whale out of the water. The picture and euphemism for Twitter downtime was born: the Fail Whale, pictured in Figure 13-1.

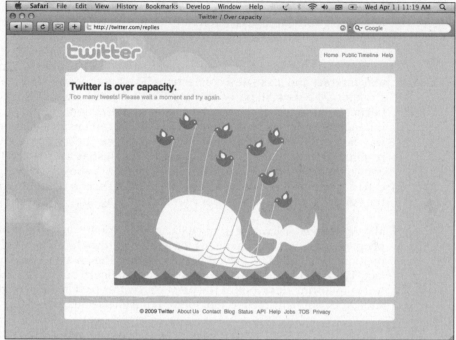

Figure 13-1:
The Fail
Whale used
to appear
when
Twitter's
traffic
exceeded
its server
capacity.

So what does all this connectedness have to do with you? If you listen to longtime Twitter users talk, you may start to feel like there are a whole lot of shared memories and assumptions that you're not part of. Don't worry. New people are joining Twitter all the time. Quite a few of the people you meet on Twitter are also pretty new and uncertain, so you shouldn't feel shy about not knowing what came before. We're just filling you in so that you have some idea how these past feel-good moments apply to you.

For one thing, Twitter's past has established the underlying tone, lexicon, and conventions on Twitter. Also, the camaraderie among Twitter users is based on trust, and if you want people to trust you on Twitter (just as you'd want people to trust you in any other circumstance), you'd be wise to always give a bit more than you expect to get back. To be effective, you need to add value to the Twitter streams of others and act in a way that inspires trust. When in doubt, try to take the high road and give someone else the benefit of the doubt. You'll be rewarded by interesting new connections, ideas, and even lifelong (virtual and real-life) friends.

Making New Connections

In life, the word *friend* can have different meanings, but on Twitter (and on most of the Internet), your connections — those you follow and those who follow you — are sometimes called *friends*. Many Twitter users naturally follow people they know and trust; over time, however, many people start interacting with strangers. Therefore, it's not unusual to hear about the new friends and real-life connections that people make on Twitter.

At first, you may have trouble believing that you will be able to comfortably interact and make new connections. Most people start out feeling like strangers at a cocktail party. Existing Twitter users may seem much too busy talking to one another to start a meaningful interaction with you right away. But most people respond well if you say hello in an unselfish and meaningful way. Some may even find you on their own and say hello; they expect you to respond to them and tell them a bit about you, just as they would in a real conversation. Well, it *is* a real conversation. All the above is why it's so crucial to spend a lot of time listening (of course we mean reading, but *listen* is the common term) to Twitter in your earliest stages.

Making friends on Twitter is much like making friends in the real world. If two people have things in common, such as a hometown or an interest (such as politics), or simply find each other fascinating, they may become friends. In fact, Twitter's interface makes it pretty easy to figure out whether someone is worth following. Just look at the person's Twitter profile page, read her bio, and check out her timeline, and follow her if she seems interesting.

The most interesting Twitter users tend to share something unique or talk about themselves on their Twitter profile pages, in their bios, at their profile URLs, or all of the above. So if you receive Tweets saying hello or welcoming you to the service, take a look through those people's profile pages and URLs to get a better feel for who they are and whether you'd want to strike up a conversation with them. Then do so, if you want!

If you thoughtfully express genuine interest in other people and what they say or do, they tend to reciprocate. In general, people love to know that you're interested in what they have to say, both in real life and on Twitter.

You can find people with whom you want to start conversations in many ways (see Chapters 5 and 6), but if you want to look for people who share your interests, you can quickly and easily find them by using Twitter Search (see Chapter 8) to see who's already talking about your interests. Laura frequently challenges new users to search for the most obscure keywords about their work or their favorite hobbies to find people they have something special in common with.

You may find sending that first Tweet to a potential Twitter connection a bit daunting. After all, what do you say to a total stranger? How do you say it? As a general rule, think of Twitter as a giant cocktail party, and try an approach similar to what you're comfortable with in real life. If you're the type of person who carefully chooses her conversations, Twitter gives you a lot of ammunition.

Take a look at people's bios, their websites, and the things that they've tweeted so you can pick your conversations carefully. If you tend to be the life of the party, have at it! Go ahead and start @replying to people and stirring up conversations. You decide what approach you want to take, because there's no single right way to tweet. You'll ultimately find that your own personal style for meeting people in real life translates pretty similarly to Twitter.

Searching for topics of interest

Conversations on every possible topic are happening all the time on Twitter, so if you want to see what people are saying about something you're interested in, search for it.

Say that you're a huge cupcake fan and want to connect with other pastry buffs, so you want to see what people are saying. You can do this simply by running a Twitter Search for *cupcakes*. (We cover Twitter Search in detail in Chapter 8.)

Figure 13-2 shows a sample search for making cupcakes. A recent search result, "Making chocolate cup cakes for the kids . . . Honest" depicts a woman who is joking around about who the cupcakes are really for. Let's say you clicked through to her profile and realized she tweets about a lot of things you're interested in. You could then follow her. If you were feeling particularly brave you could @reply to her "I'm about to make cupcakes "for my kids" — what recipe or mix do you use?" The two of you might go on from there and happen to start a relationship about your mutual love of baking cupcakes.

Or maybe you find the prospect of maple cupcakes intriguing. That user seems like a great person to ask for a recipe if you want to make them, too!

The fancy name for this is *social object theory* — the idea that two people who discover a common interest are more likely to connect better because they already share a connection to (and feelings for) that interest.

Although the original Twitter prompt (that is, the question you were supposedly answering when you published any Tweet) was "What are you doing?", in practice, a whole lot of what goes on on Twitter is really about "What do we have in common?"

Whenever and wherever you find people who have information you want or people with whom you want to interact, you may be tempted to direct-message them. Direct messaging works only if the person is following you, however, and because, in all likelihood, you haven't talked to those people yet, they're probably not following you. Start a conversation by replying to them directly ("@AliciaSue82 Wow, your maple cupcakes sound fantastic! Where'd you find that recipe?").

Figure 13-2:
Searching
for others
who are
talking
about
making
cupcakes.

On Twitter, you'll find yourself getting to know people a lot better than you might have expected. Because Twitter account profiles link to other resources and relevant information about the profile owners, and provide a series of those people's recent Tweets, you can get a pretty good sense of who people are very quickly by looking at profiles. So Twitter-based relationships often transition into relationships in real life (or, as some techies like to abbreviate it, IRL).

Attending Twitter-based events

Through conversations on Twitter, tens of thousands of smaller communities have cropped up. The Twitter-based community occasionally organizes meetups in real life — the common thread being that they're all part of a community from Twitter. As with nearly every term relating to Twitter, it should come as no surprise that these meetups are sometimes referred to as *tweetups.*

Because Twitter is just another medium by which people connect, and because the medium allows you to build relationships easily, you may not see meeting offline as such a stretch. In our experience, because Twitter connections are based on trust within a community (which you can measure by seeing who people talk to, what they say, and what they're like), meeting people offline doesn't feel as taboo as it used to.

In fact, because Twitter makes reaching out to new people so easy, some people have had great success in meeting people in the most random of places, such as at an airport in between flights during a layover.

Say that you're traveling from New Jersey to Colorado with a layover in Texas. You might send an update to Twitter: "Flying EWR to DIA, via IAH. Anyone care for a game of Scrabble during my 2-hour layover?" A fellow traveler, out of curiosity or boredom, may be searching Twitter for new people to meet and may take you up on your offer.

If you happen to be in a new town for business or to visit friends or relatives and need to get away, you may be able to find people in that city to meet for coffee or drinks. Twitter is another avenue on which you can find people, and having the ability to figure out who they are before agreeing to meet them certainly benefits you. You can not only look for common interests to talk about before meeting people (which certainly jump-starts the awkward early phases of any conversation), but also make such meetings safer by screening people before meeting up with them. Your mom was partially right about not talking to strangers, of course, but by meeting in public and by finding people you know in common, you can be a bit safer in making the jump to an offline connection.

Tweeting-Up with celebrities

At first, Jesse Bearden didn't believe that his friend Sean was getting regular updates from Shaquille O'Neal on Twitter. Anyone could be masquerading as the much-loved star. But when O'Neal (@SHAQ) tweeted he was at 5 & Diner, they stopped by to try to see him. As they got up their nerve Shaq tweeted again: "I feel twitterers around me, r there any twitterers in 5 n diner wit me, say somethin."

Next thing they knew they were in Shaq's booth chatting and snapping photos. In Shaq's words: "To all twitterers, if u c me n public come say hi, we r not the same we r from twitteronia, we connect." This kind of wide open, come-who-may style of celebrity tweetup is extremely rare, but you can still encounter versions of it if you pay close attention to what's going on with your favorite celebrities.

On January 12, 2010 a 7.0 magnitude earthquake devastated Haiti. Just 11 days later, during the Sundance Film Festival, actor LeVar Burton rallied celebrities to gather at a live event, as well as to take to Twitter, in order to raise relief funds. The in-person event attracted more than 50 celebrities including actors such as Adrian Grenier, Adrian Brody, and Ryan Gosling, snowboarder Shaun White, DJ Grandmaster Flash, country star LeeAnn Rimes, Paris Hilton, and bands like The Fray, all of whom donated and tweeted for their fans to donate to the cause.

NASA regularly hosts NASA Social (formerly NASA Tweetup) gatherings for its social media fanbase, providing VIP access to their facilities, and in many cases, the chance to meet and gree a celebrity. The long list of past celebrity speakers and special guests includes will.i.am, Bill Nye, Miles O'Brien, Neil Degrasse Tyson, and Seth Green.

In addition to impromptu tweetups, the digital-media folk on Twitter (the *Twitterati*) have organized and promoted millions of in person and online charity efforts through Twitter. The first one of these in person events to reach global scale was @twestival (www.twestival.com). In just a few weeks, the first @twestival jumped to international consciousness — and headlines the world over — by drawing 10,000 twitterers to more than 200 events in cities around the world. When all was said and done, a massive series of tweetups on February 12, 2009, raised $250,000 for charity: water (www.charitywater.org) to build safe, clean drinking water wells in developing nations. Organizers went on to organize a total of 5 Twestivals before retiring the event in 2013.

Another high profile example from 2010, the Celebrity Tweetup for Haiti, is profiled in the sidebar. As we finish writing this edition, the Twitter and Facebook fueled ALS "Ice Bucket Challenge" viral craze has raised more than $100 million in just a month for the neurodegenerative disease also known as Lou Gehrig's Disease.

Just search the hashtag #charity and you will see everyone from celebrities to family members sharing about, and asking support for, worthy charitable efforts of any imaginable type. The website TwitChange (http://twitchange.com) emerged from another Haiti relief effort in which celebrities led by Eva Longoria auctioned off their Tweets, retweets, and follows in exchange for charitable donations. Today, TwitChange is a great source for breaking news and information on social media efforts to make the world a better place.

To Follow or Not to Follow?

Everyone has his own methodology for deciding who to follow and how to follow people on Twitter. Some people tend to follow everyone they interact with, but others judiciously control their following counts. Some people diligently review who they follow and trim users who are no longer relevant to their lives, but others never look through their Following list.

There's no single "right" way to go about deciding who to follow. Assume that other twitterers use the Follow button differently from you. (Just because they don't immediately follow you back doesn't mean they're not going to in the future.) Our rule is simple: Follow people if you have a reason to follow them, not just because they're following you. (If you're on Twitter for business purposes, we have different advice for you in Chapter 11.)

To prevent spam, the Twitter team has limited the number of twitterers that users can follow to 2,000 until they have roughly that number of followers themselves. When an account that has been limited in this way reaches 2,000 followers, Twitter once again allows it to go out and follow more accounts, but within about a 10 percent margin. So if you have 2,000 followers, expect to get halted again when you're following 2,200 others, and so on.

Every user has a different response to new followers. A few @reply or direct-message their new followers to acknowledge the follow or say hi, and most do nothing at all. Heavily followed accounts may not even pay attention to their new followers for lack of time. Twitter doesn't have an official protocol about what you're supposed to do, and you'll naturally gravitate toward a routine that works for you.

Some people and businesses choose to make first contact with their new followers by sending a direct message (DM). You can write a personalized DM to say hello, thank the recipient for the follow, and mention why he may want to keep in touch. Unfortunately, although people used to more or less enjoy such direct-message greetings, the popularity of automated "thanks for following" DMs ruined it. These automated hellos ring very hollow, and a huge number of them are outright spam, inviting the new follower to do something for the account he just followed. There's no hard-and-fast rule, but unless you want to invest the time to do these hellos really well and personalize them, you probably won't gain much for your efforts. Also, it's not always possible to tell which approach your new follower prefers, so play things by ear and develop your own personal style.

As we allude to in the preceding paragraph, some Twitterers go so far as to use third-party services to automatically send "thank you" DMs to people who follow them. If you decide to use that kind of technology, be forewarned that many users hate these automatic DMs. That sort of outreach can be antisocial and irritating, and if the person doesn't like receiving DMs from new people that she follows, sending her a DM can be insulting. So use these technologies with caution.

If you really and truly want to acknowledge someone who follows you, you can also make first contact openly with a public Tweet that includes (and therefore is addressed to) that person's username. This practice is in keeping with the transparent and welcoming nature of Twitter, but it has the disadvantage of looking like "humble bragging" about each new follower. DMs are meant for private conversations, which usually happen only after you spend time to get to know someone, both in person and on Twitter.

Getting Quick Answers

Have you ever had a seemingly simple question that you can't answer with Google and that has bothered you for days and days? Well, why not ask Twitter?

If you have a solid network of Twitter friends, someone can likely answer your question. People tend to know a variety of things, or have unknown talents and knowledge bases, so go ahead and ask! You may be surprised by the answers you get.

In fact, someone probably knows what you're looking for or is having a similar conversation somewhere, whether locally or on the other side of the world. If you're awake at 5 a.m. in California trying (vainly) to remember the name of the fifth Beatle so that you can stop obsessing and go back to sleep already, someone on the East Coast or not yet asleep in Europe might have just tweeted the answer. Try a Twitter or search engine search. If it's something not easily searched on Google or Twitter, then go ahead and hop on Twitter and ask!

(The Fifth Beatle's name is Stuart Sutcliffe, according to some; you can read more about it here: `http://en.wikipedia.org/wiki/Fifth_Beatle`. So go to bed already!)

Some people consider tweeting a question whose answer you can easily search in your favorite Internet search resource impolite. Try hunting down the answer by yourself before asking your Twitter network. Some users consider it rude and inconsiderate to waste their time with silly questions, and they may unfollow you. So perhaps asking the fifth Beatle's name is poor form. You might ask your followers if they have any movie recommendations, though.

If you're about to ask someone a question about something he just tweeted, please, for all that's good and kind in this world, make sure that you first click any links provided in the Tweet. It's entirely possible the link(s) answer your question. Sounds improbable, but trust us, it happens all the time. If you have a good reason why the link didn't help — maybe your phone isn't loading it or you are worried whether it is a malicious link — mention that when you ask your question. If, in turn, someone gets lazy and asks you a question about one of your Tweets without first reading what you linked to, try to remember that people are in a hurry. Most selfish behavior simply comes from their not stopping to think about what they're doing. Be as generous and warm as possible if you respond, but don't feel that you need to respond to their question about your Tweet. If they really want to know, they can drag their mouse over to your link much more easily than they can click reply and type an actual Tweet at you. They'll figure it out if it's truly important to them.

As you're likely aware, many companies use Twitter as a customer-service tool, and are willing and ready to answer customer queries. HubSpot, shown in Figure 13-3, uses a dedicated support Twitter handle, `@HubSpotSupport`, for technical support. (In Chapter 11, we explain how businesses can use Twitter to their advantage to help, educate, and communicate with customers.)

Accessing celebrities and experts

By using Twitter, you can sometimes find quick, knowledgeable answers even to serious questions. If you're doing some research for work and want to find the most useful sources, ask Twitter. You still have to do additional normal research and fact-checking, of course, but you can definitely get pointers in the right direction much faster than you can on your own.

Twitter's popularity has made it much harder to make contact with someone who has a huge following, but it still happens. Celebrities who use Twitter have pretty much the same tools that you do. They may be drowning in too many messages to read, or they may be trying to answer a few things a day. In short, they're as accessible as they want to be on Twitter. If they have the time and see your question, you just might get an answer, especially if you respect their time by asking something relevant and interesting to them, not just something selfish about you or something that's easily looked up elsewhere.

If you want to thank a favorite author for the effect his book had on you, for example, tell him in a Tweet. If you're sharing a favorite lyric, why not include the musician's @username in your Tweet? If you have a massive crush on Louis CK (@LouisCK), as Laura does, tell him. Bear in mind, of course, that he doesn't seem to particularly like Twitter, and that he already has a zillion people tweeting at him, so he probably won't see it. Then again, who doesn't love a nice compliment?

As you can probably imagine, many celebrities and industry mavens have many, many followers, and those popular folks are often inundated with questions and @mentions. If you want to ask something of them, first go and do a search on their @usernames to see how heavy the barrage is. The heavier it is, the less likely they are to see your (or any) @mention. You can still ask, but if you don't get a response, just assume that your question is lost in the noise. Feel free to try to talk to them again sometime in the future, but if you're sending them public messages in your timeline, remember that everyone else reading your updates who follows them gets all those messages, too. In short, don't be creepy.

You'll also find many industry analysts, number crunchers, stats hounds, and fact checkers on Twitter who aren't famous but are eager to help you. With your Twitter account comes an army of experts and pundits who have research-heavy charts, graphs, and reports on a wide array of topics. People on Twitter can be very generous with their time, knowledge, and information, especially when they can see you're putting some real thought into your questions, you're asking things that aren't easily looked up, and you're otherwise making relatively helpful and unselfish contributions by using your Twitter account. After all, many of the relationships you have on Twitter are with people whom you trust and who trust you.

Twitter is a trust-based network. In the process of building connections, interacting with the community, and sharing your ideas and knowledge, you earn trust. That trust-building goes both ways. Your growing network of contacts on Twitter also earns your trust. If someone in your trusted network sends you a link in response to a question, you can probably trust that the link will take you to a page that's helpful to you. An exception occurs when someone you trust sends you a link out of the blue, with little to no context or copy explaining what it is and why. This can be a spam attack that your contact didn't send. Click with caution. And remember, always check your facts before relaying seemingly valuable, reliable, and accessible information you found through Twitter.

Checking breaking news

The real-time nature of Tweets makes Twitter an ideal resource for breaking news. If anything newsworthy happens on the local level, someone on the scene probably has Twitter and is probably telling her network about it as it happens. This usually includes real-time pictures, video, audio, and other information that covers the classic "who, what, where, and when" of breaking news.

Follow your favorite news outlet for the latest breaking news, or just keep an eye on the Twitter Trends section of the Twitter interface you're using.

Although Twitter has proved itself to be a great tool for getting live updates and eyewitness reports, traditional journalism and fact-checking still have a place. Sometimes, in the heat of an event or moment, rumors can spread as easily as facts across Twitter, so take each piece of information with a grain of salt. Depending on how much you trust the person who's providing the updates, you know how much legwork you have to do (if any) to validate her claim. By the same token, accidentally spreading false rumors reduces your reliability as a source for your followers.

Getting recommendations

Twitter's a great resource for getting recommendations from your friends and contacts. Say that you're an employer looking for a reliable office manager. A great way to start is by asking your Twitter network for help in staffing that position. In fact, your next office manager may come from your Twitter following.

Or perhaps you're looking for the best Chicago-style pizza in New York City. Ask your Twitter network for suggestions on where to go. If you have contacts in both Chicago and New York, you might have a bit of fun reading their Tweets while they argue the finer points of crust thickness, cheese selection, and topping distribution. In the end, you'll likely have a few pizzerias and restaurants to try out (and more information about your contacts' food preferences than you bargained for).

Sharing Information

One of the things that new users notice quickly on Twitter is the abundance of shared information. You'll find that people share everything — from recipes to complex presentation files — seemingly without a second thought.

Sometimes, people question the motives of those who are sharing or worry that the people who see and use the information might steal it. Addressing that concern requires a fundamental psychological shift in thinking. Part of the success of Twitter is the concept of giving up some control of the information you release to your network. To quote an old adage, "Sharing means caring." Sharing with your network increases the value that you have to that network and allows your network to grow. It also shows that you care enough about the people in your network to share what you know, what you're doing, or what you're thinking about.

Giving up control may sound a little scary, but it doesn't have to be. You've built (or are building) a network of Twitter users whom you can trust. You can control who you interact with on Twitter and what kind of network you find value in cultivating. Who you share with can be just as important as what you're sharing.

As with any online service (or any gathering of human beings, for that matter), plenty of nefarious characters are trying to do ill on Twitter. They may try to socially engineer networks, artificially build reputations, or poach information for not-so-up-and-up purposes. Although parts of Twitter are pretty self-policing, plenty of it is pretty wild west. If you're concerned about a user, either block or simply ignore him. If you're concerned about your information becoming public, protect your updates and allow only people you trust to receive your Tweets.

Another way that many Twitter users share information is linking to other websites, blogs, and Internet resources. We cover linking in Chapter 8, including how to go about linking to other sites, ways you can reduce your character count so that you can maximize the information and commentary you can include, and linking etiquette.

Chapter 14

Changing the World, One Tweet at a Time

In This Chapter

▶ Promoting change

▶ Organizing people

▶ Starting your own events

*T*witter is a great communications tool for businesses and individuals alike, and it has the potential to connect people and create relationships over a variety of discussions, interests, and geographies. When people use Twitter to grow their communities and share observations and insights on issues and situations that matter to them, interesting things start to happen. Twitter becomes a touchpoint by which users try to improve their worlds.

In this chapter, we share true stories of global and social-change initiatives that either started or were facilitated by the use of Twitter, as well as world and local events aided by Twitter. We close the chapter with a few examples that illustrate Twitter's ability to spread messages of goodwill and world improvement through its user base.

Twittering the Globe for Change

Twitter offers a platform for immediate news delivery and instant communication with millions of twitterers around the world. Chapter 12 extensively reviews Twitter as a news source; this chapter focused on the revolutionary, and oftentimes inspiring, way users have made Twitter a tool for improving the world we live in. Despite the seemingly confining 140-character limit, Twitter has become accepted for social change on both a local and global level.

Quite a few individuals and organizations have begun to use Twitter for outreach, sharing news, publicizing activities and events, raising funds, mobilizing grassroots efforts, and a number of other ways for effecting positive change. Users who know how to tap Twitter's potential for swiftly spreading their ideas are able to get rapid and powerful results.

One can call attention to issues or events by consistently tweeting relevant information in digestible snippets, as well as occasionally sending links to valuable and verifiable information. You also increase your reputation as an authority on a given topic if you write credible posts and articles and share these with your followers.

Although tweeting for social good is encouraged, be sure to watch what you tweet. Certain topics may be more sensitive than others, and what you share publicly needs to be respectful of those different perspectives.

Tweeting for the greater good

Whether you can't imagine it (or can personally remember it), it was once common to travel door-to-door requesting donations or sharing pamphlets for various organizations. Such tactics are not only dangerous, but also intrusive. Online technologies have enabled quantum leap improvements to efforts to raise awareness, funds, and social support for change.

Even after years of online digital innovation, Twitter changed the game for charity and other social good efforts entirely. Where charities once had to allocate budget to host programming to garner awareness and funds, now it's possible to employ Twitter to make a message heard, to raise funds, and sometimes, to start a movement.

From 2009-2013 one organization that made numerous "social good via Twitter" innovations was Twestival (@twestival). Twestival, shown in Figure 14-1, built on the concept of "tweet, meet, give," focused on raising both awareness and funding for nonprofits.

The first ever Twestival debuted in February 2009 to benefit a charity called charity: water (www.charitywater.org and @charitywater). Amanda Rose (@Amanda) and her team recruited volunteers around the globe who in turn organized live local Tweetup parties where individuals came together and tweeted to raise money. That first instance raised more than $275,000, enough to provide clean, safe water to nearly 14,000 people. The donations were used to build wells and other water projects in developing countries where lack of water is a health crisis.

Social change on Twitter takes many forms, often going beyond any one organization or a fundraising goal. Often Twitter simply becomes the medium for a movement to come together and influence change.

Figure 14-1: @twestival's homepage with the mission to tweet, meet, give.

In May 2014, 22-year-old Elliot Rodger went on a shooting rampage at the University of California, Santa Barbara and Isla Vista, California, injuring 13 and killing 6 before killing himself. In the wake of the violence, his manifesto, online postings, and YouTube videos came to light, suggesting that he was motivated by his desire to punish all women for romantically and sexually rejecting him. Worldwide reaction to this horrific event took on a much bigger issue: that individuals and our culture as a whole all too often treat women as objects with limited rights to control over their own bodies, and an obligation to tolerate or even please whomever feels entitled to them.

Spontaneously and very swiftly, the hashtag #YesAllWomen arose on Twitter as a floodlight on thousands of examples of everyday misogyny and violence against women. Women and men alike spoke up about the frustrating, painful, and sometimes brutal things they experienced. Within a few days, the hashtag surpassed one million Tweets. Some of the most powerful ones were collected by TIME.com: http://time.com/114043/yesallwomen-hashtag-santa-barbara-shooting.

The #YesAllWomen movement brought a massive community together quickly, raised massive awareness to a major issue, and highlighted Twitter's ability to spark a global conversation in an instant. It doesn't matter where you are or who you are, when thousands unite via hashtag to speak out against injustice we can potentially all have our voices heard.

Tweeting in politics

You can gauge the effect of an issue around the world by checking Twitter. Both the 2008 and 2012 U.S. elections employed Twitter at the core of its strategy.

Let's start with 2008. During the 2008 U.S. election campaigns, news junkies used Twitter to follow not just the issues, but also the sentiments of people from around the world: disillusionment with the administration of George W. Bush, the shortcomings of U.S. foreign policy, the rapidly deteriorating economic situation, and the rise of Barack Obama (@barackobama). In the weeks leading up to the election, Twitter even launched a page specifically for campaign-related Tweets and worked closely with Al Gore's (@algore) company Current.TV on a video-text integration of Tweets into their election-related broadcasts.

Twitter users began to follow and monitor politics in real time, bonding over some candidates, making fun of political gaffes and snafus, and overall creating a real-time political metric that instantly became a media favorite. Twitter users live-tweeted debates and stump speeches, and even less-active twitterers turned to the service to keep tabs on what was going on in the world of politics as it happened.

Staffers caught on to the fact that politicians can use Twitter to measure the buzz about them in real time. During the 2008 election, Barack Obama's team was in on the ground floor when it came to the use of Twitter as a publicity and organization tool, choosing the platform as an important way to interact with prospective voters.

The night of the U.S. presidential election, Twitter was nearly brought to its knees by millions and millions of shared concerns, excitement, questions, voting reports, and a massive buzz of connection around the events that were unfolding. Twitter's technological system took on massive traffic from all over the globe and managed not to crash, although there were time delays, especially in the SMS-to-Twitter message flow that was still popular at that time. It was amazing to share it all virtually with friends and loved ones from around the globe in real time on our phones and computers.

The reactions were varied, but no matter which side of the fence you were on, you were a part of the first, truly real-time, global reaction to a national election. Barack Obama's election victory was historic for twitterers, in more ways than one.

Twitter continued to play an important role in the 2012 campaign. Obama's 100,000 followers from the 2008 campaign grew to over 20 million by election day 2012. When the election was won, Obama perfectly captured the emotions of the moment by tweeting the words "Four more years" along with a simple image of him embracing his wife Michelle, as shown in Figure 14-2. Within hours this Tweet became both the most retweeted of 2012 and the most retweeted ever. Although that second record has been broken and rebroken since, at the time of this writing President Obama's iconic Tweet has 767,250 retweets and counting.

Figure 14-2:
@Barack Obama tweets the end of his 2012 re-election campaign.

Naturally, Obama wasn't the only one continuing to embrace Twitter. During the 2012 campaign, Obama and his opponent Mitt Romney often engaged in "Twitter duels," taking jabs at one another over the platform. This banter was even highlighted on Romney Vs Obama (@romneyobama), a Twitter account that still provides hourly updates on news involving either of the 2012 presidential candidates.

Another notable Twitter moment was touched off by Romney's "Big Bird" reference. During the October 2012 presidential debate, Romney said that he planned on cutting subsidies for PBS, even though he likes Big Bird. Within no time, "Big Bird" and "PBS" were appearing in over 17,000 Tweets per minute. The hashtag #SaveBigBird erupted, with endless Tweets on saving Big Bird. Romney's inclusion of Big Bird in his comment handed Obama fans an evocative symbol: By electing Romney, you would be killing Big Bird.

Twitter was such a major medium for the campaign that the website Mashable created an entire infographic comparing the two candidates' Twitter usage. You can view it at http://mashable.com/2012/05/25/obama-romney-twitter-head-to-head.

Tweeting during natural disasters

Twitter has also caught on as an extremely important medium for natural-disaster reporting, such as innumerable hurricanes, most notably 2012's Hurricane Sandy, wildfires, earthquakes, volcanoes, and tornados. These days, with so many people using the service, news of major weather events often break on Twitter long before the mainstream media reports it.

You can use Twitter as a sort of tracking service for weather events and other surprises across the globe. Follow weather in real time while it moves from place to place, just by watching the Tweets of people you follow.

Government agencies can find tremendous value by tapping into Twitter as a real-time system for sensing and signaling events around the globe. Because of Twitter's open application programming interface (API), programs that use Twitter's search and trends data to help people survive and thrive in future disasters are only a matter of time.

Twitter has value to individuals beyond news reporting and storm tracking, too. Twitter users can also connect with far-off family, friends, and colleagues to check on their status after a major weather incident in their area. You can use Twitter as an immediate channel to get information about what's happening and, more important, do something about it. See Chapter 13 to read about how the Celebrity Tweetup for Haiti helped raise funds after a 2010 earthquake devastated the island nation.

Tweeting to help others

As we've mentioned, using Twitter for social change goes well beyond fundraising. People also use Twitter for some very unique problem-solving: Among the more unusual projects is one fronted by user `@maratriangle`, a Twitter handle for the Mara Conservancy, who has been on Twitter since its early days and uses the service to track and catch poachers in Africa. The account has developed a network of Twitter users all over the globe who make sure no reports of poaching go unnoticed.

Twitter can effect real global change by facilitating data-sharing for professionals across borders. One teaching hospital tweeted during a live surgery to educate students who couldn't actually be at the surgery. Other people have suggested using Twitter to share medical and prescription data anonymously from doctors to pharmaceutical companies so the companies can see in real time what is being prescribed where. Twitter data has been used for disease tracking and outbreak control.

Twitter certainly has lofty potential for global connections on a large scale. So how can you use it yourself? Be patient. After you build a following on Twitter and become a respected member of a strong network, you can help rally others to a cause, or even get a hand when you need some help. Your Twitter network can help you relocate across town or across the globe, find a new job, reconnect with lost family members, and even research your history and genealogy.

Twitter to the rescue

Still think Twitter is more game than tool of change? Keep an open mind, because one day Twitter may come directly to your rescue. Sound farfetched? Believe us, it's something that has happened again and again.

The first notably dramatic example comes from 2008 when James Karl Buck was arrested in Egypt during unrest. He managed to tweet a single word: "Arrested." Friends at home got word to authorities and mobilized the help needed to secure his release. Read the story at www.cnn.com/2008/tech/04/25/twitter.buck.

In early 2014 Twitter factored into the oceanic rescue of a San Diego family when their child became sick and their ship simultaneously foundered. The young couple, Eric and Charlotte Kaufman (@CaptEricKaufman and @charlottesails), had seven years' experience sailing and living aboard their ship, and planned to sail around the world. After extensive sailing in Mexican waters around both sides of Baja, California, they set out with their two young children in March 2014, bound for the Pacific Islands and New Zealand, with months of supplies aboard. Throughout their trip, they used Twitter to send micro-updates. On March 1, 2014, Eric Kaufman tweeted "Loaded months of food and sundries onboard today. The Pacific crossing is maybe a week out."

At some point along the journey, their 13-month-old daughter broke out in a severe rash and wasn't responding to medication. This prompted a rescue effort from the Navy, Coast Guard, and California Air National Guard. Even the sailboat sent out to find them used Twitter to share updates, as shown in Figure 14-3. Although their sailboat home was lost in the rescue attempt, the family was grateful to make it home with their lives.

Using Twitter to stay alert

For the first seven years of Twitter's existence, users dictated how the social network was used to help the world. After it became a popular channel for disseminating critical information — such as during the 2011 Hurricane Irene or 2012 Hurricane Sandy — Twitter decided to invest in building its own tools.

Figure 14-3:
The California Air National Guard's 129th rescue wing tweets an update on the rescue mission.

In September 2012, the Twitter team launched "Lifeline" in Japan. This feature was intended to help Japanese users discover vital information during a crisis. To use this feature, Japanese users simply had to search their postal code on `Twitter.com`, and Twitter would then share critical information for their surroundings. For example, if there was an earthquake nearby, Twitter would display Tweets sharing updates from those regions to alert them of any crisis. The search results also displayed utility companies to provide information about gas, water, or electricity. Users can also set up notifications to receive Tweets from these accounts.

In September 2013, Twitter launched "Twitter Alerts," which expanded the idea behind Lifeline to any user worldwide. The goal of the feature was similar, helping to spread accurate information from credible organizations during natural disasters and emergencies.

You can automatically sign up for Twitter Alerts from the Federal Emergency Management Agency (FEMA), which the agency sends in keeping with its mission to help with disaster mitigation, preparedness, response, recovery, and education. Take the following steps to receive these alerts:

1. **Navigate to `https://twitter.com/fema/alerts` in your web browser.**

2. **Click the blue Activate Alerts from @fema button.**

   This button currently appears in the bottom left of the screen, as shown in Figure 14-4.

3. **After clicking the Activate button, you'll arrive at a page that either confirms or asks you to enter your country/region and phone number for alerts.**

   If you select any country other than the United States, Twitter asks you to input your mobile phone carrier.

4. **Once that information is submitted, Twitter requests you to text GO to 40404.**

   Note: If you already texted GO to this number to activate cellphone alerts (discussed in Chapter 7), you shouldn't have to repeat this step.

   You are now subscribed to alerts from FEMA. The page on your web browser will prompt you to return back to Twitter, if you so desire.

Figure 14-4: Activate immediate alerts from @fema during a natural disaster.

Organizing People Online and in Real Life

Twitter makes organizing group activities both online and in real life easy. People have used Twitter to solicit volunteers for events, rally a group around a cause, push get-out-the-vote efforts, find speakers for conferences, scout locations for get-togethers, or just have impromptu *tweetups* (a term twitterers use to refer to spontaneous real-life meet-and-greets).

Twitter helps people take online interactions into the real world. As Twitter becomes more popular and enters the mainstream, however, Twitter users may want to exercise some basic common sense when meeting people offline for the first time. Make sure to meet in groups and in public places, and tell someone where you're going and with whom. While the vast majority of the people we've met on Twitter are trustworthy, we advise you not to make rash decisions about your safety.

You can use Twitter in such a wide variety of ways because of — you guessed it — how open-ended it is. Because Twitter doesn't have any forced rules of use, beyond common courtesy (see `https://support.twitter.com`), Twitter users can craft their own strategies for how to use it.

The drive to change a nation

In the second half of 2013, Twitter became a driving force behind an online and offline campaign for change in Saudi Arabia.

Saudi women are banned from driving in their own country. Throughout the country's history, women have sought to change the ban. In November 1990, almost 50 women protested, but their efforts were unsuccessful. In 2011, motivated by the recent Arab Spring, a group of women started a social media campaign dubbed "Teach me how to drive so I can protect myself," and employing the hashtag `#Women2Drive` to focus and fuel the movement. A video was shared online of one woman, Manal al-Sharif, driving as a part of the campaign. Manal was arrested, and later released on bail.

But that didn't stop the women. In October 2013, a campaign called on Saudi women to defy the ban together on October 26 by all driving at once. The news spread on Twitter through `#Oct26Driving`. You can view Tweets from the right to drive campaign here: `https://storify.com/globalpost/the-right-to-drive-campaign-oct26driving`.

When October 26 arrived, at least 25 women drove in support. Although the ban has yet to be lifted, women involved shared positive feedback on how other drivers noticed them driving and made no fuss. They felt proud and accomplished for their efforts, and are hopeful that the continued social media support will help them one day lift the ban for good.

While the end goal of this campaign is yet to be achieved, it illustrates the power that users around the world see in Twitter. They rely on social media platforms to help spread their voices and help work towards better solutions. The `#Oct26Driving` campaign also illustrates once again how hashtags can organize people offline as well as on.

Organizing on Twitter does come with some risks. Because of the crowd mentality, Twitter opinion can turn on a dime. Everything discussed on Twitter is so real time and in the moment that something can be trendy one moment and passé the next. Take the time to set up some foundation work first — a website that has accurate information, an agreed-upon hashtag, and easily followed keyword tracking. Your potential attendees and volunteers will know that you mean business if you use such tools. Remember, you really can't own or stop a hashtag. It belongs to those who use it the most.

Organizing on a small scale

You can use Twitter to rally people around a cause at any level. We mention some bigger examples in the preceding section, such as the Twestival non-profit raising $275,000 for charity: water. But what can each of you do in your own communities?

Even if your big idea is a local one, you can take advantage of Twitter to make it happen. Twitter empowers the user to locate and organize like-minded people online around a common goal or idea. If you need volunteers to fundraise for your child's class trip or school supplies, you can probably find them through your Twitter network. If you want to start a book club, try using Twitter to find members. (A hashtag may be helpful here, as discussed in Chapter 8.)

Organizing on Twitter does help serious causes, but it doesn't have to be all work and no play. You can use Twitter as a tool to organize whatever kind of group you want, including those on the lighter side of life. Food and spirits enthusiasts have always made great use of Twitter. Thousands of thriving foodie communities socialize online, plan dinner parties, compare notes on restaurant weeks, and arrange other on- and offline excursions to celebrate their passion for food. These communities are both international and local, at the same time. They trade recipes and ingredients, solve cooking problems, and spread the word about all things food together.

Banding together for creative purposes

If you want to drum up user-generated content for your company or clients, or use that content on a website or blog, then you can often find enthusiastic participants by reaching out via Twitter. Twitter users have banded together on creative projects of all sizes, some of which were started by corporate marketers. Tyson Foods uses Twitter and its blog to generate blog comments that trigger in-kind donations to food pantries. Marketing software company HubSpot has gathered people in the Boston area — both company employees and outsiders — to "star" in musical videos about inbound marketing (a marketing strategy that encourages companies to get found by customers, contrasted with outbound marketing or pushing marketing onto customers) on YouTube, and they do it by rallying the troops on Twitter.

Creative content from Twitter is definitely not limited to commercial purposes. Twitter users have planned, written, and cast whole online *webisodes* (television-style video series based online only) via the service. When they need to change a plot or scout a location, Twitter can come to the rescue, letting interested participants help the project in real time.

In fact, when writing the third edition of this *Twitter For Dummies* book, Laura even used Twitter to conduct some research. As shown in Figure 14-5, Laura asked her followers their most outstanding moment on Twitter to fuel our book with creative stories we wouldn't know of otherwise.

Figure 14-5: Laura tweets to her audience to conduct some research for the book you're reading right now.

Do you need to organize an audio or music challenge, such as the RPM Challenge (www.rpmchallenge.com)? Twitter can help you do that, by allowing people to participate or express interest in your idea. Twitter is also a fantastic tool for collaborating on projects. You can find co-authors, lyricists, people who play various instruments, and more, just by shooting out a few strings of 140 characters into the Twitter universe.

Planning an event with Twitter

If you plan events — whether they're small, impromptu meetups or large weekend workshops or seminars — Twitter can help. You can use Twitter to find speakers, scout locations, score discounts, locate equipment, and drive attendance.

Here's how you can make the most of Twitter for your event:

1. **Create a landing page.**

   Even though you're doing most of your organizing on Twitter, Twitter itself isn't feature-heavy enough to provide all of the information to your potential event-goers and volunteers. Make the landing page, sometimes referred to as a microsite, an off-site location for signing up, recording offers of help, and generating interest. Your landing page can be a blog, a website, or an event page on a site such as EventBrite (`www.eventbrite.com`) or Amiando (`www.amiando.com`). Twtvite (`http://vite.io`) is another event planning site purposely built for Twitter that incorporates the Twitter avatars and profiles of those who sign up.

2. **Choose a hashtag (keyword) for your event.**

   Take a minute to check Hashtags.org (`www.hashtags.org`) or Twitter Search (`https://twitter.com/search-home`) to make sure that no one else is using that hashtag. A unique hashtag will eliminate confusion.

3. **When your event landing page is ready, set up basic alert tracking for your event.**

   Several free services, such as Google Alerts and the Sidekick + Zapier integration (see Chapter 8), meet your basic requirements.

   You can also use a paid media monitoring service such as that offered by HubSpot, called Social Inbox (see Chapter 8), to track your event. When you need to decide what to track as your keyword, your hashtag is a great place to start. You can also track the venue, the theme, and other related keywords.

4. **Now that you have laid the foundation for tracking interest and attendance to your event, start spreading the word!**

   Don't let talk of the event completely dominate your Twitter stream — you can lose followers that way — but make sure to highlight your event adequately. You can generate interest and allow the Tweet to get legs and be retweeted (RT'd).

If you're planning something larger than a simple two-hour meetup, make sure to keep up with who has volunteered assistance, who signs up for the event, and venues that have offered help.

Can you plan a full-blown conference by using Twitter as your main tool? Yes, you can! Planning a conference takes a little more finesse than a short business function, but it's very doable.

If you do plan to go big by organizing a large event on Twitter, keep thorough records to help you manage all the Tweets related to it. You can even use a free tool such as Evernote (`https://evernote.com`) to track what people have offered to do, who's coming, and other logistical issues. Coupled with your tracking methods, you may find planning a big event the 140-character way relatively painless.

Planning a tweetup to meet Twitter friends

Although you can plan an event with Twitter as a tool, don't forget that a huge benefit of Twitter is making offline connections with people you may not meet otherwise. If you've begun meeting other users with similar interests and want to get to know them in real life, consider hosting a tweetup.

A *tweetup* is a way to meet up with Twitter friends (and strangers) in real life. It's a way to get to know a group of people better by hosting an event. Here are four steps you could take if you want to put one together:

1. **Build an invitation list of people with similar interests.**

   Some tweetups simply set a theme or occasion and whomever is moved to attend, attends. You could do a bit more legwork and find specific users in your area who have been tweeting about your selected theme. Perhaps this would be an opportunity to gather people impacted by a natural disaster, to help discuss recovery. Perhaps it's just an opportunity to gather and discuss a new business idea. Whatever the case, you could even consider making an actual Twitter list (discussed in Chapter 3) of all the guests you are hoping will attend.

2. **Send out invitation Tweets with a specific hashtag.**

   Now that you have your list, tweet your invitation, perhaps addressing it to some of your desired attendees via direct message or @mention. Include an event-specific hashtag to encourage guests to start connecting with one another, spreading the word, and starting a conversation solely focused on the event. Aim to keep your hashtag as short as possible to make it easier to fit in 140 characters, and as specific as possible to ensure your community finds one another.

3. **Organize your actual event.**

   Plan your event as you would any event — find a location, and figure out food, drink, entertainment, and everything else needed. Use your event hashtag to gather help from your Twitter friends who plan on attending.

4. **Tweet the actual event.**

   As the event is going on, be sure to continue using the event hashtag to keep the conversation live. Make sure you physically display the hashtag, and if possible, the Tweets, at the event. After all, you have to use Twitter to communicate about the event you're hosting to meet people you met on Twitter, right? Now that you're networking with your Twitter followers in real life, you can continue hosting Tweetups and even use your hashtag between events to keep the community excited and interested.

Part V
The Part of Tens

Still feeling a bit gunshy about trying to communicate and connect with folks you don't already know via Twitter? We've got you covered at www.dummies.com/extras/twitter with ten way to approach someone using Twitter.

In this part . . .

- ✔ Discover ten Tweets you can send right now to get yourself started, with a little background on how and why to send each.

- ✔ Find ten of the coolest ways you can use Twitter, from your basic socializing to interacting with live sporting events.

- ✔ Read about ten great tools and services that you can use with Twitter.

- ✔ Review ten resources to help you go above and beyond and achieve Twitter glory.

Chapter 15

Ten Tweets to Send Today

● ●

Getting started on anything new is hard. We get it. Twitter can seem tricky or mysterious simply because you don't know quite how to begin to get yourself up and running. In this chapter, we suggest ten basic Tweets you can send right now to get on your feet.

You can send any or all of these Tweets any (or every) day on Twitter and do just fine.

Say Hello

You can try it now, if you want to. Just pull up any tweeting interface and write

Hello, world!

"Hello, world" is an old inside joke that comes to us from the world of computer programming. The idea is that when you're first learning to write software, simply getting a device to display the words *Hello, world* is a good starter project.

Why not approach your Twitter account with the same sense of simplicity? You have to start somewhere. Say hello. Yes, just *hello* is enough, and *hello, world* specifically might make someone chuckle. Be sure to add whatever else you might want to add after that, but why not just start by saying hello?

Especially for your first few Tweets, it's totally fine to just acknowledge that your account is in the awkward early stages of just getting started.

Even when you're tweeting on a regular basis, it's okay to work in some kind of a greeting here and there. Some like to share a beautiful or inspiring photo of the sunrise and simply write "Good morning." Laura likes to include a hello message when she uses a location-based app like Foursquare or Path to check into an event or a new city.

Retweet (RT) Someone

As we touch on in Chapter 5, way back when, people started noticing that more and more Tweets were worth repeating. Back then, repeating a Tweet meant copying the Tweet in some way and then editing it so that people could tell who said it first.

It's unclear who first took the really obvious and tempting plunge and changed *repeat* to *retweet*. I remember doing so, and kind of laughing at myself for it, as I shared the idea on Twitter. Most likely, lots of us arrived at the term and posted it, and next thing you know, it was a thing. Now retweeting (RTing) has its own button and everything!

To simply RT someone, find any Tweet you like and click the RT button. This will cause the original Tweet to appear in your list of Tweets in exactly the same way it appeared originally, including the name, username, and photo of the original author.

What about if you don't like the Tweet or feel you need to add more context to why you are sharing it?

One of the most useful things you can do when repeating a Tweet is add a little something about why. While that RT button sure is tempting, doing it the old-fashioned way lets you add to the conversation.

Just copy the words from the Tweet and paste them into a new Tweet. Insert the letters RT and the @username of the original writer, right before the first word in the Tweet, and you're basically there. Your added remark goes before the RT so readers better understand your take on what you're RTing. This can be a great way to answer a short question, so that anyone who sees the Tweet easily understands it's the answer to a question.

If you want to send a funny RT right now, you can use the following and just add your remarks where we've drawn an underline "blank" before the RT:

_____ *RT @Pistachio wondering if twitter is worth it . . .*

If you have to edit the Tweet to get it to fit, use MT instead of RT and readers will know you modified the Tweet while quoting it. In the example that follows, we shortened *Bradley's* to *B's* and removed one period from Ellen DeGeneres' famous Oscars selfie so that you can check to see if it's still the most famous Tweet. (As of this writing, her selfie remains the most retweeted and most favorited Tweet ever.)

Is Ellen's selfie still the "most famous Tweet?" MT @TheEllenShow If only B's arm was longer. Best photo ever #oscars pic.twitter.com/C9U5NOtGap

Answer a Question

You won't have to look too far on Twitter to find a question just waiting to be answered. Because you're starting out here, please don't be shy about coming right out and answering these questions, yes, right out loud.

Poke around some keyword searches, or accounts of friends and people you're interested in, and look for a question you feel like answering. Maybe you have a great answer to it, or maybe you just really like the question and want to contribute to the answer.

Remember that you can answer two different ways. If you click Reply and answer, your answer will appear right in the string of Tweets attached to the original Tweet, which can be a good idea and can sometimes give your voice a little more exposure than it would otherwise have.

Other times, you might want to answer using the RT trick described earlier, because it will let your readers see what you're answering without them having to click through and see what you're replying to. For example:

During morning coffee to catch up with pals/news/colleagues RT @dummies *What's your favorite time of day to use Twitter?*

Both ways are good, and it's up to you to experiment with both to help you decide when you want to use each one.

Share Something Great

Laura's two-word guide to Twitter is as simple as it gets. Be useful.

Ultimately, people are looking to get something out of Twitter. What you share, along with who you seem to be according to your profile, really does determine whether or not they connect with you, and having connected, whether or not they ever engage.

At least once a day, try to share at least one great thing. It could be an inspiring quote, a photo you took, a link to a great article, or even an idea you have that others might find useful. Suggest something you really love — a book, song, movie, TV show, or performer — and say what you love about it.

Have you read something recently that contained data or statistics that surprised you? Go find the URL for what you read, and share it using the sample Tweet that follows:

The stats in this article kind of blew my mind. What do you think? http://
(insert your article's URL here)

If possible, always try to link to a URL that lets the reader find out more.

Say Thank You

Did you know that just being more grateful on a regular basis can help make you a happier person? Why not put that into action right in your Tweets?

Taking the next logical step from "Share Something Great," when sharing an article you really appreciate, it's nice to thank the person who wrote it. There are lots of others you could thank, and ways to thank them, once you really start thinking about it.

You could thank someone specifically, recognizing them for their work. You could thank a group of people generally: your friends, your family, your church, your employees. Go ahead and send a thank you Tweet right now, using this sample:

I'd really like to thank _____ for _____.

Another way to approach this kind of Tweet is to simply share something you're grateful for and say a bit about why you feel that way. Reading well thought out grateful Tweets makes me genuinely feel good.

If you're stuck trying to put this one into action, grab a pen and paper and jot down a list of answers to this "fill in the blank" prompt: "Today, I'm grateful for _____."

Now pick one (or more) favorite from your list and make it into a Tweet you can send right now:

Today, I'm grateful for _____.

Ask a Question

This one can be a little harder in the beginning because it can take a while for people to start following you and a bit longer than that for them to feel comfortable actually responding to you out loud.

Try to be okay with that. Not all questions are asked to be answered. Maybe you can ask a question that's simply meant to get people thinking. Maybe just ask a funny one that will give folks a chuckle.

To start, ask a really simple question that's also bound to be on other people's minds, like, how did you like that show last night? Here, we use @Pistachio's favorite TV show (she has an enormous crush on comedian @LouisCK), but you should choose one you watch:

Did you watch @LouieFX last night? What scene was your favorite? #LouieFX

Search for your show's username using Twitter or Google search, and then look at the show's Twitter profile page to see if there is a hashtag they suggest. That way, you're more likely to connect with other fans talking about the show.

If it really bothers you that you might not get an answer to a wide-open question, try addressing your Tweet to someone you are already connected to on Twitter by including their username in your message.

Before you do this with a total stranger, try to think about what kind of question they might enjoy answering. Celebrities, politicians, journalists, authors, and the like get tons of repetitive questions that aren't fun (or in some cases, even possible due to volume) to answer. Don't be that guy.

Put a # On It

#Hashtags. Love 'em or hate 'em, they're having a huge impact. Hashtags not only changed how we use Twitter to discover things and discover one another, but also changed how we use Facebook and how we talk, and as of this rewriting they show up everywhere you could imagine, from hand-drawn signs to billboards, radio, television, and print.

Hashtags are seemingly everywhere these days. Pick one that really speaks to you and join in the conversation. Look at trending topics, Twitter searches, your favorite TV show, or any number of other places to find a hashtag conversation you want to add to. Then, use that hashtag in a Tweet that contributes to what is already being said. A word to the wise: one, possibly two hashtags is usually plenty. Don't give in to the temptation to pack your Tweets full of hashtags, because all the hyperlinks and # signs get messy in bulk.

Don't get nervous about how to add a hashtag to your Tweet. It's really as simple as typing # (Shift+3 on most Western keyboards) before any word or even any set of letters and numbers. Just avoid punctuation and spaces, because anything that follows any punctuation or space will not automagically be included in the hyperlinked hashtag that results when you add a # before a group of letters and numbers.

Here is a sample Tweet that you can use to talk about your experiences following any given hashtag:

I'm really getting a lot out of the conversation at #_____. Now following people I found there.

Thanks @BryanCook for inspiration here. The conversations he mentions all hinge on following a relevant hashtag: https://twitter.com/BryanCook/status/475852050887360513

Tell Us About Someone

Twitter is such an awesome way to discover interesting new people that the ability to find, curate, and share interesting people is, in and of itself, a really smart way to establish and grow a Twitter presence.

It's part of the reason guys like @ChrisBrogan and @Garyvee have the massive audiences that they have earned. Each of them goes out of their way to recognize and draw attention to interesting people they come across. Think about those you genuinely admire — and what you like about them — and then share that. You might use the sample Tweet that follows:

Looking for more information about _____? @username always has interesting things to say about it.

This isn't about kissing up to famous people, and it's actually better for your readers if you're shouting out folks they've never heard of before.

Be Human

Sometimes the very best Tweet is the very simplest one. Just be human. Respond appropriately to a human situation on Twitter. You might say "congratulations" or "get well soon." "I'm sorry" is really nice to hear when it's appropriate because either you've made a mistake or they've experienced something unpleasant.

Here is text you can use to congratulate someone in a Tweet:

Congratulations @username for _____.

Shout out to Becky McCray who is a master of this: https://twitter.com/BeckyMcCray/status/475856763577585664

Don't Tweet at All

You might think this is a copout, but it's actually a really, really, really important point about using Twitter. Often the best Tweet you can possibly send is no Tweet at all. Pause and invest time in reading, really reading, all that is going on around you on Twitter. You might be amazed.

Run some searches. Follow a hashtag. Drop by the profile page of an old friend, a colleague, a family member, or a favorite TV show, sports team, or company, and read back a few pages worth of Tweets.

Why include this tip in a list like this? We can't say enough about how important it is to spend time listening, especially when you're just getting started. We also know it's hard to read tons of Tweets without thinking of something you yourself want to say.

We were inspired to include this section in this chapter by @LeapingWoman: https://twitter.com/leapingwoman/status/475851679129038849.

Chapter 16

Ten Cool Ways to Use Twitter

. . . .

*Y*ou can use Twitter for much more than keeping up with your friends and family. Whether you use it to stay on top of your industry, breaking news, or tidbits from your favorite shows and celebrities, Twitter has many cool and diverse uses. And yes, you can even find out, or tell the world, what's for lunch. The possibilities are endless. In this chapter, we introduce you to ten cool ways you can use Twitter.

Socialize and Network

Across the wide universe of Twitter users, one of the most popular uses is simply chatting and keeping up with family and friends. As fun as it is to follow "famous" accounts, the most engaged people on Twitter largely use it to keep up with their various social and business circles.

Twitter is extremely powerful for networking because Twitter actually mimics how people build trust — gradually, through random interactions over time, and without anyone confronting them and asking for stuff.

Routine, random, not-that-important interactions weave the fabric of community that holds the world together, in real life and on social networks alike. Twitter's environment of random interactions makes discovering new people with shared interests pretty easy, and helps you gradually learn what interests them.

On the go, it's really easy to stay in touch with someone and follow up later by simply exchanging usernames with someone. Later on, you can find her again, recommend her to someone else, send her an @Mention, or just check in on her last few days before sending her an email.

Follow Breaking News

Twitter continues to grow as a resource for breaking news. Over and over again almost since the beginning, major emerging world news events often break first on Twitter and are then picked up by the mainstream broadcast media. Very few aspects of the entire media business remain untouched by Twitter.

Sourcing standards for journalism still apply, of course, and you can easily lose what really has happened until a definitive account is posted on a major news site, such as *The New York Times* or CNN.

Find, Follow, and Fan Celebrities

Celebrities from all walks of life have discovered that they can forge a direct connection with their fans by using Twitter. This gives them a chance to trade some of their time and privacy, on their own terms, in order to attract attention to what they are working on. A quick look at the top 100 most followed accounts on Twitter per Twitter Counter shows how dominant celebrities — and their fan bases — have become on the site. Visit `http://twittercounter.com/pages/100`.

Not sure who to follow? Connect with your favorites in two dozen categories, including athletes, musicians, and world leaders, by checking out Twitter's Popular accounts page, `https://twitter.com/who_to_follow/interests`.

It's likewise a great idea to simply search Twitter or Google for the Twitter accounts of musicians, actors, business leaders, authors, and others you admire or respect. If at first you don't succeed, check their websites and Facebook pages for a mention of their Twitter account.

Musicians so dominate as Twitter celebrities that they merit additional detail here. As we go to press, seven of the ten most followed Twitter accounts are musicians. Katy Perry (`@KatyPerry`) and Justin Bieber (`@JustinBieber`) have been trading places as the most-followed account for the past couple of years. They're so popular that the third most popular account (`@BarackObama` — you know, the leader of the free world) trails behind both by about 10 million followers! The other five musicians in the top ten are Taylor Swift (`@TaylorSwift13`), Lady Gaga (`@LadyGaga`), long-time twitterer Britney Spears (`@BritneySpears`), Rihanna (`@Rihanna`), and Justin Timberlake (`@JTimberlake`).

If small time music celebrities are more your speed, remember that tens of thousands of recording artists at all levels are making innovative use of it. Check out this Twitter list published by Ross Barber (`@ElectricKiwi`) for 16 independent musicians featured in the #GoIndie advice series: `https://twitter.com/ElectricKiwi/electric-kiwi-goindie/members`.

Whatever kinds of celebrities you decide to follow, be a little picky to get a great quality stream of Tweets coming your way. Remember that it's not enough that someone you dig is tweeting, because tweeting extremely well is a bit of an art. Find the person's account, click through to her profile page, and read recent Tweets. Take a look at the media she tends to share, and think about whether this will add to your Twitter experience.

Participate in Live Media: Sports and Television

Although Twitter has made major impacts across the entire media landscape, the most extreme examples often come from live media.

Never before was it so simple for audiences to connect with one another while they are all watching an event unfold together. Live sporting events, season premieres and finales, awards shows, and reality television contests all have avid Twitter fan communities you can find and watch in real time.

The producers of such programs know this. They make smart use of it by showing hashtags onscreen, or even having on-air talent ask people to tweet using a specific hashtag. While hosting PBS' *A Capitol Fourth,* Washington, D.C.'s annual July 4th concert and fireworks event, Tom Bergeron (@Tom_ Bergeron) repeatedly asked viewers to tweet their thoughts on the show using the hashtag #July4thPBS.

Hashtags like #SpoilerAlert and #NoSpoilers refer to the idea of spoilers. Put simply, if reading the wrong Tweet before you've watched your favorite show or played back a digital TV recording of the game can mess up the experience for you by ruining the surprise, then that Tweet is a spoiler.

Our advice? Stay far away from social media of all types if it's really important to you not to hear the score or the shocking plot twist before you get to watch.

Engage with Shared Media: Books, Movies, and More

Although books, movies, and similar forms of timeless media can be experienced and shared live via Twitter, in most cases it's less likely that a mass audience is experiencing them in unison as with live and televised events. Let's look at how that makes the sharing experience a little different.

Authors and readers alike have discovered new books to read and recommended books to others on Twitter. Famous writers, such as Neil Gaiman (@NeilHimself) or Paulo Coelho (@PauloCoelho), actively engage fans around the world. Some of the most famous writers currently active on Twitter include Judy Blume (@JudyBlume), Margaret Atwood (@MargaretAtwood), and Stephen King (@StephenKing). Authors have done Twitter chat book tours, landed publishing deals, released serials one chapter at a time, or even developed stories one line at a time using Twitter. Others release serials one chapter at a time on Twitter. One service, 140Story (@140story), actually uses Tweets to write stories.

However you look at it, Twitter is full of readers. When you start listening, you'll find book clubs, writing groups, and more. And when you begin contributing, you'll often discover a phenomenal amount of instant connection and support available on both sides of the pen through Twitter.

It's been years since a major motion picture was released anywhere without at least some thought being given to how Twitter could help research, connect with, and grow the movie's audience. From movie posters with hashtags to stars talking about the release on their personal accounts, there are dozens of ways to promote a new movie using Twitter.

It's not all marketing. Fans have done incredibly creative things with Twitter, like Geoff Todd's @OnePerfectShot account, which posts a single frame from each movie, selected for how well it captures the spirit of the entire film.

By now you also know that wherever there's celebrity, Twitter accounts are sure to, well, follow. Chances are good your favorite filmmaker, director, critic, or actor is tweeting. You can follow the Internet Movie Database — better known as IMDb (@imdb), the American Film Institute (@AFI), and any major film studio, and of course, you can always "thank The Academy" (@TheAcademy) even if it's just by simply tweeting at them.

Optimize Your Lifestyle

If it's a section in the Sunday *The New York Times*, there's something interesting happening on Twitter about it. Fashion? Yep. Arts? Of course. Travel? Are you kidding? Here are some examples to get you thinking about how to use Twitter to dive deeper into the lifestyle stuff you love most. Within the category of lifestyle, food stands out the most as a great way to use Twitter. If we've all heard it once, we've all heard it a thousand times: "Twitter is just a bunch of people sharing what they had for lunch." Although that's a gross oversimplification, there's a good reason the idea is so widespread. Twitter is a great way to share photos, tips, recipes, and food reviews quickly and easily online — so easy, in fact, that often folks share while still immersed in eating the meal itself.

Yes, good food can be truly gorgeous when it arrives from the kitchen. A striking image of that plate may be well worth sharing. But, don't make your eating companions pay for your social media excitement by ruining the flow of conversation or the dining experience itself. Etiquette goes a long way here. "Hey, mind if I snap a quick photo to share later, before I dig into this?" Then put the phone down, look others in the eye and savor your food. There's plenty of time to upload your photos later on when doing so won't frustrate or bore your companions.

For many of us, food and beverage are inseparable aspects of our lifestyle choices. Probably in part due to Gary Vaynerchuk's (@Garyvee) early popularity and success, there is no shortage of wine experts, websites, and apps actively using Twitter to help you find and consume wines you will love. Twitter wine pioneers like Rick Bakas (@RickBakas) and Paul Mabray (@PMabray) of VinTank (@VinTank) are still cranking away, and you can now find most wine publications and vineyards on Twitter in one form or another.

Because drinking in its many forms is an inherently social activity, it's no surprise that alcohol enthusiasts of all types come together on Twitter. You can learn lore and share ideas about your favorite fine spirits, craft beers, vintage cocktails, and pretty much anything else you use to wet your whistle. Heck, whiskey alone even has a whole flight of hashtags to its credit, including the popular #WhiskeyFriday.

Where better to savor this fine food and beverage but some exotic destination? Perhaps because Twitter is so ideally suited to mobile use and sharing experiences, travel brands were amongst the earliest to embrace it. That trend has continued. Airlines, trains, car companies, and more all use Twitter to keep their corporate finger on the pulse of a lot more than just brand perception. Some airlines, like Southwest (@SouthwestAir), have taken it one step further and use Twitter to track flow at various airports, monitor problems in real time, report delays, and so on.

You can connect with many travel-focused companies using Twitter. If you lose a bag or are experiencing flight delays, some airlines, like JetBlue (@JetBlue), are trying to reach out and help customers through Twitter. You can even find cab companies on Twitter that offer more innovative ways to find a ride once you're on the ground, especially if you have an iPhone. Uber (@Uber), Lyft (@Lyft), and Hailo (@Hailocab) are great examples of this.

Someone has to pay for all these lifestyle indulgences, so we'll round out this section with a quick look at personal finance. From scammy foreign exchange traders to the bona fide financial press, the old saw about "people with money don't talk about it" does not apply on Twitter. Not as widely known as the @Mention and #Hashtag functions, adding a dollar sign ($) to the front of a string of letters will also create a hyperlink to a Twitter search containing similar Tweets. It's how the financially minded cite stock ticker symbols on Twitter. So whether you're invested in Apple ($AAPL) or Zillow ($Z) or anything alphabetically in between, now you know where to look for breaking stories that might affect your holdings.

Support Charities, Causes, and Education

Charities have raised money and forwarded their missions right on Twitter. Causes and even whole political movements have gained steam, accessed global audiences, and been more able to organize. Kidney and marrow donors found. Missing persons searches quickly mobilized and spread, ad hoc emergency responses coordinated.

If communication can make it better in some way, there are probably some pretty cool ways to use Twitter to further any mission.

Charities and causes find Twitter an easy way to get word out about their passions. People use Twitter to raise awareness and money for a wide variety of international causes and charities. The ease of use makes it appealing to many agencies and groups.

The world of education is no different. Teachers tweeting their lessons. Students tweeting questions about their homework. Schools using Twitter to communicate with their communities, quickly getting out information and cutting down on the cost of mailings. Conference attendees sharing insights and links from the conference, creating a virtual community for remote colleagues. These are just a few of the ways Twitter is woven into education.

To cite just one example, classes with a Twitter-fueled *back channel* (ideas, observations, questions, and comments coming from the audience) have even been taught at colleges and universities around the world, including the esteemed Harvard business and law schools.

Plan and Promote Events

The immediacy and reach Twitter allows can really help you get your next conference, party, or social-networking event off the ground.

Often, great event promotion hinges on your use of a hashtag to bring the event community together. This helps participants connect with one another, which is one of the greatest values an event can provide. This also helps remote participants follow along even if they don't know who is going to be at your event, or who will share the best takeaways and media from it.

Pick a good hashtag for your event well in advance, and publicize it along with other crucial information like your date, time, and venue. A good hashtag is short enough to remember and spell correctly, unique enough to filter out the noise, and most of all it is agreed upon and used widely among the people at the event or following along remotely.

Do some test searches before you finalize your choice. You want to be sure the one you pick isn't already being used by someone else. Then, promote the hashtag everywhere and anywhere having to do with your event, from the website, to social platforms, and to physical signage.

Two of the easiest ways to get participants to use it? Post it front and center onstage or at the podium, and project live streams of Tweets that use the hashtag during your event. Don't worry: There are tools like Tweetwall (http://tweetwall.com) that allow moderation and that can put a little delay into your display and help you reduce the chances of abusive Tweets getting through.

Find Inspiration and Personal and Professional Development

Want to stay abreast of advances in your industry, learn a new skill, lose weight, or get inspired? Look no further than Twitter for a surprising array of options to help you.

Have you heard of Twitter chats? These may seem mysterious at first, because they're a form of convening and conversing that emerged as a result of Twitter itself as Twitter first got popular. At the core, what's happening is that a group of people are deciding to all communicate with each other at a set time by all looking at the same set of Twitter search results.

They do this by picking, using, and following a given hashtag. #JournChat, started by @PRSarahEvans, is widely considered to have been the first. Hundreds, if not thousands, have followed suit. Depending on your industry, a weekly or biweekly Twitter chat might be a great way to hone your skills and stay on top of recent developments. Sometimes a chat interviews a guest expert.

Trying to achieve something specific? Stating and sharing your self-improvement goals is a time-tested method of making sure you will follow through and have the best possible chance of attaining them. In the world of fitness alone, people are tweeting their activity level with tools like Fitbit (@Fitbit), sharing their workouts with apps like Runkeeper (@Runkeeper), and even tweeting their weight on their Withings (@Withings) scales.

At the moment, hashtags from #100HappyDays to #100Pushups give you a peek into very specific self improvement efforts that are popular. More timeless hashtags (if a hashtag can ever be considered timeless) to check out include #coaching, #selfimprovement, #happy, #fitness, and #inspiration.

We want you to feel inspired to grab Twitter by the horns and go do something #awesome in this world. Trust us, the world needs that special thing that only you can see it needs. Now go unleash some of it!

Invent New Uses of Twitter

Twitter, more than any other online social media platform, is a system that has been constantly shaped and reshaped by the patterns, habits and conventions its users have developed. All the cool ways to use Twitter that we just described came from someone very like you dipping their toe in and trying something that then became something, that evolved into something else, that totally became a thing.

We would be remiss in our duties if we did not challenge each and every one of our readers to riff on the basic tunes we have laid out for you in this book. Get out there and be bold. Play around. Try things that might not work. Go do something #awesome with Twitter.

Chapter 17

Ten Twitter Tools and Services

You need the right tools to get the most out of Twitter. New tools, services, websites, and applications are created for Twitter users every day, so the list of tools that you can choose among is always growing. To help get you started, we want to tell you about a few of our favorite examples, which give you a fun sampling of the different ways you can use Twitter.

Each time we tried to come up with a list of the top ten tools, we realized that it wasn't possible; too many great innovations are being built on Twitter's platform. Popular new tools emerge all the time, and, of course, the best tool for you really depends on your needs. That being said, the following tools are the best that we've found right now (although that could change by the time this book is published).

TweetDeck

https://tweetdeck.twitter.com

Type: Desktop client and Chrome application

TweetDeck is a free desktop application, owned by Twitter, that gives you the tools you need to keep track of large numbers of people in your Twitter stream. It allows you to put people in groups, keep permanent search windows open, publish and schedule Tweets, monitor who's talking to you (or about you), and much more. It does all this in a customizable interface, showing multiple streams of Tweets next to one another in real time. This means your Tweets come down the stream as they're sent; there's no need to ever refresh the application.

If you want a free and easy way to monitor and manage your personal Twitter presence, try TweetDeck. Your experience with this desktop application will be even better if you use a large monitor and keep the program up and running.

Seven essential types of tools

The Twitter ecosystem is really complex. It can be overwhelming. A short way to make sense of it is to think about seven essential types of tools that almost any Twitter user should try. Here are some of the best examples of each type:

- **Networking (Wefollow, justunfollow):** Your network is *the* most important thing about Twitter. Using tools to find, follow, unfollow, and keep track of your connections will help you customize your network with the right types of people.

- **Desktop client (TweetDeck):** A desktop client is dedicated software on your computer that makes interacting with Twitter easier.

- **Mobile application (Twitter app):** A mobile application is dedicated software on your smartphone or tablet that makes interacting with Twitter easier.

- **Search and listening (Twitter Search):** Search Tweets in real time, monitor keywords and hashtags, and subscribe to search results.

- **URL shortener (Bitly):** Make links fit into 140 characters; keep track of what you've linked to; and preferably keep some kind of records of how many people clicked, repeated, or also shortened the link.

- **Multimedia sharing and content creation (Twitpic, Canva):** Embed and share links to photos, video, or audio to make your Twitter stream a whole lot more than a bunch of text.

- **Publishing and measurement (Buffer, Topsy, Twitter Counter):** Schedule Tweets for a future date and discover how fast you're growing your following, how influential a certain topic is, and how much engagement your Tweets are getting.

Hootsuite

https://hootsuite.com

Type: Business dashboard

If you want a corporate solution that lets multiple users monitor and schedule posts to multiple accounts, you should look at Hootsuite. This tool displays all your Twitter accounts in a single interface and lets companies assign individual Tweets to employees for follow-up.

It's common to include a full disclosure in your profile if you have multiple people tweeting for your company or if you have a ghost tweeter tweeting for you. For shared accounts, authors often sign the end of their Tweets with a caret (^) and their initials. This isn't a rule, just a guideline. Make sure you take a look at other users' Twitter profiles to get a feel for best practices in your particular industry.

Social Inbox

http://hubspot.com/products/social-inbox

Type: Business dashboard

If you want a corporate solution that lets you connect your Twitter account with smart information about your customers and prospects, you should look at HubSpot's Social Inbox. With this tool, you can see exactly whom you're interacting with, whether it's a prospect, a customer, or a person who has never interacted with your company before. This tool should take care of most of your company or organization's Twitter needs, from monitoring users in your database to scheduling Tweets ahead of time to measuring the actual return on your investment. The tool offers a browser plugin, which means you have access to many of its features, like seeing which Tweets come from customers or prospects, right in your browser when you're using Twitter.com.

If you're tweeting for a business or organization, make sure that you're measuring more than just followers and retweets. It's also important to measure the number of clicks of your Tweets and the number of resulting prospects or revenue. Measuring these pieces will help you see the big picture and discover exactly which Tweets are performing best so you can tailor any future Tweets based on what your audience prefers.

Twitter App

iOS: https://itunes.apple.com/us/app/twitter/id333903271

Android: https://play.google.com/store/apps/details?id=com.twitter.android

Type: Mobile app

Want to tweet from anywhere? If you have a mobile device, the official Twitter iOS or Android app is the way to go. Find it in the App Store on your Apple device or in Google Play on your Android device.

Check your carrier's data charges before using Twitter's mobile app. Twitter may be free, but some of the associated data usage may come with hidden costs if your device isn't on an unlimited-data plan.

Wefollow and justunfollow

http://wefollow.com

www.justunfollow.com

Type: Networking

These websites let you see who you're following, who's following you, and which follows are mutual, all in a nicely tabbed, avatar-based list. You can fix any follower/following discrepancies right from the site interfaces. These sites help you follow people who better match your interests.

Don't unfollow people just because they don't follow you back. Twitter doesn't require you to follow someone back, and you never know whether that user may just have missed you. Try saying hi with an @reply to see whether you can get to know that person better.

Twitter Counter

http://twittercounter.com

Type: Measurement

If you want to see how your following has grown over time or how many followers you had on a specific date, make sure to check out Twitter Counter. With this tool, you can even compare how many followers you've gained over a six-month period with how many Tweets you sent per day during the same period.

Don't harp on how many followers you do or don't have. What's most important is that you're tweeting valuable content, connecting with like-minded people, and learning along the way.

Bitly

http://bit.ly

Type: URL shortener

This free and easy website lets you shorten, customize, and track the links you send out on Twitter. Bitly automatically generates a short link with a random mix of letters and numbers so that it fits better in a 140-character

Tweet. However, you can always customize the link you've automatically received so it fits better with your personal branding or better describes what the link actually goes to. The stats you see with Bitly links include daily and hourly click stats to identify spikes in click-throughs, the networks your Bitly link was shared on, and the countries in which people were clicking most.

If you add a plus sign (+) to the end of any Bitly link, you can see click stats for that link, whether or not you created the link. Brittany, for example, added `http://bit.ly/bleaningblog` as a link in her Twitter bio to showcase the blog posts she's written. If you add + to the end of this link in the website address bar and press Enter, you'll be able to see stats about how many clicks it got over time. If you add a Bitly link to your Twitter bio, you'll be able to see how many people are clicking the link to find out more about you.

Buffer

`https://bufferapp.com`

Type: Publishing

Buffer suggests fully crafted Tweets to you based on who you follow and what topics you generally tweet about. When you choose to add these suggested Tweets to your queue, Buffer schedules them at staggered times based on a schedule you preset; that way, you never need to worry about overlapping. You can use Buffer on its website or download the mobile application from the App Store or Google Play.

Staggering your Tweets and spreading them out throughout a week will help you avoid seeming spammy. Make sure you're scheduling a varied mix of content topics and formats, including images, quotes, and articles.

Canva

`www.canva.com`

Type: Visual content creation

If you're not naturally design-inclined, Canva is a great free tool to help you craft a beautiful header and other tweetable images without learning any fancy design skills or programs. This tool is essentially plug-and-play, optimizing sizes for the exact dimensions you'll need on Twitter.

Because Twitter now displays images automatically, you'll find that more and more people are using them to increase engagement on individual Tweets. When you tweet articles, try attaching an image from the article in your Tweet and see whether you get an increase in clicks and retweets.

Topsy

http://topsy.com

Type: Measurement

This website shows you how many mentions a certain hashtag or Twitter handle had in the past hour, day, week, or month. You can see which days or hours had the most mentions and which Tweets were the most popular.

If you're at an event that's using a specific hashtag, plug this hashtag into Topsy to see how influential it is. You can also compare hashtags side by side to see how an event's influence performed.

Chapter 18

Ten Resources for Twitter Glory

· ·

After reading *Twitter For Dummies,* you should know how to set up and navigate the Twitter interface, make connections, tweet interesting content, use the latest shortcuts, and even promote your business or cause. That should make you a pro, right? Well, the thing is, Twitter is continually changing to adapt to its fast-paced, technology-loving users. That being said, it's important to keep up with the latest and greatest Twitter trends even after you've finished this book. Here are the top ten resources for any next-level Twitter user.

The Official Twitter Blog

https://blog.twitter.com

Type: Blog

What better resource is there for finding out about Twitter than Twitter itself? If you choose to subscribe to this blog, you'll discover the latest trends on Twitter, feature updates, acquisitions, and unique ways to use Twitter. If you're interested only in Twitter's announcements or want to know more about live events on Twitter, you can browse the blog by tag to get the content that's most appealing to you.

#twittertips

https://twitter.com/hashtag/twittertips

Type: Hashtag

Hashtags are great ways to find out more about a specific topic. Why? Anyone in the world can tweet great resources, quotes, and other items in real time. The hashtag #twittertips happens to get more than 250 mentions per day, representing tips from top social media influencers and other active users.

If you filter this hashtag by top Tweets instead of all Tweets on Twitter.com, you'll find the most retweeted tips. Because #twittertips consists of 140-character opinions, you'll be able to see how Twitter's best practices can be modified and adapted to users' needs and preferences.

"How to Write a Tweet: 8 Formulas to Get You Started"

http://blog.hubspot.com/marketing/tweet-formulas-to-get-you-started-on-twitter

Type: Blog article

If you're looking for more tips for crafting Tweets, like those in Chapter 15, this blog article is for you. This article discusses eight best practices to put to use. These eight formulas are perfect to have in your back pocket so you can send unique Tweets.

You can find lots of other Twitter how-tos elsewhere on HubSpot's blog using search (http://blog.hubspot.com). More free HubSpot Twitter resources are available in its library (https://library.hubspot.com), its Grader tool (https://marketing.grader.com), and its Academy (http://academy.hubspot.com).

Twitter Chat Schedule

http://tweetreports.com/twitter-chat-schedule

Type: Networking

One of the best ways to really see what Twitter can do is to jump in with both feet. There's no better way to immerse yourself in Twitter than to try a Twitter chat. These real-time discussions can be a little overwhelming on your first try but get much easier with time. A typical Twitter chat starts and ends at a designated time, usually lasting for about an hour. The basic gist is that during a Twitter chat, every participant follows a pre-selected hashtag so that they will all see one another's Tweets. To speak up during the chat, you simply tweet like you normally would, and you include that hashtag in each of the Tweets that you want to address to everyone else in the chat.

Following the chat can be as simple as opening a browser tab and going to `https://search.twitter.com`. There, you type in the designated hashtag. Refreshing this page shows you the various chatters' Tweets as they post them. Don't forget to refresh!

How these chats often work is that the chat leader or moderator asks a question by sending a Tweet that starts Q1 (to signal this is the first question) and includes the hashtag. Anyone who feels like answering this question starts his Tweet with A1 (to signal which question they are answering) and includes the hashtag in his Tweet. A Q & A chat like this may go through anywhere from five to fifteen questions over the hour period. There may also be a lot of general commenting and interacting with other Twitter chatters, which is done simply by including the hashtag in your Tweets directed to the chat.

Sometimes there will a special guest featured on the chat because they are a subject matter expert. You might want to open an additional browser tab to the guest's profile page (`https://twitter.com/`*username*) so that you don't miss any of the expert answers amongst all the other answers being offered by participants.

No matter the specific format, just follow along by reading Tweets that contain the hashtag, and by offering your opinions by including the hashtag in your Tweets. When the hour is over, you'll find that you've gained a few new followers and learned a ton, simply from interacting with strangers, building relationships, and forming a community

The resource listed here is a schedule of all the Twitter chats that occur all over the world so you can find a chat that's relevant to your interests.

If you're interested in participating in a Twitter chat, set up a third-party app such as TweetDeck or Hootsuite (see Chapter 17) so that you're monitoring your Twitter stream, @mentions of your Twitter handle, mentions of the chat hashtag, and direct messages next to one other. That way, you won't miss a mention, and your experience will feel less hectic adrenaline-inducing.

Twitter Support

`https://support.twitter.com`

Type: Help center

Have you ever called a support line to get help with a product or service? Twitter also provides a great help center for users ranging from beginners to exceptionally advanced. This resource shows you how to report spam and other violations, what to do if you can't log in, and more. Twitter Support has its own Twitter handle, which you can follow at `@Support`.

Mashable's Twitter Category

http://mashable.com/category/twitter

Type: Blog category

Because Twitter is always changing, it's important to stay up to speed on all the little changes. Mashable, a popular social media and tech blog, has an entire category dedicated to Twitter updates. Here, you'll find articles about the latest Twitter trends, feature announcements and updates, and much more. Because the category has more than 7,500 articles, you have enough reading material to last for months or maybe even years.

@Twitter

https://twitter.com/twitter

Type: Twitter account

Here's an obvious resource that we couldn't forget: Twitter's own Twitter account, @Twitter. If you follow this account, you'll see all sorts of interesting Twitter data, examples of unique ways to use Twitter, general Twitter entertainment, and more. This account is not only fun to browse and retweet, but it's also a great source of communication with Twitter. If you ever have a question, try tweeting it to @Twitter and see what happens.

Tweetup Meetup Groups

http://tweetup.meetup.com

Type: Networking

Tweetups give you the opportunity to move your online connections offline for real-life interaction and connection. Usually at a tweetup, you get a name tag with your Twitter handle. You can put Twitter handles to faces as you walk around meeting all those recognizable avatars in the flesh. Tweetups don't exclude tweeting, of course. The majority of tweetup attendees use their smartphones to live-tweet the event on a specific hashtag. This resource shares a list of tweetups you could attend in person. Go on — give it a try!

"Everything You Need to Know to Successfully Live-Tweet Your Event"

`http://blog.hubspot.com/marketing/live-tweet-events`

Type: Blog article

We mention live-tweeting in the preceding section. This blog article provides everything you need to be a successful live-tweeter. Some of the basics to take note of are preparing before the event by knowing the event's hashtag and drafting some Tweets in advance. During the event, it's important to use the event's hashtag in every single Tweet you send, listen for 140-character sound bites to tweet, and take pictures so you can post them live.

After the event, it's a good idea to make a Twitter list of event attendees or compile a list of the best Tweets and include them in a blog post so you have even more content to tweet about.

@Dummies

`https://twitter.com/dummies`

Type: Twitter account

Finally, we suggest that you follow the official Twitter account for *Twitter For Dummies,* 3rd Edition. We'll be tweeting all sorts of Twitter tips year-round to help you achieve Twitter glory. Have a question about the book? Want to take your Twitter skills to the next level? Send an @mention to `@Dummies`, and we'll see whether we can help.

Glossary

· ·

@: (at symbol) @ both indicates a username and activates a link to that user's profile. When used preceding a valid Twitter @username, it creates a hyperlink to a popup version of that user's profile.

#: (pound or number symbol), which is used to create a hashtag (see hashtag).

^: (caret symbol) This symbol is usually appended to the end of a Tweet preceding the initials of the person sending the Tweet. The caret and initials taken together are known as a Cotag.

$: (dollar symbol) When used along with a stock ticker symbol creates a hyperlink to other Tweets containing that stock symbol.

@mention: An @mention is when you "mention" someone in one of your tweets. By placing the @ symbol (traditionally used in email addresses) before a user's handle, you can tag that person in your Tweet, and the user is notified in the Mentions section of his account. If you tweet "Love this new blog post by @anum," for example, Anum is notified. Many people use @mentions to converse on Twitter.

@reply: An @reply is when you respond directly to a user on Twitter. This tweet can be seen in user streams by you, the person you're responding to, and anyone who follows both of you. On your Twitter profile, you'll notice there is a "tweets" and "tweets and replies" section. Anyone who clicks the latter can see all your tweets.

@username: This is how you are identified on Twitter. Always used with the @ symbol preceding it.

AFAIK: Acronym for *as far as I know.*

avatar: See profile photo

bio: The 160 character self-description that Twitter users can add to tell the world a bit more about who they are.

block: The action of preventing a user from seeing your Tweets while also preventing yourself from seeing that user's @mentions or @replies directed at you.

bot: An account run by an automated program. You can find good bots, such as the ones that pull in all breaking-news headlines from a media outlet. You also can find bad bots, which put out only generic Tweets, usually filled with links to marketing or porn sites. These bots often have a generic "hot chick" avatar or an uneven follower/following ratio, meaning that they're following hundreds or thousands of people but have only a few following them back.

by: Appended at the end of a Tweet, usually indicates who the author of, for example, a URL shared in a Tweet is.

cc: carbon copy. Generally used before one or more usernames inserted in a Tweet so that those users see the Tweet on their @Mentions tab.

direct messages (DM): Private messages sent to specific Twitter users in your network. Only you and the recipient of the messages can view them. Before you can send a DM to a user, that user must be following you.

Discover: This refers to the tab on Twitter.com where you see Tweets you might be interested in because they were favorited by people you follow. The submenu on this tab contains Tweets, Activity, Who to follow, find Friends, and Popular accounts.

favorite: (v) To mark a Tweet as something you like by clicking the star next to the word favorite. (n) As a noun, it also refers to the Tweets you have marked in this way. Sometimes abbreviated fav.

feed: A constantly updating list of updates from everyone you're following that is visible to you at `https://twitter.com`. Unlike Facebook, which uses an algorithm to update your Timeline, Twitter simply updates your feed with every Tweet published by the accounts you follow, arranged in order by the time of Tweet.

follow: The action you take to subscribe to an account's updates. When you follow someone on Twitter, you see her published Tweets in the mix of Tweets that you see in your feed on `Twitter.com`. Follow is used as both a verb (to follow) and a noun (new follows). Followers are the accounts that have subscribed to yours. Following is the act of subscribing to someone's account as well as the state after you subscribe.

Follow button: (also, the Following/Unfollow button) The button marked Follow that appears on every user's profile page, as well as in a number of different places in the Twitter interface where you are being shown information about a fellow user. Follow buttons can also appear on any third party website as a way to promote and simplify the process of following an account. Note that most times that you are logged into Twitter and see a Follow button for a person you are already following, the button instead says Following, and changes to Unfollow when you mouse over it.

FollowFriday: Started in January 2009, on Follow Friday you see the hashtags #FollowFriday and #FF used as a way to recommend other Twitter users to your followers. The idea here is that you're giving them suggestions of accounts to follow. Every Friday, you'll likely see an uptick in people using #FF. This hashtag is a great way to find people to follow.

followback: Refers to a subculture of Twitter that abuses anyone who automatically follows back any account that follows theirs. Also referred to as #teamfollowback, they promote the practice of following accounts until they follow you back, and then unfollowing them, as a way to artificially increase their own follower count.

follower: Someone who follows you on Twitter and sees your updates in her feed. When someone follows you, you're not obligated to follow that person back (but you can!). See also feed.

geolocation, geotagging: Refers to the class of location-based apps (Foursquare) and features (add location to Tweet) that let you share when you are at specific geographic places like businesses and parks.

hacking: Gaining unauthorized access to someone else's computer or account, sometimes by way of a guessed, stolen, or phished password. In common usage, one would refer to an account as having been hacked. This is more likely to happen to a celebrity or brand account, but can happen to average users, especially when they give their password up to a phishing attack.

hashtag: A word, several words, or any set of letters and or numbers preceded by the # symbol. When you type a # immediately in front of any combination of letters and or numbers (not symbols or spaces), it automatically becomes a "hyperlink" to the Twitter search results for that combination of letters and or numbers. For example, typing #inbound into any Tweet at any time automatically creates and inserts a hyperlink to https://twitter. com/hashtag/inbound. Hashtags function as keywords that pull a set of Tweets together into one stream that can be followed using any search tool.

header photo: Large, horizontal, and rectangular photograph that you can add to your Twitter profile page to beautify, inform, or just give people a sense of what you care about.

Home: The main page that you see when you first sign onto Twitter.com, or when you click the Home tab in the upper left hand corner of the screen from anywhere on Twitter.com. Tweets displayed on your home page are also known as your Timeline.

HT (hat tip): A way to give credit to someone for an opinion, article, or reference to a Tweet. The Tweet "Reading this @Buzzfeed article. HT @bleaning for sending!" shows that the user is enjoying a BuzzFeed article that Brittany shared.

impersonation: Creating a Twitter account to trick other users into thinking it is something other than what it actually is. Impersonation is a violation of Twitter's terms of service (TOS) and can get you banned from the service. Not to be confused with parody accounts, which are permitted, and which must be clearly marked as parodies to avoid suspension.

list: A list is a subset of Twitter accounts that you can create in order to recognize, monitor, or share a particular set of Twitter accounts. Lists can be private or public. Public lists can be viewed and subscribed to by others.

Me: The tab on Twitter that takes you to your own profile page from where you can view your own Tweets, bio, numbers of followers and followings, lists, and so on.

metrics: A way to measure your influence on Twitter. There are built in metrics (see Chapter 10) to see your success on Twitter. A basic example would be looking at the increase in your follower account over time.

mistweet: A Tweet that you sent in error, either because you sent it to the wrong person or because you accidentally sent a direct message (DM) as a public Tweet. Either way, it's a Tweet you regret sending.

mobile Twitter: `https://mobile.twitter.com` A version of Twitter's website that works well on mobile devices.

MT (modified Tweet): This is a tweet that is altered from its original version. Sometimes, users retweet your Tweet but need to modify it to stay within the 140-character count. An example is "MT `@anum`: [contents of Tweet]."

Notifications: The Notifications tab is where you can see a stream of how other Twitter users are interacting with you and your Tweets. The Notifications menu item on the Notifications tab displays by default when you click the Notifications tab, and shows you all new followers, replies, retweets, and favorites. The Mentions menu item on the Notifications tab shows you only Tweets that are addressed to you, not the other types of notifications.

oauth: Oauth is the term to describe the process of letting a third party software have access to your Twitter account, better known as "Login with Twitter." The third party does not see or get to keep your password, but once you have oauthed a third party app to your Twitter account, it is able to access your account until you revoke that authorization. Only click the Login via Twitter button for apps you trust.

OH: Acronym for *overheard,* used to anonymously quote something funny that you heard.

Phishing: Phishing describes the act of trying to trick someone into giving up his username or password.

pinned Tweets: Users are permitted to pin one Tweet to the top of their profile page timeline, so that anyone visiting their profile page is likely to read it.

Popular accounts: Specific accounts, sorted by categories like music, sports, and news, that have been editorially selected by Twitter employees as accounts you may want to follow. Not to be confused with Who to Follow, which displays a mix of users you specifically may like following based on who you already follow, and who you have most recently followed.

Private/protected accounts: These are normal Twitter accounts, except that the owner of the account has elected to make her account private or "protect" her Tweets. You can only see the Tweets posted by someone with a private account if she specifically gives you permission to follow her. You may request to follow a private account, but you will not see anything until the owner of the account manually approves your request.

profile: The page on Twitter.com where your account and Tweets appear. To see anyone's profile page, insert the username into this URL: `https://twitter.com/@username`. There is also a pop up version of your profile that appears when someone clicks once on your username in a Tweet.

profile photo: Also known as your avatar, this is the small square photo that appears on your profile page; on every Tweet you send; on other people's Tweets when you favorite, retweet, or reply to them; and anywhere else in the Twitter interface where your account appears.

promoted products: In Twitter's advertising program, it is possible to pay for promoted accounts, promoted Tweets, and promoted trends. Collectively these are known as promoted products.

PRT: An acronym for partial retweet that is used to indicate that while you are retweeting someone, you have left out much of the original Tweet. Differs from a modified Tweet in that more of the original Tweet has been left out

RLRT: An acronym for real life retweet. Basically a fancy term for "quote," a RLRT is when you publish to Twitter something someone said in real life.

RT: Acronym for *retweet,* Twitter's equivalent of quoting. You can retweet in two ways:

> ✔ If you come across a Tweet that you want to share with your audience by giving credit to the original user, type RT at the start of a new Tweet, put the twitterer's username in @reply format, and copy the contents of the Tweet. This type of retweet looks like this: "RT @pistachio Boston — outdoor skating party this weekend, Sunday at 1pm. DM me if interested." By putting RT at the front of the retweet, you also make sure that everyone can see your Tweet, because some members choose to turn off @replies that aren't directed at them.

✔ You can share someone's Tweet by clicking the Retweet button below the original Tweet. You share the Tweet in its full form with your own followers, and it appears in your feed.

Keep in mind that retweeting, because RT is added in front of the Tweet, adds characters to a Tweet and may force it over the 140-character limit. If that's the case, you may want to use the Retweet button, which automatically shares the full tweet in its original version.

short code: In the U.S. and many other countries, 40404 is a texting or SMS short code that lets you send and receive commands and Tweets from Twitter. To find your local short code, look for your country and your mobile carrier on the list at `https://support.twitter.com/articles/20170024#`.

SMS: Acronym for short messaging service, often used as a synonym for text message or texting.

social capital: This refers to the trust, goodwill, thought leadership, and other intangible assets that you earn by participating positively within the Twitter community. It also refers to what you spend when you ask for favors and promote certain events, products, or services.

spam: Unwanted Tweets promoting a product or pressuring someone to take an action. These may be @mentions, DMs, or just general Tweets. Just like spam on email and other Internet tools, Twitter spam is useless content, usually trying to sell you something, that can clutter up your @mentions, Twitter searches, and hashtag searches. Luckily, spamming on Twitter is harder because you can simply not follow anyone, and because Twitter works hard to remove accounts that are trying to take advantage of others and violating their terms of service (TOS).

spammers: These are users on Twitter who start their Twitter accounts simply to auto-follow and auto-tweet at people and otherwise create spam.

text commands: Aso known as SMS commands. These are specific characters that you can send via text message to 40404 or your local Twitter short code in order to control your account. You can review Twitter's text commands at `https://support.twitter.com/articles/14020-twitter-sms-commands`.

Timeline: The set of Tweets you see on your home page on Twitter. Synonymous with feed.

timestamp: The element in any Tweet interface that shows a date or period of time ago that a Tweet was published. The timestamp contains an active link to the URL or permalink for each individual Tweet, and clicking it takes you to a separate web page containing the Tweet and any interactions with it.

trends or trending topics: Trending topics or hashtags represent the most active subjects being discussed on Twitter. Any person, place, thing, or idea that many users are tweeting about at once can become a trend. You can find trends on the left side of your Twitter home page, and you can even tailor what trends you see based on your location and who you follow.

trolls: People who abuse the service by spamming users with off-topic Tweets and other erratic behavior. Trolling is a form of harassment on the web.

TT: Acronym for translated tweet used in place of RT or MT when you are re-sharing a Tweet that was written by someone else in a different language

tweeple or tweeps: Quite literally, this means "twitter people" or "twitter peeps." Some Twitter users say tweeps to refer to the Twitter community overall, whereas others use it to refer only to those in their networks.

tweet: A 140-character update on Twitter. Tweet when it's a noun, tweet when it's a verb. Your 140-character updates on Twitter are called Tweets, and you can also say, "I tweeted."

Tweet button: Any button that starts or finishes the process of writing and publishing a Tweet. These can be found on third party websites as well as in various places on Twitter.com and third party Twitter client apps.

Tweetaholic or Twitterholic: Someone who's addicted to Twitter. The term should not be confused with Twitaholic.com, a metrics site that measures the relative popularity of Twitter users.

Tweetstorm/Twitterstorm: An outburst of many Tweets in a row.

tweetup: A pun on *meetup* that refers to a gathering of Twitter users organized through Twitter. A tweetup can be a get-together for Twitter users who happen to be in the same town for a concert or festival, locals who want to try out a new restaurant or bar, or even a late-night meeting of karaoke enthusiasts.

Twitpic: One of the most popular third-party applications built on Twitter's API. Twitpic lets you upload a photo, often from the camera on your cellphone, to Twitpic (www.twitpic.com), which automatically sends a Tweet that links to the picture and provides the caption of your choice.

twitter: The social network used to share 140-character updates. It can be used as a verb ("I twittered that") but not a noun. Don't say "twit" — "send a twit" is never correct. Instead, you "send a Tweet."

Twitterverse/Twittersphere: Everything about Twitter, taken collectively, including all of the Tweets, people, tools, applications, and services.

unfollow: The opposite of follow. Anyone can opt to stop following you on Twitter at any time, and you can stop following anyone else at any time. When you are following someone, the text on the Follow button changes to the word Following. When you mouse over the word Following, it turns red and displays the word Unfollow. For the most part, this happens with any Follow button, whether on `Twitter.com` or a third party site, as long as you are logged into your Twitter account in that same browser. Be careful about aggressively following or unfollowing users because it is a sign of gaming for followers that may trigger Twitter's automated TOS monitors.

URL/URLs: Acronyms for "universal resource locator" and often referred to as a link. A URL is the series of characters starting http:// that instruct a web browser which resource to load and display to you. Although link and URL are used interchangeably, they are not quite the same. A link is anything that you can click to take you to a new URL.

verification: The process Twitter uses to make it clear that an account prone to being spoofed is actually what or who it claims to be. Verification adds a small blue verification badge to the profile page, and next to the username wherever it is displayed. Verified users also have slightly different account features to help them manage a high traffic Twitter account.

Verified accounts: The small blue badge on a particular Twitter profile page or near the username of an account simply designates that yes, Twitter employees have checked to ensure that the account is in fact what it purports to be.

via: Appended at the end of a Tweet, may indicate where someone found an article, or indicate who provided a particular resource.

Who to follow: Found as a menu item on the Discover tab, the Who to follow tab shows you a group of Twitter accounts you are likely to be interested in based on your actions and following choices. This list is specific to your account and generated by a software algorithm, and should not be confused with the Popular accounts tab, which is editorially selected and shown to all users. You will also see Who to follow accounts displayed in a sidebar box sometimes, depending on where you are in the `Twitter.com` interface.

Index

• U •

• V •

About the Authors

Laura Fitton: Laura "@Pistachio" Fitton has had a long, crazy, wild ride with Twitter, which she hopes continues for many years to come. Laura is credited with convincing Guy Kawasaki and thousands of tech execs that Twitter would have real business value. She founded the first Twitter for Business consultancy, Pistachio Consulting, in 2008 and has been speaking professionally about the business use of Twitter since 2007. In addition to co-writing all three editions of *Twitter For Dummies*, she was the sole founder/CEO of the venture-capital funded tech startup oneforty.com, acquired in 2011 by HubSpot. Today Laura serves as HubSpot's Inbound Marketing Evangelist.

Laura is a warm and engaging keynoter, has lectured at HBS and MIT-Sloan, and has been quoted in dozens of national publications including BusinessWeek, Forbes, Fortune, Newsweek, and *The Wall Street Journal*.

Laura is a magna cum laude graduate of Cornell University's eclectic College Scholar program. In "past lives," she studied science writing with Carl Sagan, rock climbed, cooked and sailed on a schooner, raised a niece, ran a hobby farm, traveled, and lived abroad.

She also raised $25,000 for Charity:Water (www.charitywater.org) in December 2008 in the first ever "donate by tweeting" charity campaign, @Wellwishes. Laura lives in the Boston area with her two daughters and two dogs.

Anum Hussain: Rising from the media and journalism world, Anum quickly realized her content and communication skills had a home in the world of marketing. While at HubSpot, she has written countless blog posts, e-books, and reports on Twitter effectiveness and strategy that have been viewed by over 1.2 million readers.

Anum also ranks among the top ten speakers at the annual INBOUND conference. Her 2013 presentation featuring optimal social media tips and tricks has over 80,000 views on SlideShare.

Anum graduated summa cum laude from Emerson College, and her early career strides have been recognized by organizations such as MITX and MPAC. When she's not working, she enjoys spending time with her family, eating cookie cakes, and talking about Harry Potter.

Brittany Leaning: After being forced to use Twitter by a college professor, Brittany soon found herself "Leaning" into the social media site for good.

Since then, she's directly managed social media strategy and execution for brands such as HubSpot, Vermont Teddy Bear, PajamaGram, and Hoodie-Footie, developing an obsession for driving real business results through Twitter along the way. She believes that Twitter is a tool beyond personal enjoyment — it connects students with teachers, organizations with donors, job seekers with employers, and so much more.

When she's not tweeting up a storm, Brittany enjoys writing and designing content, with a large cup of coffee in her hand.

About the 1st and 2nd Edition Authors

Michael E. Gruen: Michael E. Gruen continues to serve in interim COO/CTO/CEO roles with tech startups. Michael graduated cum laude from Hamilton College as a Senior Fellow with a BA in Computer Science. He lives in New York City and in the off-hours, races taxis on his road bike through the city streets.

Leslie Poston: Leslie Poston has since moved from New Hampshire to New York City, where she is a Social Media Editor for McKinsey. When she isn't watching or playing sports (especially hockey and UFC/MMA), playing piano, hiking, sailing, skiing, supporting local bands, playing with her Rottweiler, or working, Leslie can be found on Twitter, meeting new people and making connections with the world.

Dedication

This book is dedicated to . . . *you*.

We hope, above all things, that *you* will go do something #awesome with Twitter. Something you already have in you right now, just waiting to get out and help the world. Ready? Set? Go!

Authors' Acknowledgments

Writing and publishing this book has always been a team effort. The three of us would most like to thank Michael Gruen and Leslie Poston for all their contributions to the 1st and 2nd editions. We're incredibly grateful to the Twitter community and its most innovative users whose experiments shaped Twitter itself. We thank every @dummies follower, Amazon.com reviewer, and everyone who tweeted, shared, or otherwise commented on *Twitter For Dummies*.

Turns out writing a book involves an incredible amount of time, collaboration, and support. If it were not for our wonderful editors and production team, this book would not have come together as quickly as it did. Thanks to Sarah Hellert, Kathy Simpson, and Michelle Krasniak (3rd edition), and continued thanks to Kelly Ewing, Beth Taylor, Jodi Jensen, Andy Cummings, Mary Corder, Mary Bednarek, Laura Miller, Elizabeth Kuball, Steven Miller, Mark Burstiner, and Jennifer Webb (previous editions).

Many thanks to our acquisitions editor, Steve Hayes, for getting this project started and for sticking with it over the years, and Chris Webb and Ellen Gerstein tirelessly explaining Twitter to their colleagues and introducing Laura to Steve. Special thanks to Alexa Scordato (@alexa), Alex Howard (@digiphile), @mdy, and Caroline McCarthy (@caro) for their help on previous editions.

Anum wants to thank her co-authors: Laura for her invitation to contribute to this book and Brittany for endless Saturday afternoons writing in random Starbucks across Cambridge. She'd also like to thank her mother. She once scolded an uncooperative — and incredibly rude — airline official for his poor customer service with threats of her daughter shaming him on Twitter. Anum hopes this gives her an entire book to make her case next time someone tries to rip her off! #LoveYou.

Brittany wants to thank her co-authors for a fun and challenging few months. Laura for introducing her to the Dummies world, and Anum for being her work-partner in crime. She would also like to thank her friends, family, and colleagues for supporting her throughout this process. Finally, thanks to Elaine Young, the college professor who first got her started with Twitter.

Laura sends love and thanks to her co-authors, mentors, friends, readers, and everyone who has shared, commented on, or read her various writings, social posts, speeches, and interviews over the years. Most of all, Laura thanks her daughters Sammi and Zoe. You two are my everything.

Publisher's Acknowledgments

Executive Editor: Steve Hayes

Project Editor: Sarah Hellert

Copy Editor: Kathy Simpson

Technical Editor: Michelle Krasniak

Editorial Assistant: Paige Newman

Sr. Editorial Assistant: Cherie Case

Project Coordinator: Emily Benford

Cover Image: Front Cover image: ©iStock.com/ Dominik Pabis